How to Become an Entrepreneur in a Week

How to Become an Entrepreneur in a Week

The Value of 7-Day Entrepreneurship Courses

Edited by

Lise Aaboen

Professor, Department of Industrial Economics and Technology Management, Norwegian University of Science and Technology, Trondheim, Norway

Hans Landström

Professor, Sten K. Johnson Centre for Entrepreneurship, Lund University, Sweden

Roger Sørheim

Professor, Department of Industrial Economics and Technology Management, Norwegian University of Science and Technology, Trondheim, Norway

Edward Elgar
PUBLISHING

Cheltenham, UK • Northampton, MA, USA

Published by
Edward Elgar Publishing Limited
The Lypiatts
15 Lansdown Road
Cheltenham
Glos GL50 2JA
UK

Edward Elgar Publishing, Inc.
William Pratt House
9 Dewey Court
Northampton
Massachusetts 01060
USA

A catalogue record for this book
is available from the British Library

Library of Congress Control Number: 2020931979

This book is available electronically in the **Elgar**online
Business subject collection
DOI 10.4337/9781788979283

ISBN 978 1 78897 927 6 (cased)
ISBN 978 1 78897 928 3 (eBook)

Printed and bound by CPI Group (UK) Ltd, Croydon, CR0 4YY

Contents

v

Figures

Tables

Contributors

Lise Aaboen	Norwegian University of Science and Technology (NTNU), Norway
Vegar Lein Ausrød	Aarhus University Incubator, Denmark
Olga Belousova	University of Groningen, the Netherlands
Andreu Blesa	Universitat Jaume I, Valencia, Spain
Chiara Cantù	Cattolica University, Italy
Sílvia Costa	University of Groningen, the Netherlands
Servane Delanoë-Gueguen	TBS Business School, France
Aard Groen	University of Groningen, the Netherlands
Jeppe Guldager	Aarhus University Incubator, Denmark
Jarna Heinonen	University of Turku, Finland
Carlos de las Heras-Pedrosa	University of Malaga, Spain
Ulla Hytti	University of Turku, Finland
Patricia P. Iglesias-Sánchez	University of Malaga, Spain
Arne Jacobsson	Linköping University, Sweden
Hans Landström	Lund University, Sweden
Eric Michael Laviolette	TBS Business School, France
Carmina Jambrino Maldonado	University of Malaga, Spain
Laura Martínez	Universitat Jaume I, Valencia, Spain
Gunn-Berit Neergård	Norwegian University of Science and Technology (NTNU), Norway
Aniek Ouendag	University of Groningen, the Netherlands
María Ripollés	Universitat Jaume I, Valencia, Spain
Antonella La Rocca	Rennes Business School, France

Claus Andreas Foss Rosenstand	Aalborg University, Denmark
Emilee Simmons	University of Leeds, UK
Roger Sørheim	Norwegian University of Science and Technology (NTNU), Norway
Pekka Stenholm	University of Turku, Finland
Christian Tollestrup	Aalborg University, Denmark

1. How do you become entrepreneurial in one week?

Lise Aaboen, Hans Landström and Roger Sørheim

SETTING THE SCENE

Entrepreneurship has become a catchword in academia. Education in entrepreneurship has expanded from a business school offering to an education offered to students within many other disciplines. Moreover, entrepreneurship scholars are extensively involved with course development and pedagogical initiatives, and new ways of teaching have been developed featuring new methods and overarching ideas about what an entrepreneurship education should entail (Fayolle, 2013; Katz, 2003; Neck and Corbett, 2018; Vesper and Gartner, 1997). Thus, universities offer a broad range of entrepreneurship education programmes, courses, cross-disciplinary activities, co-curricular activities and students' clubs for entrepreneurship with business plan competitions, internships, grants and venture creation activities (Levie, 2014; Morris et al., 2014). The pedagogy of entrepreneurship education and course curricula have evolved significantly. Now, entrepreneurship activities include everything from traditional case solving, simulations, games and student enterprises which only exist during the course, to more advanced pedagogical approaches, such as internships, consultant businesses and new technology-based venture creation. Typically, entrepreneurship education activities are categorised into (a) education which intends to wake dormant entrepreneurs; (b) stimulation activities for supporting a process from idea to business plan; and (c) incubation activities to ensure that start-ups can survive independently (Jansen et al., 2015).

In this book, we will focus on one such activity: activities aiming to make students more entrepreneurial through week-long courses, camps and/or summer schools. A brief explanation of a start-up weekend is 'an event for young entrepreneurs (and those who want to be one) to work creatively in a low-risk, high-energy atmosphere and develop ideas into small businesses' (Hiss, 2018: 64). We have witnessed first-hand that such activities have increased significantly in practice over the last five years. An early description of such initiatives involves the three camps described by Bager (2011): a student camp aimed at developing student ideas, a student camp aimed at company innovation, and a student camp aimed at university commercialisation. Bager's (2011) article demonstrates three shortcomings typical of articles describing short initiatives. First, such articles focus on describing the camps. Second, the outcomes of the camps are unclear. There is no information regarding what 'very positive' refers to. Even though it is assumed that students have increased their understanding and self-efficacy, this is not explicitly assessed. Third, Bager (2011) shows that, even if the three camps have divergent aims, there are still common denominators in short initiatives. Typically, students work in teams to solve a challenge in a specific location with facilitators.

This book overcomes the shortcomings in the literature exemplified by Bager (2011), and we will collect examples of such short initiatives from various countries and contexts. The ultimate aims of the book are: (1) to provide examples of short initiatives from European research-based universities which show what activities they use, how they have developed and how they seek to contribute to the entrepreneurial activities at their universities; and (2) to initiate a discussion which will improve the quality of one-week initiatives and advance the research frontier of such initiatives beyond a pre-test/post-test of entrepreneurial mindsets and intentions. In the entrepreneurship education literature, authors sometimes differentiate between 'entrepreneurship' education and 'enterprise' education. For instance, Rae et al. (2012: 382) use the definition 'enterprise' when they describe 'students learning to use the skills, knowledge and personal attributes needed to apply creative ideas and innovations to practical situations' while 'entrepreneurship' is used to describe 'the study of enterprise and entrepreneurs, including the practical and academic knowledge, skills and techniques used in being an entrepreneur'. However, the words tend to be used interchangeably (Hannon, 2005), and following this trend we primarily use the term 'entrepreneurship' in the present book.

The book has been developed in the following way. An invitation to contribute chapters to a book about short entrepreneurship education initiatives was sent out in the early spring of 2018. Based on the extended abstracts submitted, chapters were selected. The selection process took into consideration the geographical context and content of the initiatives as well as the inclusion of different types of initiatives in order to provide a European view of short entrepreneurship education initiatives. Once the book proposal was approved, the authors of the selected extended abstracts were invited to submit full paper drafts of their chapters. A first round of reviews was provided by the editors. After the submission of the second drafts of the chapters, the chapter authors performed a review of each other's chapters so that each chapter received a review from the authors of two other chapters. Furthermore, the chapter authors were invited to a seminar in Trondheim where they acted as discussants on each other's papers. This seminar provided valuable comments for the chapters and a common understanding of what the book was about. The third drafts of the chapters were reviewed by the editors, and the fourth draft was the final draft for most chapters while a few received additional minor comments.

CONTENT OF THE BOOK

The book consists of three parts: Part I: Skills, competencies and awareness among students; Part II: Start-ups and entrepreneurs from the university; and Part III: Entrepreneurial citizens. Part I includes initiatives which focus on instilling an entrepreneurial mindset in students or inspiring the students to entrepreneurial thinking through teamwork. The result is often a pitch or presentation about how the students solved a challenge. In initiatives in Part II, the intended result is to contribute to the 'third mission' of the university by preparing students for careers as entrepreneurs. Part III describes initiatives which are part of collaborations between universities. Such initiatives are often influenced by the collaborations they are based on and often have a regional or societal goal for their activities. Below, we introduce the parts and chapters of the book.

Part I: Skills, Competencies and Awareness among Students

The Workshop for Innovation and Entrepreneurship (WOFIE) was a four-day workshop designed to provide students with a tangible understanding of innovation and entrepreneurship at Aalborg University, Denmark. It was targeted towards second-year master's students from all disciplines at three campus locations, and every year approximately 300 students passed the course. The workshop included a large group of facilitators and was based on a WOFIE guide map focusing on the dimensions of unique, verify, business and convince. The chapter provides a description of how the workshop developed between 2008 and 2017. In particular, the chapter emphasises the informal aspects of organising entrepreneurship education initiatives before, during and after WOFIE was offered.

The Innovation Camp is a mandatory three-day course introducing nursing students to the need for innovations in healthcare at the Norwegian University of Science and Technology, Norway. In order to meet the new national learning objectives for nursing students, the Unit for Nursing collaborates with an organisation for youth entrepreneurship, the municipality, the hospital and a national centre for entrepreneurship education. During the course, the students attend lectures and work in teams to develop innovative ideas which are presented to a jury at the end of the course. In particular, the chapter focuses on the particularities of the healthcare context.

SEMIS is a mandatory four-day course for instilling entrepreneurial competencies in the first-year master's students at TBS Business School, France. The teamwork, which follows a design thinking methodology, is based on challenges in the areas of boldness, excellence, openness and responsibility. The course culminates in a pitch contest. In particular, the chapter focuses on the use of internal university challenges for short entrepreneurship education and the opportunity to build a learning community by inviting university professors from all disciplines to join the initiative as coaches.

The Leeds International Summer School (LISS) is an international summer programme at the University of Leeds in the UK. The programme use lectures, teamwork, daily reflective journals and field trips to help students understand the skills, attributes and abilities of entrepreneurs as well as how entrepreneurship can be used as a vehicle to bring about social change. In particular, the chapter focuses on how the initiative becomes an environment in which faculty can experiment with new ways of teaching and PhD students can get teaching experience.

Part II: Start-ups and Entrepreneurs from the University

Sommarmatchen is a summer programme for verifying research results and moving projects closer to market in order to create an awareness of entrepreneurship as a career path at Linköping University, Sweden. During the programme, students are matched with a research idea and after an initial week of crash courses in such activities as cold calling, the students work with the idea during the summer and deliver a report and a presentation. In particular, the chapter focuses on the planning and organisation needed in order to accomplish successful matches between students, researchers and research.

Entrepreneurship for Research Professionals is an elective course for PhD students from all disciplines at the University of Turku, Finland, aimed at widening their career perspectives from academia to business life. The course demonstrates the entrepreneurial process and consists of pre-readings, a ten-hour learning camp, a learning diary kept for two weeks, and a wrap-up session. In particular, the chapter focuses on the importance of teamwork, entrepreneurial action and time scarcity for this group of students.

VentureLab Weekend is a three-day extracurricular learning event for bachelor's, master's and PhD students from all disciplines. The event aims at the development of entrepreneurial competencies and business ideas into well-developed business models and investor pitches at the University of Groningen, the Netherlands. During the event, workshop activities are combined with working with peers, and the numerous activities include feedback, working and coaching. The organisers work extensively with national and international partners. In particular, the chapter elaborates on the event's participant-centred approach.

PIE 17-088 is an extracurricular initiative at the University of Malaga in Spain which trains students in competencies related to entrepreneurship as a differentiating factor in being more competitive in the labour market. In the initiative, students choose between a hackathon, team building, practical cases with entrepreneurs and role playing. The organisers then determine which training activities seem most attractive and effective. In particular, the chapter emphasises the importance of experimentation and stakeholder involvement during the development of entrepreneurship initiatives in higher education.

Part III: Entrepreneurial Citizens

Pursuing Entrepreneurship is an extracurricular course at Aarhus University in Denmark where students learn how to pitch and apply the Lean Startup methodology tools and understand that ideas develop in interactions between people. Three institutions – Aarhus University, VIA University College and Business Academy Aarhus – have collaboratively committed to the goals of 7000 students receiving extracurricular entrepreneurship education, 2500 students signing an incubator contract and 350 students starting an officially registered venture. Pursuing Entrepreneurship is part of the plan to reach these goals. During the two-week course, participants develop their ideas through workshops and videos which the participants receive through text messages. In particular, the chapter focuses on the blended learning resulting from the use of both workshops and videos and how the tracking of the videos enables the organisers to follow the engagement of the students during different parts of the course.

5UCV-E2 is an extracurricular course which coaches students in entrepreneurship and nurtures their adaptive capabilities at five universities simultaneously in the region of Valencia, Spain. The collaboration of the five universities is coordinated with the help of Dirección General de Economía, Emprendimiento y Cooperativismo of the Valencian regional government and the Santander International Entrepreneurship Centre to help the universities in carrying out and designing the programme. During the programme, students work in teams facilitated by student tutors and local entrepreneurs following worksheets during seven sessions. In particular, the chapter focuses on the activities which have been carried out to foster collaboration between the participating organisations. 5UCV-E2 is one of seven extracurricular activities carried out by the same consortium.

ComoNExT iStart Academy guided the participants through the lean start-up process using lectures, teamwork and mentoring for five days in Lomazzo, Italy. The extracurricular course was part of an Erasmus+ Key Action 2 (KA2) strategic partnership project. The project consortium consists of universities, incubators, research centres and business angels from Turkey, the United Kingdom, Greece, Portugal, Belgium and Italy and aims to contribute to growth, jobs, social equality and inclusion through a lean-training, innovative, multidisciplinary digital entrepreneurship platform. In particular, the chapter focuses on how the network among the actors in the consortium enabled the ComoNExT iStart Academy.

LESSONS LEARNED ABOUT SHORT ENTREPRENEURSHIP EDUCATION INITIATIVES

All short entrepreneurship education initiatives covered in the book are based on a process the students go through during the initiative to experience the activities and reach the intended result at the end of the programme. The initiatives detailed in Part I all focus on idea development leading to a presentation at the end, while Part II provides examples of initiatives in which the focus is on a somewhat later stage of venture development. In some of the initiatives, the process itself is designed to simulate the entrepreneurial process of finding a business opportunity using elements from, for instance, design thinking. In other words, being guided through the process and learning, for instance, how to pitch are important concrete goals of the initiative. At the student level, the initiatives also present goals such as developing and nurturing capabilities, developing competencies, creating awareness, introducing transformative learning and providing an understanding of entrepreneurship, which are more difficult to evaluate (Table 1.1). Most of the initiatives also have goals at the university, regional and national levels which they want to reach or contribute to. These goals have included meeting national learning objectives of providing entrepreneurship to all students or a certain number of students and creating jobs and growth.

The measured results presented in the chapters are mostly quotes from surveys and interviews regarding student satisfaction and perceived learning. Given the short time frame of the initiatives, it may be difficult to detect new capabilities, competencies and transformative learning even though an initiative may have provided a student's first inspiration in that direction. Similarly, in terms of the goals regarding jobs and growth, it may be that the initiative, together with other efforts, makes a change, but it will be difficult

Table 1.1   *Target students and goals*

	Audience/Students	Goals
WOFIE, Aalborg University	Master's students from all disciplines	Tangible understanding of innovation and entrepreneurship
The Innovation Camp, Norwegian University of Science and Technology	Third-year nursing students	Fulfil new national learning objectives; Introduce the need for innovation in healthcare
SEMIS, Toulouse Business School	All first-year master's students	Instil entrepreneurial competencies
LISS, University of Leeds	International undergraduate students with no previous knowledge of entrepreneurship	Understand the skills, attributes and abilities of entrepreneurs as well as how entrepreneurship can be used as a vehicle to bring about social change
Sommarmatchen, Linköping University	Students from all disciplines; Previously, primarily engineering and economics	Awareness of alternative careers; Moving research results one step closer to the market
Entrepreneurship for Research Professionals, University of Turku	PhD students from all disciplines	Widen students' career perspectives from academia to business life
VentureLab Weekend, University of Groningen	Bachelor's, master's and PhD students from all disciplines	Development of entrepreneurial competencies and business ideas into well-developed business models and investor pitches
PIE 17-088, University of Malaga	Students from all disciplines	Training in competencies related to entrepreneurship as a differentiating factor in being more competitive in the labour market
Pursuing Entrepreneurship, Aarhus University	Students from all disciplines	Learn how to pitch, apply Lean Startup tools and develop an understanding that ideas develop in interactions between people
5UCV-E2, University of Valencia	Students from all disciplines for the teams and students with entrepreneurship backgrounds as tutors	Develop and nurture adaptive capabilities
ComoNExT iStart Academy, Catholic University of the Sacred Heart	Students from all disciplines	Contribute to growth, jobs, social equality and inclusion through a lean-training, innovative, multidisciplinary digital entrepreneurship platform

to isolate the effects of the particular week of training. Even if a former participant starts a business later, it will be difficult to know that it was because of a particular initiative. However, providing an initial awareness of entrepreneurship or guiding students through a useful process may be valuable, more attainable within the timeframe and easier to measure. We found it interesting to notice that these initiatives are sometimes used to meet new national learning objectives of introducing all students to entrepreneurship. The format provides the opportunity to experiment with the content, but there is also a risk that entrepreneurship may be perceived as an add-on rather than an integrated part of curricula. We also noted that at least two of the initiatives used the course to try out new ways of teaching and to provide teaching training to new faculty and faculty from disciplines other than entrepreneurship. In this way, an initiative may become a way to improve entrepreneurship teaching in other courses as well.

The short entrepreneurship education initiatives tended to be extracurricular except for the initiatives in Part I, all but one of which were mandatory. A common denominator for the mandatory initiatives was that they all wanted to ensure that all students become equipped with the tools needed to develop an opportunity. The initiatives in Part III are based on consortia of universities and other actors. The activities which take place in order to make the collaboration work and to enable the initiatives are important for these initiatives. However, the other initiatives also mention external actors, for example, an organisation for youth entrepreneurship as well as local entrepreneurs and technology transfer offices. It also seems important that an organisation sponsoring the initiative is well connected in the university. Some initiatives are organised by centres which are semi-independent from the regular faculties (Table 1.2). This enables them to connect with all parts of the university without being dependent on as many structures. However, it also makes it particularly important for them to anchor the initiative in the organisation so that they are able to access students and resources. For instance, it is mentioned by one initiative that the local teaching environments sometimes 'forgot' to communicate the initiative or planned study tours, which prevented their students from participating because the local teaching environments did not see the point of innovation and entrepreneurship for their students. Another example regarding organisational anchoring is that the organisers of some of the initiatives previously held important positions in entrepreneurship-related activities and thus had the legitimacy necessary to organise the initiative and access all students as well as important decision-makers in the university.

The pedagogical approaches used were mostly experiential learning in which the students worked on a project in groups with mentoring and

Table 1.2　　　*Organisation of the initiatives*

	Organisation
WOFIE, Aalborg University	Guide map, script and video links to ensure that the event was run consistently in all locations; Supporting Entrepreneurship at Aalborg was the formal coordinator; Informal network which has organised similar initiatives since WOFIE
The Innovation Camp, Norwegian University of Science and Technology	Organised by the nursing faculty in collaboration with an organisation for youth entrepreneurship, the municipality, the university hospital, a centre for entrepreneurship education and a student organisation for entrepreneurship
SEMIS, Toulouse Business School	Organised by two professors who previously held positions in the university entrepreneurship system
LISS, University of Leeds	Organised by the Centre for Enterprise and Entrepreneurship Studies
Sommarmatchen, Linköping University	Organised by the Technology Transfer Office
Entrepreneurship for Research Professionals, University of Turku	Organised by the Entrepreneurship Unit on behalf of the graduate school
VentureLab Weekend, University of Groningen	Organised by the University of Groningen Centre of Entrepreneurship as part of their entrepreneurship funnel; Many international partners and collaborations
PIE 17-088, University of Malaga	Organised as a project at the University of Malaga; External collaborators for some of the activities
Pursuing Entrepreneurship, Aarhus University	Organised by the Aarhus University Incubator; Collaboration between three Danish universities; Funded by the region and the European Social Fund
5UCV-E2, University of Valencia	Organised by a collaboration between five Valencian universities, the regional government and the Santander International Entrepreneurship Centre
ComoNExT iStart Academy, Catholic University of the Sacred Heart	Part of an Erasmus+ KA2 strategic partnership project; The project consortium consists of universities, incubators, research centres and business angels from Turkey, the UK, Greece, Portugal, Belgium and Italy

attended lectures to learn the tools they needed during their project (Table 1.3). There were also excursions to local entrepreneurs, reflection diaries and short movies on SMS to complement the experiential learning. There are rather traditional pedagogical approaches used in these initiatives. However, we noticed some attempts to think differently, such as the use of the movies to measure the engagement of the students and the effort to include the students in designing the entrepreneurship education. We find it interesting that the pedagogical approaches are so similar in the different initiatives, given that they are designed for different students, for different goals and in different contexts. There seems to be an emphasis on teaching the students how to use tools such as design thinking or lean start-up rather than on specific content. Furthermore, the initiatives do not seem to be connected to the other courses at the institutions of which they are part. For the extracurricular courses, it may be natural that they are more connected to the other extracurricular activities of the university. For the initiatives which are part of the curriculum or even mandatory it could perhaps be possible to connect to other courses and thereby contextualise the content of the initiative and/or prolong the learning of entrepreneurship. Another interesting observation is that the majority of the activities seem to take place at the university and in interaction with other students and faculty. Except for talking with potential users as part of the design thinking and lean start-up processes, very little of the experiential learning seems to be connected to the 'real world'. It seems to involve more 'classroom' exercises preparing students to carry out similar activities in the 'real world' later. Initiatives in which students work on developing research ideas for the commercial market seem to be an exception.

Table 1.3   *Pedagogical approach in the initiatives*

	Pedagogical approach	Extracurricular/curricular	Contact with external actors
WOFIE, Aalborg University	Changed from a creativity-based approach to a business-based approach; Group work using design thinking-based framework	Elective course	Judges and expert panels
The Innovation Camp, Norwegian University of Science and Technology	Group work to develop an idea for solving a challenge following the framework provided by the organisation for youth entrepreneurship	Curricular and mandatory	The stakeholders providing the challenges
SEMIS, Toulouse Business School	Group work to develop a solution to a challenge provided by the university based on design thinking	Curricular and mandatory	Experts and potential users

	Pedagogical approach	Extracurricular/curricular	Contact with external actors
LISS, University of Leeds	Lectures, teamwork, daily reflective journals and field trips	Extracurricular, summer	Local entrepreneurs and organisations
Sommarmatchen, Linköping University	NABC framework; Crash course, independent work and presentation	Extracurricular, summer	Researchers
Entrepreneurship for Research Professionals, University of Turku	Pre-readings, ten-hour learning camp, learning diary for two weeks, and wrap-up session; Develop idea based on interest; Lean start-up; Motorola reflection tool	Elective course	Potential users
VentureLab Weekend, University of Groningen	Workshop moments are combined with working with peers moments, and there are numerous active moments, such as feedback, working and coaching	Extracurricular	Coaches from the local ecosystem, panels and potential users
PIE 17-088, University of Malaga	The students choose between a hackathon, team building, practical cases with an entrepreneur and role playing	Extracurricular	Some activities take place in the entrepreneurs fair
Pursuing Entrepreneurship, Aarhus University	Develop idea through kick-off, development with videos using the NABC framework and a workshop for reflection	Extracurricular	Test the idea on potential customers
5UCV-E2, University of Valencia	Teamwork using worksheets together with student tutors and local entrepreneurs to develop a business model	Extracurricular	Local entrepreneurs
ComoNExT iStart Academy, Catholic University of the Sacred Heart	Lectures, teamwork and mentoring; Virtual learning environment (VLE); Lean start-up	Extracurricular	Mentors, tutors, experts and potential users

CHANGING THE SCENE

The development of short entrepreneurship education initiatives so far seems to be fuelled by external pressure to provide entrepreneurship to more or all students. The traditional structure of universities does not seem entirely suitable for these initiatives. The development of the initiatives has, therefore, often been conducted by freestanding units with entrepreneurship competency or faculty together with external collaboration partners with the same competency. Even though the use of freestanding units, ad hoc teachers and practitioners as facilitators has enabled the introduction of these initiatives, it also hampers the initiatives during their further development as it makes the initiatives loosely coupled with the competency and management structures of the university. The lack of embeddedness in the university structure prevents the initiatives from benefiting from the continuous pedagogical development which faculty conduct in regular study programmes. Simultaneously, the traditional programmes are not benefiting from the learning activities used in the initiative.

The time span provides less time for reflection, so the experiential learning is rather limited compared with a full course or a study programme in entrepreneurship. It is possible, therefore, to discuss whether entrepreneurship education has actually been provided to the students of these short initiatives. It is, of course, connected to the goals, but it may be wise not to set goals beyond providing awareness of entrepreneurship. Furthermore, student satisfaction provides leverage in negotiations, and the offering of tools which are popular and common provides legitimacy to the initiative. However, in isolation, the short entrepreneurship education initiatives currently in use run the risk of becoming simply fun events during education, also known as intellectually comfortable 'McEducation' (Hytti, 2018).

For the future development of short entrepreneurship education initiatives, we suggest increased contextualisation so that initiatives are relevant for the students who are attending instead of one-size-fits-all add-ons. In other words, we suggest that initiatives could be different depending on the students they are targeting and the context in which they are developed. One step in accomplishing this may be that more initiatives use the short initiatives as test beds for new ways of teaching and for educating faculty in entrepreneurship education. Furthermore, we suggest that opportunities be provided for continuing to work on the ideas developed either as part of thesis work, in courses or in extracurricular initiatives. Moreover, we suggest that the initiatives could become integrated parts of disciplinary courses. In this way, the initiatives will become less standardised and homogeneous over time as well as more embedded in the university and the education provided by the university.

ACKNOWLEDGEMENT

The authors would like to acknowledge the financial support provided by Engage – Centre for Engaged Education through Entrepreneurship.

REFERENCES

Bager, T. (2011), 'The camp model for entrepreneurship teaching', *International Entrepreneurship Management Journal*, **7**, 279–96.

Fayolle, A. (2013), 'Personal views on the future of entrepreneurship education', *Entrepreneurship & Regional Development*, **25** (7–8), 692–701.

Hannon, P.D. (2005), 'Philosophies of enterprise and entrepreneurship education and challenges for higher education in the UK', *Entrepreneurship and Innovation*, **6** (2), 105–14.

Hiss, F. (2018), 'Talk, time, and creativity: Developing ideas and identities during a start-up weekend', *Language & Communication*, **60**, 64–79.

Hytti, U. (2018), 'Critical entrepreneurship education: A form of resistance to McEducation', in Karin Berglund and Karen Verduijn (eds), *Revitalizing Entrepreneurship Education. Adopting a Critical Approach in the Classroom*, Abingdon: Routledge, pp. 228–40.

Jansen, S., T. van de Zande, S. Brinkkemper, E. Stam and V. Varma (2015), 'How education, stimulation, and incubation encourage entrepreneurship: Observations from MIT, IIIT, and Utrecht University', *The International Journal of Management Education*, **13**, 170–81.

Katz, J.A. (2003), 'The chronology and intellectual trajectory of American entrepreneurship education', *Journal of Business Venturing*, **18** (2), 283–300.

Levie, J. (2014), 'The university is the classroom: Teaching and learning technology commercialization at a technological university', *Journal of Technology Transfer*, **39** (5), 793–808.

Morris, N.M., D.F. Kuratko and C.G. Pryor (2014), 'Building blocks for the development of university-wide entrepreneurship', *Entrepreneurship Research Journal*, **4** (1), 45–68.

Neck, H.M. and A.C. Corbett (2018), 'The scholarship of teaching and learning entrepreneurship', *Entrepreneurship Education and Pedagogy*, **1** (1), 8–41.

Rae, D., L. Martin, V. Antcliff and P. Hannon (2012), 'Enterprise and entrepreneurship in English higher education: 2010 and beyond', *Journal of Small Business and Enterprise Development*, **19** (3), 380–401.

Vesper, K.H. and W.B. Gartner (1997), 'Measuring progress in entrepreneurship education', *Journal of Business Venturing*, **12** (5), 403–21.

PART I

Skills, competencies and awareness among students

2. WOFIE: Workshop For Innovation and Entrepreneurship

Christian Tollestrup and Claus Andreas Foss Rosenstand

WOFIE was a grand, scalable and flexible workshop on innovation and entrepreneurship. It had a four-day workshop format offered to all master's students from all study programmes across campuses, faculties and institutions at Aalborg University, Denmark. The programme ran the week before Easter from 2008 to 2017 and has had a long-term impact, spawning several new entrepreneurship teaching initiatives.

DESCRIPTION OF WOFIE

WOFIE (Workshop For Innovation and Entrepreneurship) was a four-day workshop that ran for nine years, from 2008 until 2017, at Aalborg University. The overall focus of WOFIE was to provide students with a tactile understanding of innovation and entrepreneurship.

Aalborg University was founded in 1974 as a problem-based learning university where students could formulate and reformulate problems (research questions) during group-based semester projects within their disciplines. Aalborg University is now a full university with more than 20 000 full-time students and more than 3000 full-time scientific employees (including 850 PhD candidates) located at three campuses in Denmark: Aalborg, Esbjerg and Copenhagen.

At the time WOFIE was initially developed in 2007, part of the goal-contract between Aalborg University and the Danish government stated that all students during their master's programme should be offered teaching in entrepreneurship. At the university, a cross-disciplinary group of researchers and staff with experience and knowledge in innovation and entrepreneurship teaching was formed to advise university management on an execution format. A central unit called SEA (Supporting Entrepreneurship at Aalborg University) was the formal coordinator of the initiative. SEA's aim was to support the cross-disciplinary network amongst the relatively few researchers at the university interested in entrepreneurship, and they had the opportunity to connect and organize independently of the university governance through study boards, departments and faculties.

From the very beginning, it was clear that the number of experienced research-based teachers with adequate competences within the field of entrepreneurship was quite low (less than 15 at Aalborg University back in 2007) compared to the number of students, so offering conventional teaching to all master's students within the existing university governance was not possible. Instead of offering voluntary courses for all master's programmes, where perhaps fewer than half of the students would attend, WOFIE was offered to all master's students as a grand coherent, scalable and flexible four-day workshop across the three campuses supported by a video conference system. It was offered across all faculties: Humanities, Medicine, Social Sciences, and Engineering and Science. Even students from University College Northern Jutland were invited to attend the workshop at the university campus in Aalborg. The workshop was equivalent to two ECTS (European Credit Transfer System) and ran from Tuesday to Friday the week before Easter in the spring semester. It primarily targets second-semester master's students with a total potential of 800 to 900 students. Just under half the students applied, and around 300 students attended at least 80 per cent of the course-time and passed every year.

To deal with the technical and logistical challenges of running a workshop across locations, high-quality video links between the locations provided live feed of lectures in any location to the other locations, including teachers asking online questions across the campuses to illuminate a coherent impression. In the first year (2008), there were five locations used at the Aalborg campus, which resulted in quite an expensive set-up regarding professional video-meeting equipment and tech man-hours; however, from 2009 onward, WOFIE managed to run with one or two locations at the Aalborg campus, plus one at Copenhagen and one at Esbjerg. In the beginning, the video links were quite challenging, and an expert team was required to support them; however, in the end, the quality of a Skype connection was sufficient.

While WOFIE was a solution to offering innovation and entrepreneurship teaching to all master's students, it is self-evident that this 'totally out of university governance workshop' introduced a myriad of challenges, reflections and unique practices, including logistic, financial and administrative obstacles. But more importantly, from a pedagogical and learning perspective, organizing and executing an interdisciplinary and flexible workshop of this scale was the main challenge to be addressed.

The format, approach and theoretical basis changed over the years from primarily a creativity-oriented approach to an innovation and business-oriented approach. The main change was implemented in 2010 when WOFIE was restructured as a new version where the flexibility embedded in everyday innovation and entrepreneurship was incorporated into the pedagogical format.

The practical organization was based on dividing the participants into groups of seven to eight students, mixing them so that the interdisciplinarity was maximized. The groups were divided into clusters consisting of six to eight groups. Each cluster was assigned a cluster-supervisor who closely supervised the cluster's teams during the full workshop. The three locations were connected via video links, allowing instructions, lectures and so on to be executed from any location. However, each location did have a local 'host' (location master) as back-up, if, for example, a cluster-supervisor became ill.

WOFIE

The four-day workshop was based on a combination of a forecast of the process from ideation to business proposal and the freedom for participants to navigate themselves. This provided a platform where supervisors and students could adjust the process, progression and individual groups' actual needs of tools, taking into account their previous process, current state and concrete circumstances regarding their project ideas. This could lead to either skipping an activity and moving into future activities or returning to iterations of the process, thus taking into account the open-ended and unpredictable (flexible) nature of an innovation and entrepreneurship development process. This freedom of navigation was based on a prerequisite that all supervisors and students have a common platform for making decisions regarding process, tools and methods. This platform was the guide map (Table 2.1).

Each year, a mandatory introduction day was offered to key facilitators, including all supervisors, to walk through the guide map. On this day, the specific programme of the year was reviewed, and some exercises ('energizers') were rehearsed. Both new and old facilitators took part in the introduction day because lessons from each year were used to improve the following year. To this end, there were new and relevant perspectives for both new and old facilitators.

In short, the WOFIE guide map (Table 2.1) is essentially an activity matrix based on the notion that the overall movement in process goes from focusing on a unique, verified idea (innovation) to how to create a valuable business that others can believe in (entrepreneurship).

The thinking behind the guide map's structure reflects a progression from innovation to leveraging and idea into a business. If we break down the flow even further, the initiation of the workshop is oriented towards open and iterative ideation and creativity exercises. The underlying assumption is that there are many sources of inspiration for ideas. The WOFIE approach is not dependent on a single, disciplinary, theoretical framework; the methods and

Asynchronous Learning Activities	WORKSHOP FOR			
	INNOVATION		ENTREPRENEURSHIP	
	Day 1: Unique	Day 2: Verify	Day 3: Business	Day 4: Convince
UNIQUE	Ideation	Value	Business Concept	Desire
VERIFY	Need	Research	Critique	Potential
BUSINESS	Business Idea	Market	Organization	Strategy
CONVINCE	Pain	Cure	Profit	Presentation

Table 2.1   WOFIE guide map

approach embrace several starting points. The four levels of activities on Day 1 illustrate the various starting points.

In practice, the workshop started out using the plenum instructions on open ideation since it worked rather well at the beginning of the workshop to get traction in the development, and it created a sense of big-scale activity. But from midday on Day 1, there were no plenum instructions, allowing supervisors to use the guide map to instruct students. Four focal pedagogical points, emphasizing significant activities with different purposes each day, formed a suggested structure (Table 2.1).

On Day 1, 'Unique', the emphasis was on ideation activities to support the purpose of creating something unique. The main tools were different ideation techniques to identify problems and potential ideas for solutions. The 'Ideation' box primarily involves creative techniques for open ideation. This can lead to unexpected ideas and does not discriminate between solution-oriented ideas and problem-oriented ideas. So, an idea for a problem is an equally valid starting point as an idea for a solution.

The 'Need' box is more problem-oriented and encourages participants to investigate and explore what needs existing solutions are already addressing. This can inspire or result in the identification of opportunities to consider existing problems and needs from different angles.

The 'Business Idea' box aims to elevate the thinking to a higher level of abstraction and, at the same time, to look at ideation from a business perspective, resulting in, for example, ideas for new business models. This prompts participants to reflect on the reason for addressing problems or needs: What are the mission and vision?

The 'Pain' box asks for the relation between problem, idea and relevance to the target group. So, no matter what the sequence of building content has been, the objective is to reflect on the coherence and consistency.

On Day 2, 'Verify', the emphasis was on research activities to support the purpose of verifying that the proposed product or service actually was unique and valid. The main tools were research methods and ideation targeted on elaborating the core idea and identifying the innovation potential. Moving from Day 1 to Day 2, there was a slight shift from a more open, creative approach to a more innovation-oriented approach with more depth and precision to all four types of activities.

If we look at the Unique level, 'Ideation' turns to 'Value', inspired by design and innovation literature where you look for new angles, not necessarily the invention of a new product or technology, to create innovation (understood as a successful product on the market). The point was to move beyond the invention emphasis by addressing other factors that may create innovation. These were factors like product, processes, technology, supply, organization, user experience and services that may represent opportunities to add value to the original business idea for the potential customer.

On Day 3, 'Business', the emphasis was on organizational activities to support the purpose of value creation through the product or service. Moving from Day 2 into Day 3 was a major shift from innovation to entrepreneurship. The approach no longer revolved around development and ideation-oriented activities, but rather execution, organization and realization of the idea. The participants had to consider stakeholders on the supply side, not only the customers and user perspectives from the previous innovation phase. This introduced new elements, such as risks, motivation and financing from the different stakeholders' perspectives. Forming a business plan to tie the proposed activities and stakeholders together was a central activity on this day.

On Day 4, 'Convince', the emphasis was on presentation activities to support the purpose of accounting for the potential that a unique and verified business could lead to. The final move from Day 3 into Day 4 shifted the emphasis to the desired future and communication thereof. Themes, such as 'potential', investigated the opportunities the business idea represents, for example, the scalability of the market and possible new versions of the product or service for future development. All the activities on this day focused on clarifying what the essential value of the business idea was, both at present and in the future. This culminated in a presentation in the form of a pitch in front of 'to-be-investors' that evaluated the proposed business and its potential.

For the pitch on the final day, the groups had to deliver a PowerPoint presentation for a maximum five-minute oral pitch at 2:00 pm. The presentation was supported by the WOFIE guide map under the presentation activity through two methods: rehearse the pitch and complete presentation. In short, both pitch and slideshow could follow the four 'Convince' activities (pain, cure, profit and presentation). Many pitches were conducted and evaluated in order to select a first, second and third place out of approximately 70 groups. For this, three voluntary judges were recruited for each cluster; supervisors and other facilitators were excluded from this because they might have biased preferences based on their involvement in the process.

The WOFIE judges were instructed during the last day and were given an evaluation table where they had to give 1 to 5 points (5 as best) for ideation, verification, business and presentation, individually. The four aspects correlated with the focal points for each day of the workshop and were equally weighted. For each aspect, an interpretation and disclaimer were made clear to the judges in an attempt to align the evaluation between different clusters and locations. For example, 'Ideation' was described as 'Innovation in product, service, organization, supply, etc. — do they know where the "new" part is? Primary focus on the concept — not considering the commercial aspect and realism. Is the idea innovative/a mix of different technologies that have not previously been connected — is it new/unique?'

The evaluation of these aspects was at the discretion of each judge, with two to four judges in each cluster. The group with most points (max. 20) was appointed cluster-winner, and they moved on to the second round where two location winners were appointed. These location winners (for example, eight in 2011) continued to the third and final round, where first, second and third place were appointed. The judges were only assigned to one of the three rounds, so they were not biased by listening to the same pitch twice. Moreover, a student's choice award was granted. The prizes varied from year to year, depending on external sponsors.

REFLECTION

WOFIE Version 1: The Synchronous Set-up (2008–2009)

To address control and pedagogy, the first version of WOFIE was based on an already known platform (the 'Creative Platform') developed for teaching innovation with a focus on facilitating creativity. This format was already working to manage larger workshops with a maximum of 100 students. In this format, instructions were given in plenum, one instruction to all participants simultaneously. This pedagogical format relieved the participants of the need to worry about process and progression. In creativity theory and approach (Chikszentmihalyi, 1990), the lack of processual awareness is meant to facilitate participants' creativity freedom.

An example of an instruction from the Creative Platform is 'use the next ten minutes to generate individual ideas and write them on Post-It notes'. This might be followed by an instruction, such as 'use the next twenty minutes to cluster the group's ideas written on the Post-It notes'. To execute this on a larger scale, a number of tools and roles were used to ensure each location followed the same progression in a synchronized manner. For each location, one location leader was responsible for plenum instructions for the activity and for keeping deadlines. The cluster supervisors were available for follow-up questions about the instructions and detailed questions regarding ideas. Three expert panels were available for consultation on different topics; experts were available for feedback on proposals (businesspeople) and assistance in searching for information (librarians or experts on the theme of the workshop).

The tools were lectures and inspirational talks from entrepreneurs and researchers, an instructional slideshow and a detailed script describing the process in steps. The script outlined the precise timing and tools or techniques used for each step. The location leader used the instructional slides to manage each cluster and make sure the detailed script was followed. This also ensured synchronization between locations.

The script led all the groups through ideation and maturation of ideas over the four days of the workshop. By Day 4, most of the students' time was spent preparing the five-minute pitch of the final proposal for a product or service-based business idea.

WOFIE Version 2: The Agile Set-up (2011–2017)

The organizational structure with external experts and judges was successful and, therefore, did not change in the second version of WOFIE. However, evaluation of the first set-up through questionnaires to students, cluster supervisors and location leaders pointed to a couple of major drawbacks, identifying the synchronous approach as the source of the problems.

First, students were expected to engage in an activity based on a plenum instruction given by location leaders using supporting slides. The level of instruction was, therefore, relatively practical and aimed for the lowest common denominator, taking diversity and potential lack of skills into consideration. This provided a relatively non-advanced level of instruction and tools. Secondly, the plenum instruction also meant abrupt interruption for all groups regardless of their progression and current needs. Thirdly, the detailed script on which the instructions were based meant a fixed, predetermined process that did not take iterations, delays, hiccups in the process or any other aspect into consideration. This left the experienced cluster supervisors somewhat frustrated because the structure did not fit the demand for agility in an entrepreneurial process.

The process of innovation and entrepreneurship is inherently open-ended (Cross, 2007; Sarasvathy, 2008) and thus cannot be prescribed precisely in a step-by-step format that predicts the process and outcomes of each step. This meant that the original WOFIE format was inconsistent with the content and approach. Moreover, it conflicted with a problem-based learning model, where it is important to reflect upon and reframe the problem and select adequate tools for the academic solution process. The process was not transparent, and students gained very little learning and insight into the innovation and business development process.

The evaluations (online questionnaires) from the WOFIE Version 1 in 2008 indicated the focus was too much on innovation; the creativity and ideation techniques inherent in the approach were too predominant. In 2009 the entre-preneurship aspect was slightly improved, but mostly on the technical set-up (video links) which was quite challenging in the beginning. The change did not have enough focus on the pedagogical process, which led to too tight a sched-ule that stressed the participants, resulting in a student satisfaction rating of only 45 per cent and 46 per cent for the two first years on a 1–5 scale where 4 and 5 were considered 'satisfied' (Rosenstand and Tribler, 2012).

In WOFIE Version 1, the tools provided and the structural format impaired the communication and process. The students were not empowered to choose another tool or process if they found it more suitable that what was instructed. This led to a large revision in 2010. WOFIE was cancelled that year while the team completely revised the set-up. WOFIE Version 2 was introduced in 2011, and student satisfaction rose to 68 per cent (Rosenstand and Tribler, 2012).

Based on the evaluations of the first version, the 2011 edition of WOFIE was completely redesigned using two main principles (Tollestrup, 2011):

1. Allow for asynchronous and flexible processes between groups.
2. Provide qualified progression suggestions for supervisors in a scalable manner.

The first principle led to the development of the WOFIE guide map (Table 2.1) to replace the detailed script. The second principle moved the responsibility for process progression from location leaders to supervisors and subsequently empowered the students to select processes and tools.

Evaluation and interdisciplinarity
WOFIE was post-evaluated through questionnaires every year. Except for the abovementioned change from a phase-oriented (WOFIE Version 1) to an agile learning and teaching process (WOFIE Version 2), these evaluations only resulted in incremental improvements. An initiative such as WOFIE is a pedagogical challenge, due to the interdisciplinarity and number of students, supervisors, location managers and experts. In the beginning, WOFIE was known for its interdisciplinarity, and this was given as a reason why students

should choose it. However, we learned a quite simple fact: interdisciplinarity is troublesome. An interdisciplinary setting can be very effective regarding both innovation and entrepreneurship. Forced interdisciplinarity creates a situation in which students have to select, prioritize and combine perspectives inherent in their individual disciplines from the very beginning, which often results in new and, therefore, innovative perspectives of real-world problems. In this way, the pedagogy is case-based learning (Rosenstand, 2012), which reframes conventional problem-based learning.

As mentioned, Aalborg University was founded as a problem-based learning university where students could formulate and reformulate problems (research questions) addressed during group-based semester projects within their disciplines. The difference we experienced at WOFIE was a decoupling of the inherent disciplinary perspectives on the framing of problems. In other words, in normal problem-based learning at Aalborg University, the coupling of working-method and problem was a task for the students; at WOFIE, the students had to add the extra dimension of coupling a selection, prioritizing and combining different disciplinary perspectives inherent in their study programmes, meaning that the everyday inherent disciplinary blind spot (the eye of the beholder) in a study programme was illuminated during WOFIE. To this point, WOFIE could be characterized as an interdisciplinary problem-based learning course—also termed case-based learning because the student's point of departure was oriented towards an innovative and entrepreneurial case before they oriented towards a problem. The problem could simply not be formulated before the disciplinary perspectives were selected, combined and prioritized.

A core competence of early-stage, knowledge-based entrepreneurs is to account for vision through communication: they have to convince key stakeholders to participate in a venture towards a land of fortune that has never been visited before. At a four-day workshop like WOFIE, there is no room for actually making proof of business—actually showing some 'gold grains' from the 'gold in the mountain at the Promised Land'. Entrepreneurs depend on investments from other stakeholders in terms of knowledge, resources and time, and they only get this if they can communicate convincingly. Because knowledge-based entrepreneurship always has some dimension of a new type of value creation and capturing, entrepreneurs cannot simply refer to existing businesses. At WOFIE, key stakeholders were represented by judges during the evaluation of the students' pitches on the final day.

Regarding entrepreneurship, interdisciplinarity is a strength: every business can benefit from design thinking, digital competences, business knowledge and so on. However, most importantly in the context of WOFIE, it forces students to communicate in a common language that cannot only be understood by students and teachers within their own discipline. With the diversity in disciplines, there is a need for common ground and common denominators. This applies both to students and facilitators (supervisors, experts, and technical and administrative staff). The diversity of supervisors and experts was also addressed. Moreover, a refresher was needed for old facilitators after a year. The high percentage of returning facilitators resulted in a growing body of facilitators across departments and faculties. Many of the key facilitators also helped recruit new facilitators from their own network with the requisite open attitude to innovation and entrepreneurship. However, some supervisors could not cope with the agile format of WOFIE Version 2; they felt they were not in control, and thus out of their pedagogical comfort zone.

Origin, Organization and Roll-out Challenges

During the ten years the WOFIE initiative ran, it proved its viability and value. The concept has even been exported to Australia, where miniature versions of WOFIE and its guide map have been implemented (McDonald et al., 2018); this was possible because one of the developers of WOFIE, Professor Frank Gertsen from Aalborg University, implemented the problem- and case-based workshop there as a guest professor. However, WOFIE was not without challenges that had to be addressed from the very outset. There are two main aspects we want to highlight as paramount to WOFIE's success.

Interdisciplinarity
Following the reflection on evaluation, interdisciplinarity is a key aspect of innovation and entrepreneurship. The discipline-neutral central unit of SEA and its network, the few researchers from the university who were interested in entrepreneurship, worked as a facilitator for the initiative; SEA being a neutral stakeholder in terms of disciplines meant that no research environment 'owned' the initiative and the organizational responsibility. This probably prevented internal competition related to avoiding tasks or obtaining funding. As the researchers interested in entrepreneurship at the time were relatively few and dispersed, and the majority of the researchers were already looking outside their own field of expertise for collaboration, the foundation for collaboration was high. When researching design, innovation, creativity and entrepreneurship, there is an acute awareness of the need for collaboration between disciplines in order to achieve innovation (Buijs, 2012).

In the beginning, WOFIE was constituted by an interdisciplinary steering committee across university faculties with researchers with a common research interest in innovation and entrepreneurship, plus a university library representative. The members of the steering committee also took part in the development, implementation and execution of the pedagogical concept. The interdisciplinary team that formed the steering committee was almost unchanged for the entire duration of WOFIE, and the participants later created more initiatives together with SEA, forming a group of 'usual suspects' regarding interdisciplinary innovation and entrepreneurship teaching activities. This group of researchers were willing to ignore the usual university governance (silo functions for sub-optimizing) in order to achieve a level of collaboration that ensured a higher quality of the combined work.

Organizational ownership

Without the rector's agreement with the ministry, WOFIE and its impact would probably never have happened. A governance like WOFIE could only coexist with a university institution because it was anchored in SEA outside existing study boards in a political steering committee and a pedagogical coordination board, and had the rector's full support. Today, SEA still exists as an important part of a new organizational unit, Aalborg University Innovation, where it is a key part of the university strategy; for many years, WOFIE was the 'Innovation and Entrepreneurship Flagship' and the biggest project in SEA regarding time and money.

In a way, WOFIE demonstrated that there are so many other ways of organized learning across common boundaries of universities. The organization ensured shared ownership among the researchers who contributed to WOFIE across organizational borders (courses, study programmes, departments, faculties and locations); however, over the years, a lack of political ownership was experienced, apart from the rector. Many study boards and semester-responsible teachers composed an organizational immune system for WOFIE because they could not see how innovation and entrepreneurship were important to their students. Consequently, the local teaching environment 'forgot' to communicate about WOFIE, or they, for example, planned other selectable, non-mandatory but attractive extracurricular activities, like study tours, which they highly recommended over WOFIE. First, the rector tried to promote WOFIE by mailing everybody at the university, and it had a positive effect the first year; however, somehow this activated the immune system even more. Therefore, it was agreed that the steering committee would be changed into a coordination board, referring to a new political steering committee where faculty deans and selected heads of department were represented. Retrospectively, we learned that, due to the immune system of a historically disciplinary divided organization, it is important and beneficial to have an organization like this from the very start, where both political and research/teaching ownership are ensured.

Uniqueness

WOFIE died, but the DNA is still alive in new initiatives. WOFIE Version 2 ran until 2017 when funding for extracurricular activities dried up due to national regulations. But, at the same time, innovation and entrepreneurship had gradually been integrated into many study programmes and entrepreneurship master's programmes were even created. Pedagogical key stakeholders from WOFIE were involved in the development of the master's programmes, where experiences from WOFIE were used. Moreover, the interdisciplinary network of WOFIE developers and supervisors is still utilized today in innovation and entrepreneurship activities at Aalborg University. To this day, WOFIE still has a pedagogical impact, although the workshop is no longer running.

WOFIE created some interesting spin-off initiatives in various forms of new educational courses and programmes. Key stakeholders from WOFIE were involved in the study design and execution. These courses and programmes have helped foster ideas that have turned into businesses. The initiatives are presented in 'scale', ranging from a two-week workshop to a two-year master's programme.

The User-driven Creative Academy (U-CrAc) was one of the first spin-offs founded in 2011 by key WOFIE stakeholders from the Department of Communication. The main inspiration was the interdisciplinarity in the set-up. It is a two-week course module offered to multiple university programmes and one college programme. Students are mixed in interdisciplinary groups and work on relatively open problems and cases from companies. In a sense, it is a two-week version of the first half of the WOFIE set-up. The emphasis is on user-oriented research and ideation to create product and service inno-vations, with interdisciplinarity enriching and challenging the students to see different perspectives on ideation and innovation. With access to real users and stakeholders, there is a drive to create something useful and interesting. This initiative is still running, and occasionally ideas from this workshop turn into real products on the market: TubusOne, for example, was based on an idea from this course for a communication tool for individuals with mobility disabled arms and hands.

Advanced Integrated Design II: Business Development is a three-week course module for industrial design students organized by a key stakeholder from the Department of Architecture, Design and Media Technology. It was inspired by the informal evaluation of WOFIE by external experts. This module gives students ten working days to design, develop and manufacture 20 units of a product to be sold on Day 11. This provides enormous intrinsic motivation to face customers. In its first run in 2018, the first business was created based on a product from the course: a lamp, now sold at stobt.dk.

New Venture Creation is an initiative founded by stakeholders from the Department of Business. The initiative is a semester offered to all third-year master's students across the full university who are interested in creating a business. It was inspired by the interdisciplinarity of WOFIE and its focus on entrepreneurship. Approximately 25 per cent of the business ideas generate revenue before the semester ends, and 35 per cent enter the AAU start-up programme to be developed further.

The National Academy for Digital Interactive Entertainment (DADIU) is a semester that selected master's and art students across universities and art schools in Denmark can apply to. Six game development teams with approximately 16 students are accepted each year; two teams are placed in Aalborg and four in Copenhagen. The module has resulted in several start-ups in the gaming industry, such as Bed Time Games, which has produced several surreal, nonsense-genre games with millions of downloads.

Finally, stakeholders from four departments (Communication, Business, Center for Industrial Production, Architecture and Design) and the SEA unit responsible for organizing WOFIE formed a new interdisciplinary group in 2012 with the purpose of creating a new master's programme with a hands-on approach to entrepreneurship. The group built on their experience developing WOFIE across several organizational units, finding common ground on a theoretical, practical and organizational level based on the high level of trust between members of the group.

The initiative is called Entrepreneurial Engineering: a two-year master's programme at AAU offered to technical bachelors. It again leverages interdisciplinarity to facilitate innovation and entrepreneurship. Several projects from the programme have become businesses; for example, Artland App was based on a master's thesis project and secured its first funding two weeks prior to the exam.

Entrepreneurial Engineering brings together creativity from the Creative Platform at the Department of Business; a user-driven approach from the Department of Communication; a proposal-oriented design approach from the Department of Architecture, Design and Media Technology; and finally an entrepreneurial approach from the Department of Material and Production. Together, these form an action-oriented, interdisciplinary approach to teaching entrepreneurship that is directly inspired by the years of creating and running WOFIE.

Finally, the researchers connected to WOFIE formed the Digital Disruption Consortium as a platform for interdisciplinary research activities; the group helped, for example, the LEGO Brand Group regarding disruption. Moreover, this group has attended several ISPIM conferences, where they have co-authored interdisciplinary papers. They recently published a book, *Investigating Disruption—A Literature Review of Core Concepts of Disruptive Innovation Theory*, which 'shares knowledge collected from 2015 and onward within the Consortium for Digital Disruption anchored at Aalborg University' (Lundgaard and Rosenstand, 2019: 5).

REFERENCES

Buijs, J.A. (2012), *The Delft Innovation Method: A Design Thinker's Guide to Innovation*, The Hague: Eleven International Publishing.

Chikszentmihalyi, M. (1990), *Flow: The Psychology of Optimal Experience*, New York: Harper Perennial.

Cross, N. (2007), *Designerly Ways of Knowing*, Basel: Birkhäuser Verlag AG.

Lundgaard, S.S. and C.A.F. Rosenstand (2019), *Investigating Disruption: A Literature Review of Core Concepts of Disruptive Innovation Theory*, Aalborg: Aalborg Universitetsforlag.

McDonald, S., F. Gertsen, C.A.F. Rosenstand and C.H.T. Tollestrup (2018), 'Promoting interdisciplinarity through an intensive entrepreneurship education post-graduate workshop', *Higher Education, Skills and Work-Based Learning*, **8**, 41–55.

Rosenstand, C.A.F. (2012), 'Case-based learning', in N.M. Seel (ed.), *Encyclopedia of the Science of Learning*, Berlin: Springer Science & Business Media.

Rosenstand, C.A.F. and N. Tribler (2012), 'WOFIE, linear to agile learning design', in *Design for Learning 2012*, paper presented at the 3rd International Conference Exploring Learning Environments, Copenhagen, Denmark, April.

Sarasvathy, S.D. (2008), *Effectuation: Elements of Entrepreneurial Expertise*, Cheltenham, UK and Northampton, MA, USA: Edward Elgar Publishing.

Tollestrup, C. (2011), 'Large scalable workshop for innovation and entrepreneurship', paper presented at the International Conference on Engineering and Product Design Education, City University, London, Design Society, September.

3. Innovation camp for nursing students: igniting an entrepreneurial spirit in three days

Gunn-Berit Neergård and Antonella La Rocca

The innovation camp described in this chapter is addressed to third-year nursing students at Norwegian University of Science and Technology (NTNU). It aims to introduce students to the need for innovation in healthcare and to enable future nurses to identify tasks that require innovation in their everyday work. This is done by providing students with real-life challenges from external stakeholders. The camp, which is a mandatory part of the bachelor's degree in nursing, is a three-day, action-based course run at the very beginning of the first semester.

DESCRIPTION OF THE INITIATIVE

The university that hosts the innovation camp is NTNU, the largest university in Norway. It has nine faculties and 341 study programmes; health is one of its strategic research areas (NTNU, 2018b). The innovation camp for nursing students at NTNU is inspired by a government document (NOU, 2011:11) highlighting the need for innovation as a strategy for increased knowledge in the healthcare sector. Nurses are the largest group of health professionals, both in Norway and globally, and they are expected to participate actively in the development of the healthcare system. In Norway, these expectations have been formalized as new learning objectives for nursing students (Kunnskapsdepartementet, 2018). The nursing faculty at NTNU has initiated the innovation camp to meet the changing learning objectives. The draft of the new guidelines for Norwegian education within health and social sciences states that future nurses should have insight into the effect of innovation in healthcare services. Furthermore, they should be able to identify and convey challenges related to the quality of systems or tasks that require innovation and to contribute to these processes (Kunnskapsdepartementet, 2018). Given NTNU's focus on 'innovative solutions to complex health challenges', the camp also addresses key challenges in the healthcare sector.

Table 3.1　　　Stakeholders involved in the 2018 camp

Organization	Activities and Role in the Camp	People Involved
NTNU Department of Public Health and Nursing	Initiator and executor	Four nurse faculty
Organization for youth entrepreneurship	Initiator and facilitator Provided a camp template	One manager and two advisers
Municipality	Provided real-life challenge Acted as mentors and jury members	Two council members and one nurse
University hospital	Provided a real-life challenge Acted as mentors and jury members	One nurse
Centre for Entrepreneurship Education	Provided a real-life challenge Acted as mentors and jury members Lectures: being a health entrepreneur; opportunities in nursing; pitching; teamwork	Three PhD students and former entrepreneurs One professor and one assistant professor
Student organization for entrepreneurship	Mentors	Four student entrepreneurs
MedTech start-up	Lecture (Skype): Being a nurse entrepreneur	One nurse entrepreneur

The three-day camp described in this chapter was first introduced in 2017 as part of the nursing education programme offered at NTNU. The camp was initiated in collaboration with an organization for youth entrepreneurship. External stakeholders were involved due to their position in local healthcare and entrepreneurship education, as listed in Table 3.1. A municipality, a hospital and a national centre for entrepreneurship education provided the groups with real-life challenges. These three stakeholders presented their assignments, served as mentors and jury members, and awarded prizes to the winning teams. The nursing faculty deemed the camp a success, and arranged new camps in 2018 and 2019, following the same set-up as in 2017.

The Camp Approach

Norwegian nursing education spans three years and leads to a bachelor's degree in nursing. Participation in the innovation camp is mandatory for the 204 third-year nursing students at NTNU as part of a ten-credit course called 'Nursing Third Year'. Some of the topics in this course include quality improvement and service innovation, health service development and welfare technology. The learning objectives related to the activities at the camp are to gain knowledge about 'research and development relevant for nursing', as well as to develop skills to 'use principles of quality improvement and patient safety in their work'.

To obtain credits for the Nursing Third Year, the students must write an assignment as well as attend 80 per cent of all lectures and other educational activities, such as participating in the innovation camp. Students who miss more than 20 per cent of classes must compensate with additional work. The students are evaluated through a written examination (NTNU, 2018a). A list of books, articles, reforms and reports constitute the material that students are supposed to read as theoretical underpinnings for Nursing Third Year. This curriculum includes two Norwegian books[1] relevant to the innovation camp. In addition, the innovation camp relies on a poster (Table 3.2) developed by the youth entrepreneurship organization. This poster presents a work process through 11 steps, starting with understanding the assignment, then searching for new ideas, choosing an idea, developing the idea and finally presenting it. Each step has different tasks and tips to help the students in their progress towards a clearly formulated idea. The students are encouraged to use this poster for organizing their work.

Other written documents in the camp included the programme, a team-contract template, a score sheet for the jury, a list of all students, a list of mentors and their mentoring slots, as well as an empty implementation plan for students to fill out. The implementation plan should describe the students' idea and their targeted audience. In no more than 300 words, the plan should also address the feasibility in terms of actions to be implemented and the related costs. The students have to list their 'unique selling point', as well as explain how they intend to communicate their idea. In the final part of the plan, they evaluate their satisfaction with the teamwork. Some, but not all, teams use the team-contract template to formalize their expectations to one another.

Activities

The class is divided into three main groups (A, B and C), and each group is split into ten smaller teams. Table 3.3 presents the camp programme. The first day starts with a welcoming plenary session, followed by work in teams, and closes with a new plenary session. Day 2 has an open schedule. The nursing faculty assigns rooms to all teams so that they can meet at the university campus and work on their assignments. Day 3 is designated for pitching. Juries select three winners based on evaluating criteria provided by the nursing faculty, listed in Table 3.4.

During the 2018 innovation camp, Group A received their assignment from the municipality, who asked the students to work on the following questions: 'If you were a user [of health and welfare services], what would you wish for? If you were the relatives of a user [of health and welfare services], what would you want?' The students were free to focus on either

Table 3.2   The poster provided by the youth entrepreneurship organization

	Step	Main Focus	Task 1	Task 2	Task 3	Tips
UNDERSTAND	1	The assignment	Everyone reads the assignment	Read it together		For whom? Where? Why? What?
	2	What do the stakeholders want help with?	Think alone	Everyone in the group: How do you understand the assignment?	Discuss	
	3	Do you have the same understanding of the assignment?	No? Go talk to a teacher	Yes! Go on		
IDEA HUNT	4	Find ideas that can provide solutions	Write down all the ideas you came up with	Everyone in the group presents their ideas	Write down the ideas that the group decide on	YES-phase. There are no bad ideas or questions. Talk to your mentors
	5	Gather knowledge	Gather knowledge	Discuss the ideas with your supervisors	Combine ideas. Make new ideas	
CHOICE	6	Find the best ideas	Choose favourite ideas	Everyone in the group presents one to two chosen ideas		Check: Do your ideas solve the assignment? If yes: Keep working on the idea. If no: Discard the idea
	7	Evaluation	By now, you should have 5–10 ideas that you are to evaluate	Keep your idea if the idea is innovative and if the solution is feasible	Discard the idea if it is not new or feasible	
	8	Place the idea in a diagram	Place the idea in a horizontal line, from impossible to feasible	Place the idea in a vertical line between 'seen before' and innovative		
	9	Choose one idea!	If you disagree or if it is hard to choose: Vote!			
PRESENT WORK	10	From idea to a business model	Develop the idea	Name and describe the idea. Who is the target audience? What is the purpose of the idea? Can it connect to earlier ideas? How to implement it?	Fill out a description of the idea in a paper. (The implementation plan for students)	This is what you will be handing over to the jury
	11	Create the presentation	Convince the audience and jury that you have the best solution			Get feedback from a teacher

one or both questions and to choose among all health and welfare services provided by the municipality. The municipality created an assignment with open questions to facilitate creativity among the students. This was a consequence of providing a too narrow assignment in 2017, where all students came up with very similar solutions. Students were encouraged to use their own private and professional experiences. The winners of Group A won a day at the municipality where they pitched their idea in front of the mayor's staff and had dinner with representatives from the board of the chief municipal executive.

Group B got their assignment from the hospital. This assignment was also broader than the 2017 edition. The hospital described four present and future challenges: (1) the increasing number of hospitalized patients; (2) the non-corresponding increase in the number of the hospital's employees; (3) how to manage and 'utilize' user participation; and (4) how to maintain their long-term outstanding performance. The document compiled by the hospital asked, 'How could we [the hospital] find good solutions to these challenges so as to reach our ambitions? You can choose the challenge(s) you would like to focus on'. The hospital further listed three stakeholders to keep in mind while addressing the challenge(s): the health minister, the population of Norway, and the employees at the hospital. In addition to the nurse faculty criteria, the hospital listed five criteria to assess students' solutions, namely the ability to identify a challenge, identify a target group, make use of unconventional methods, describe useful solutions and to hold an engaging and convincing pitch. Winners from Group B won a meeting with decision-makers at the hospital to present their ideas to see if the idea was viable and to get valuable feedback.

Group C was asked to solve a challenge by a national centre for entrepreneurship education. This assignment relied completely on the students' own experiences and motivations. The students were asked to identify and select a problem within the health sector and then to find one or two potential solutions. They received a template with six main takeaways and nine subsections as a framework for exploring the challenge. The template was designed to let the students work on defining the problem, describing the profile of the stakeholder experiencing this problem and quantifying the entity of the problem. Students were asked to describe and categorize current solutions and their shortcomings, as well as the new solution and key resources needed to create it. Further, the problem needed to be explained in relation to timing and current societal trends. The groups also had to explain potential ways of selling the solution and exploring the financial consequences of implementing it. Finally, students needed to list the individuals contacted during the project. Indeed, contacting relevant stakeholders in the sector was a condition of completing the assignment. Winners from Group C were awarded free guidance from a student mentoring service specialized in entrepreneurship and won a visit to the University's Venture Creation Program to present their ideas. In addition, all winning groups were awarded cinema tickets by the faculty of nursing.

How to become an entrepreneur in a week

Table 3.3   *Programme, Days 1–3*

		Time	Activity	Stakeholder Participating
Day 1	Plenary Session	08:15–09:15	Welcome to the innovation camp.	University staff, Department of Public Health and Nursing.
			The story of a health entrepreneur.	A health entrepreneur/PhD candidate, Centre for Entrepreneurship Education.
			Creative brainstorm, cooperation and team building.	University staff, Centre for Entrepreneurship Education.
		09:15–09:45	Assignment from the municipality.	A representative from the board of the chief municipal executive and a municipality nurse ambassador.
			Assignment from the hospital.	A nurse/quality adviser at the hospital.
			Assignment from the Centre for Entrepreneurship Education.	A nurse/PhD candidate, Centre for Entrepreneurship Education.
	Work	10:00– 15:00	Teamwork in groups. The faculty has booked rooms for teamwork. Mentoring is available from 11:00.	In total, three mentoring boards, one for each group (A, B, C). Each board consists of (at least) one representative from the assignment-stakeholders, one member of the nursing faculty, and one representative from the youth entrepreneurship organization.
	Plenary Session	15:00–15:45	Lecture about entrepreneurial opportunities in nursing, locally and globally.	A nurse/PhD candidate, Centre for Entrepreneurship Education.
		15:45–16:00	Entertainment from a student choir.	
	Work	16:00–17:00	Possibility for further teamwork in groups. The faculty has booked rooms for teamwork.	
Day 2	Work	09:00–17:00	Independent work on assignments. The faculty has booked rooms for teamwork.	A student entrepreneurship organization provided mentoring as an optional service for the nursing students.
Day 3	Plenary Session	08:15–09:15	Lecture about being a nurse entrepreneur.	A nurse entrepreneur presenting via Skype.
			Lecture about pitching.	An entrepreneur/PhD candidate, Centre for Entrepreneurship Education.
	Work	09:15–12:15	Work in teams to prepare a pitch.	
	Pitching	12:30–15:00	Each team pitching their idea in front of their own groups, A, B and C. Each group is located in different rooms and has its own jury. Each team has ten minutes in total for pitching and Q&A. A winner in each group is awarded at the end of the session.	Each jury consists of (at least) one member of the assignment stakeholder and one member from the nursing faculty. Representatives from the youth entrepreneurship organization participate in some juries. In total, three or four persons in each jury.

Table 3.4   *Evaluation criteria for the jury*

The group has clearly defined the problem and described and quantified the problem in a good way.
The group has clearly described and categorized potential solutions to the problem that exists today and potential issues with these. The group has clearly described its own idea for a solution.
The group has described the key resources necessary to solve the problem.
The group has explained whether the problem has been a constant issue or if it is caused by something in particular.
The group has described potential ways of selling its solution to the market and showing its economic consequences.
The group presents in a convincing and engaging way.

REFLECTION ON THE INITIATIVE

Some reflections on this initiative draw primarily on the experience and evaluations of the participants collected through 44 semi-structured individual interviews. Seventeen nursing students (11 female and 6 male) were interviewed both before and after the 2018 camp. Ten stakeholders (8 women and 2 men) were interviewed after the camp: four of these were nursing faculty (Anne, Lisa, Wendy and Sofie), two were representatives from the centre for entrepreneurship education (Marcus and Marion), one represented the youth entrepreneurship organization (Linn), one the student entrepreneurship education, acting as a mentor (Johan), one represented the hospital (Emily) and one spoke on behalf of the municipality (Mary). Most students and stakeholders had no or very limited previous experience in entrepreneurship. The respondents represented all stakeholder organizations that were involved in the camp, selected based on their willingness to participate in the project. All interviews were sound-recorded and transcribed, and all respondents' names disguised.

Among the reflections and evaluations collected, we have selected two aspects that, if addressed better, can improve the quality and effectiveness of the camp and similar initiatives. These aspects regard: (1) theoretical background and learning objectives, and (2) incentives and work efforts. In addition, we reflect upon (3) the development of an entrepreneurial spirit among nurses.

Reflection on the Camp Approach and Learning Objectives

The design of the theoretical and pedagogical approach of the camp has generated some controversy. The camp was designed to be related to a specific curriculum called Nursing Third Year. However, we found that stakeholders had no clear awareness of the content and aim of the curriculum. Anne, one of the organizers of the camp, said that the students were supposed to learn and use a framework for improvement processes presented in their textbook, as listed in the curriculum. However, neither students nor nursing faculty members, such as Wendy or Lisa, or other stakeholders, such as Marion or Emily, captured this information. Lisa said that there was room for improvement regarding the use of the curriculum. She missed a theoretical foundation in the planning and execution of the camp; to complement the action-based learning, 'the students should learn some terms, and the understanding of what they mean, and perhaps be tested in this with an exam'.

There was no consensus across stakeholders or students on the learning objectives for the camp. Student 12 puts it like this: 'I don't feel that the requirements were crystal clear ... The way I interpreted it ... we only needed to come up with an idea that could ...work in one way or another'. Our respondents reported on a variety of potential learning objectives that were important for each of them. Linn, the young entrepreneurship adviser, hoped students would learn a new way of working. Ann and Marcus highlighted a sense of achievement tied to creation and teamwork. Hospital nurse Emily wanted students to learn how to ask questions and argue their opinions, while nurse faculty Sofie focused on opportunity recognition. In terms of takeaways, some students felt they learned a lot about 'entrepreneurial processes'. Others, such as Student 10, said they learned how to find new ideas, but not how to implement them. Anne said the learning objectives of the camp required huge effort by the students, making them 'ready to act' in innovative processes: 'So, they are not only getting out of here with knowledge, they must know how to use that knowledge'. Student 1 disagreed, saying that the camp learning objectives required limited commitment from students: 'I didn't feel like that was a very high course requirement'. Johan, representing a student entrepreneurship organization, criticized the reliance on templates: 'There could have been a stronger emphasis on the problem, especially the value aspect of [solving] the problem'.

From these statements, we can see that neither the curriculum nor the learning objectives of the camp were clearly stated. This led to a variety of interpretations regarding the aim of the innovation camp. Some thought the learning objectives were set by the university; others perceived the requirements from the different stakeholders as learning objectives. This signified different learning objectives for the three different groups of students. To avoid negative effects in future camps, the nursing faculty should discuss and agree about the aim of the camp with invited stakeholders, and a clear set of learning objectives for all students, as well as a well-chosen curriculum, should be clearly communicated to the participants before the start of the group activities. A learning objective statement should be possibly combined with a rubric, a document that articulates the expectations for an assignment by listing the criteria and describing levels of quality from excellent to poor. This is a critical point for the success of the initiative, as a lack of clarity in learning objectives may affect the students' work efforts, as we will reflect upon in the next section.

Reflections on Incentives and Work Efforts

The second aspect that has generated some frustration, especially among students, is the incentives and work efforts. Based on observations and interviews, we know that several teams finished their work and submitted their implementation plan on the first day of the camp, not returning to campus on Day 2. Students explained this as a conscious choice not to invest too much effort in the assignment. Student 1 told us that her group thought the assignment was impossible to finalize in the time available: 'So, we scaled down our own expectations'. Thus, the students, although assigned with real-life problems, experienced the assignment as unrealistic and adjusted their workload accordingly. As one student put it, they felt they were not willing to 'turn the world upside down in one and a half days of teamwork'. Thus, some students' approach was to invest minimum effort in completing the task and take the rest of the time off. The fact that the camp was a non-graded activity reinforces such an attitude.

Student 1 explained how the work effort was a challenging team decision, as 'some students simply want to pass, while others wish to excel'. This student's team wrote a team contract, stating that they wanted to finish the work during the first afternoon: 'I think the time limited us. We agreed that this [assignment] was too big'. Several of her peers shared the feeling of being overwhelmed. Many interviewees repeated the sentence 'we only got three days'. Stakeholder Marion observed that unclear learning objectives could be an explanation for the varying work efforts. Students were unsure of what to focus on and seemed stressed about writing a half-page implementation plan. Marion told the students to choose an idea they believed in and were passionate about, as the jury did not expect to see a solution in three days. Nevertheless, some students chose the easiest pathway to hand in their implementation plan. In contrast, Student 5 was part of a team who met and worked during Day 2. She criticized the incentives put in place by the organizers, saying that grading or better prizes would have affected the students positively: 'We would have gone a lot further. We thought about it; this [assignment] was not even "accepted/not accepted". We just needed to do something'.

The organizers of the 2018 camp have already reflected on these issues and told us that, in the 2019 camp, they plan to replace the Centre for Entrepreneurship Education with a new stakeholder in the healthcare sector to allow all students to work with a potential employer, broadening the view of the job market as a nurse. They will also change the way mentoring is organized, providing a coach on Day 2 as well, which will probably have a positive effect on the work efforts during the second day, and thus on the outcomes of the camp itself.

Another aspect that emerged during the camp and that requires attention in future initiatives is the perceived lack of relevance of the entrepreneurship topic to nursing students. Indeed, students struggled to relate the camp activities to their future roles as nurses. Student 10 was confounded before the camp started: 'I certainly didn't think that our profession was going to start innovating'. Moreover, faculty member Wendy said, 'There is very little tradition to run a business in our [profession]'. The distance between the disciplines of entrepreneurship and nursing was a hot topic among both students and stakeholders. Building on this, students and stakeholders highlighted the mandatory participation as essential. Post-camp, Student 14 said, 'If [the camp] wasn't mandatory, there wouldn't be many attendees. Maybe not even myself. Still, I think it is important that we have had this experience … that we were enlightened to see opportunities, not having to wait around for others to solve the problem'.

We would like to highlight a specific characteristic of nursing students' life that might influence their level of involvement in the camp. Sofie explained that many students work shifts as nursing assistants: 'They have their priorities, and … many of them work alongside their studies. They have their obligations'. This is an aspect that substantially differs from other camps where practice is usually brought into theoretical study programmes and as such constitutes an element of novelty for students. Nursing students, paid for practising their future work, must find added value in the camp if they are to dedicate their time and effort to it.

As a final reflection on this issue, we would like to mention that we collected several nuances in desired work incentives. Some students simply loved to work on their idea (Students 10 and 13); Student 13 really wanted to win, and Student 12 disliked the competitive element. Student 1 was disappointed by the prizes, in contrast to Students 6 and 17 who would have worked harder if they had known they could win cinema tickets. As some longed for grading (Student 5), others praised the current solution, arguing that grades would increase stress and hinder creativity (Students 15 and 16). As we can see from the diversity of the students' feedback, it is difficult to envision an incentive and evaluation system that would satisfy all students. However, a form of evaluation (although different from the usual grading system to keep the activity distinct from a standard course) and the attribution of prizes that are of value (also symbolic) to students is advisable.

In sum, unclear communication of learning objectives, a sense of unrealistic time in which to perform the tasks, a lack of explanation of the relevance of entrepreneurship for future nurses, competition with practical and paid work, and ineffective incentives among students have shown a negative impact on work efforts and learning outcomes of students. Organizers should address these issues carefully.

Reflections on the Formation of an Entrepreneurial Spirit

Creating an entrepreneurial spirit among future nurses was quite a challenge for the stakeholders of the innovation camp, as most students had little or no prior knowledge or experience of entrepreneurship. We know from the previous reflections that several students entered the camp with scepticism towards entrepreneurship. Student 14 told us that while some students felt negatively about the camp, thinking it was only arranged 'to fill the schedule', others stated the importance of the topic, asking their peers to 'open their eyes'. Thus, there were nuances in the students' expectations of the camp before it started. While some students (12, 14, 16 and 17) had unclear or low expectations regarding the camp, others (Students 1, 8 and 15) were excited. Student 8 explained his eagerness by seeing himself as a participant in the development of healthcare and the nursing profession:

> I think this can be a good initiative … Our teachers have been good at pointing out that we, as nurses, must take some responsibility for the development within our own profession … it is us who have the experience and competencies and we have to use these, instead of letting others do it for us.

From this, we can see that some students were motivated to learn entrepreneurial skills to use in their future roles as nurses, while others did not see the relevance of including entrepreneurship in their study programme.

However, post-camp, more students clearly expressed a positive association towards entrepreneurship. Something happened in those three days that made them change their minds. Student 1 understood more about the relevance of entrepreneurship in her own context: 'I have seen more of what innovation is, and that it is needed in the health industry'. Student 12 learned that there is a huge potential to contribute to the challenges in healthcare: 'It gets clearer to me that anyone can be a part of it. You do not have to be a politician or a … researcher … anyone can have a good idea'. In other words, the students saw a closer link between the fields of nursing and entrepreneurship. Furthermore, they pictured themselves as potential actors in change processes: 'We have to get used to change; we need to change the way we think, the way we work' (Student 1). Student 6 said that she wanted to have her eyes 'wide open' when graduating as a nurse, 'not simply [taking] for granted that this is the way it is, and that's what we got'. In other words, she and several of her peers expressed a readiness to challenge the status quo to improve healthcare.

From the previous paragraph, we see that the innovation camp may have an impact on students' view on their future work: from striving to be good nurses given the current conditions, to trying to improve conditions in order to become even better nurses. A related aspect of this reflection is the challenge of maintaining this mindset after graduation when entering institutions as nurses. Several stakeholders expressed concerns regarding the possibility of succeeding with entrepreneurial initiatives in real life. Nurse faculty member Sofie reflected upon how the culture in a hospital ward or nursing home could differ from a training situation in nursing school. She had her doubts as to whether the entrepreneurial spirit of the students would be applicable in practice: 'It all depends on the door you face in real life. Whether it is open, and if it is easy to walk through, or whether it is closed, and you face a wall, where it is impossible to do anything'.

The challenge and importance of developing a certain confidence in future nurses was also part of our reflection regarding learning objectives. Some stakeholders wished for students to learn to speak up for themselves. We can cite Emily, representing the hospital, who said that having a reasoned opinion would be the most important learning outcome of the camp: 'If you want to be heard, it has to be well-founded'. Marion, the PhD student, agreed. As a former health tech entrepreneur, she had dealt with hierarchical tensions in healthcare, seeing that doctors often got the final word in discussions. Her opinion on this matter is clear: 'if the nurse says that there is a problem, everyone should listen, [understanding] why this is a problem for the nurse ... the doctor cannot decide what is a problem or not for the nurse—because they are not nurses, right!' From her longstanding frustration with healthcare hierarchy, Marion was convinced that nurses need support to learn how to speak up in the highly hierarchical environment they may face. She asked the students to be prepared not to accept 'no' for an answer. Several students report having gained more confidence during the camp, picturing the need to detect and pursue challenges in healthcare as an important part of their future role as nurses.

LESSONS LEARNED AND LESSONS TO SHARE

We have reported on the weaknesses and points of strength of this initiative, which have led to some learning points for the following editions and for other institutions that intend to start an innovation camp for nurses. First, we recommend clarifying the theoretical background and learning objectives of the camp. Given the unfamiliarity of nurses with entrepreneurship, it is likely that a sort of more tangible 'framing' would be more reassuring. Clearly stating the aim of the camp, an explicit set of learning objectives, as well as theoretically founded educational material, may help the students understand and better appreciate the purpose of the activities they are performing.

Furthermore, this may affect their time management and performance. More tangible framing does not mean renouncing the flexibility inherent in this camp, which has allowed stakeholders (professionals in the sector) to integrate learning objectives considered compelling for changes in the sector to take place. Rather, we think that this approach, oriented towards practitioners' experience in the healthcare sector, should be emphasized as it helps make the camp compelling (not simply mandatory). Involving stakeholders shows the relevance of entrepreneurship in nursing, and it is likely to affect learning incentives and the efforts participants put into the task.

Furthermore, grading students' performance in the camp should be considered to motivate students and stress the importance of the project. There is a need to find a good balance between an ambitious and feasible assignment for the time allotted so as to avoid the sense of unrealistic expectations that is likely to affect students' experience of the camp negatively. To place more importance on the process and not just the final solution, one could develop an intermediary milestone where students present and explain the reasons for their discarded ideas. The end result could also be made more tangible than a pitch, for instance, by handing in a prototype or a written action plan for the next few months, or by sketching a business plan. However, more in line with the principles of action learning, a short reflection paper could be delivered after the final presentation, once feedback has been received from the stakeholders involved.

Finally, an important part of the camp is to develop an entrepreneurial spirit. This new mindset of students might be fragile when facing the established hierarchies and organizational structure of healthcare institutions. It would be interesting to foster the entrepreneurial spirit of students through continuous training throughout the Nursing Third Year course.

THE UNIQUE ASPECTS OF THE INITIATIVE

The camp event examined in this chapter has several characteristics of a typical innovation camp, but it is unique in that it features the specific context of healthcare, addressing students with no previous exposure to innovation or entrepreneurship studies. It is offered by an academic institution to students who will become an important part of the healthcare sector, namely future nurses.

In order to highlight the unique aspects of the event as a tool to promote and sustain innovation and entrepreneurship in healthcare, we need to look at the background of the initiative. Nursing education in Norway has attracted increasing attention and is under transformation as a consequence of the societal changes impacting the healthcare sector. Growing demand for safe, high-quality, cost-efficient and effective services had led to constant pressure for change and transformative innovation in healthcare (Eriksson and Ujvari, 2015; McCline et al., 2000). There is a widespread conviction, based on rather extensive research, that there is a need for a bottom-up approach to innovation in order to achieve transformative innovation in healthcare. 'What's needed is innovation driven by doctors, nurses, administrators, entrepreneurs, and even patients who are devising new solutions to daily challenges' (Govindarajan and Ramamurti, 2018: 98).

Since nurses are one of the main categories of staff in healthcare, they are also an important target for entrepreneurship education. However, until now, there has been little emphasis on the inclusion of entrepreneurship in nursing education (Boore and Porter, 2010). In the past, entrepreneurship in nurse education has been overlooked because of other priorities in the healthcare domain, such as acceptance, standardization and prescription (Robinson, 2008). However, over the last few years, nursing education has empathically embraced interprofessional education, which has also led to the recognition that nurses should 'accentuate their talent in building and sustaining relationships within their health care systems' (Embree et al., 2018: 61).

There are several ways in which entrepreneurship could be included in nurses' education programmes. However, we believe that the complexity of the healthcare system in which future nurses will have to operate makes the camp described in this chapter an approach that can help foster entrepreneurship in healthcare. Indeed, the camp is a good arena for nurses to prepare for transformative innovation in healthcare in two ways: first, by developing the individual entrepreneurial attitude and skills of the future nursing personnel, and second, by improving the understanding of the organizational context and how it affects the innovation process in healthcare. This two-sided potential effect of the innovation camp is in line with findings of prior research in healthcare.

Healthcare systems are complex due to several reasons clearly identified in previous studies. Among these is the need for a multiplicity of actors and roles involved in a patient pathway and the related need for relational coordination to make it as smooth as possible for patients (La Rocca and Hoholm, 2017). Healthcare is a system that is extremely dependent on the dynamics of relationships among providers of care, in particular when innovation or new solutions are introduced. Rather than focusing solely on the origin of an innovation (opportunity discovery), studies of innovation in the healthcare sector have placed great attention on the processes related to putting innovation to work and the effects of innovation.

Several studies have observed that a change – a new technological solution, service or process – is likely to impact different categories of care professionals and their existing care practices (see, for example, Nicolini, 2007). The tension between the 'established' and the 'new' has been at the focus of several researchers studying innovation in healthcare contexts as it is where controversies arise (Hoholm et al., 2018). La Rocca and Hoholm (2017) observed the controversies that a relatively simple, newly introduced communication technology brought to an established system of practice, both internally to the focal hospital and between the hospital and the various health institutions with which it connected. That study showed that a simple and limited change brought to the surface latent tensions between doctors and nurses in hospitals but also that change can lead to issues of jurisdiction over certain tasks when these are spread among different healthcare actors, which is highly relevant for the role of the nursing personnel. In that particular case, the authors observed how nurses working in the hospital had different evaluative criteria in relation to discharge decisions that clashed with the criteria applied by nurses working at the primary level of care.

This line of research offers indications as to the role of local practices, according to which the same professionals (nurses in this case) receiving similar education and training can develop different ways of doing the same task. An effective collaboration among different actors requires avoiding the temptation of imposing one's own way of doing on others. Recognizing and understanding one another's work practices becomes crucial because of the presence of 'interconnected practices'. If the healthcare system implies interconnected practices, innovations in health context are inevitably 'networked', which puts the attention on the dynamics of interorganizational relationships, including power issues (La Rocca, 2018).

Overall, prior research on transformative innovation in the healthcare context suggests that there are two aspects that seem to be important for innovation processes in healthcare. One aspect is the generation of new ideas and opportunities by individuals; the other is the organization and management of the process of translating and putting the innovation to work locally. We find that the first aspect is often emphasized as the objective of initiatives that aim to enhance the innovation (creational exercises that aim to promote innovativeness), while the second aspect tends to be underplayed. Both aspects are challenging, but the second has been more emphasized in recent research as it has been shown that the pathway of innovation is anything but downhill once the brilliant entrepreneurial idea is found. The camp event we examined has the potential to affect both aspects positively.

The two aspects are interwoven, both in nursing practice and in the innovation camp event. If nurses lack a legitimate voice in a hierarchical system with a clear power asymmetry in favour of doctors, there will be no, or only limited, space for nurses to contribute new ideas. The formation of an entrepreneurial attitude for nurses thus goes through an empowering process, which means acquiring more awareness of their role and potentialities. The benefits of a sense of empowerment have been observed and documented: empowered nurses tend to feel more committed to their job, resulting in a higher level of performance (Leggat et al., 2010). However, it has also been observed that 'nurses often do not feel empowered to use their expert knowledge to devise innovative solutions that improve patient outcomes' (Goodyear-Bruch et al., 2017). A key to harnessing the power of nurses is to deliver educational content that improves leadership and influence skills, instilling confidence in nurses to lead change (Goodyear-Bruch et al., 2017). However, there is more than the creational part. To make innovations happen, the innovations have to be translated into local contexts, which requires a collective organizational effort.

The innovation camp described in this chapter has all the characteristics of an experimental healthcare arena in which to exercise both aspects: creating new solutions and finding ways to put solutions into practice by interacting with relevant healthcare actors of the solutions proposed. In a protected environment, such as an innovation camp, nursing students can anticipate and experiment with creational exercises and organizational issues related to innovation processes. A camp representing the real healthcare sector can accommodate the plurality of perspectives and voices that are always present in initiatives that aim to change existing practices. Such an initiative also shows participants the need to confront different perspectives and find a way to resolve or conciliate diverging perspectives and interests. Developing an awareness and understanding of the need for entrepreneurship, and the factors shaping the outcome of innovation processes in healthcare, is important for nursing staff because they can be active subjects of innovation initiatives or exposed to transformative innovations taking place in the current organization of healthcare.

The unique feature of the innovation camp is that, besides fostering traditional entrepreneurial skills, the camp permits participants to experiment and experience the importance of learning to communicate change and be inspired to question the existing framing of healthcare. We think that initiatives of this format, if well prepared, have the unique potential to infuse a mindset favouring innovation at the individual level while, at the same time, favouring the development of insight into the effects and hurdles of transformative innovation. It seems important that future nurses are confronted early in their study programmes with the challenges that their profession involves, challenges that go far beyond medical-related issues.

Unlike other innovation camps, which are traditionally more business-related and thus more generalist, this camp for future nursing personnel sheds light on the complexity of a sector like healthcare. If the camp has to be realistic and propose realistic challenges, it inevitably has to involve multiple stakeholders. The inevitable tension among different stakeholders should be accommodated in the camp as an important and valuable part of the learning experience. The innovation camp analysed in this chapter has only marginally and implicitly addressed this issue thanks to the initiative of individual instructors and not as part of the design of the camp.

We think that the camp could benefit from making use of stakeholders in order to create a more vivid debate around the selected challenge(s) and show the multiplicity of voices and positions around the challenges, which often contrast one another. The camp could thus become even more effective if various stakeholders with respect to innovation in the healthcare system were more directly involved. This refers to GPs, specialists, and various healthcare workers (in the private and public domain) who could be more actively involved. Direct involvement of other stakeholders in the innovation process is bound to make the 'contrary force' (Hoholm, 2011) more vivid in the experience of the participants and thus enhance the experiential learning of the organizational aspect.

In the same vein, the camp was clearly inspired, from a pedagogic point of view, by action learning, but the approach has not been fully followed or applied. Action learning means 'learning by developing ideas (plan) and testing them out in action (act), observing the consequences (observe), reflecting on the observations (reflect), questioning and, as a result, developing further ideas which, in turn, are tested out in practice and so on' (Bourner and Simpson, 2014: 127). If future organizers aim to exploit the benefits of action learning, they should consider following this approach in a more consistent way, in particular by including stakeholders in the preparatory phase and properly illustrating the principles of this approach to students and instructors.

To conclude, comparing the camp experience with previous studies on innovation in the healthcare sector, it appears clear that the role of practitioners, or academics with experience in healthcare, is fundamental to making the experience compelling and relevant for future nurses. The camp is a unique means to make the work of nurses different and possibly more attractive, which, given the potential shortfall of healthcare workers estimated by the European Commission, is a priority of policy makers. If governments are to guarantee an adequate level of care to all users, they have to work hand-in-hand with education institutions to create learning experiences as close as possible to real practice. We hope that the experience reported in this chapter can inspire institutions to introduce entrepreneurship in the curriculum of nurse training in various forms, such as the camp event examined in this chapter. However, if tangible results are to be achieved, we would also argue for the need to extend the exposure of nursing students to the topic of entrepreneurship beyond a one-off three-day educational event.

NOTE

1. Kristoffersen et al. (2016, Chapters 4, 6 and 7). Orvik (2015, Chapters 1, 2, 5, 6, 7, 9, 10, 11, 12).

REFERENCES

Boore, J. and S. Porter (2010), 'Education for entrepreneurship in nursing', *Nurse Education Today*, **31**, 184–91.

Bourner, T. and P. Simpson (2014), 'Action learning and the pedagogy of professional doctorates', *Higher Education, Skills and Work-based Learning*, **4** (2), 122–36.

Embree, J.L., Wagnes, L., Hendricks, S., LaMothe, J., Halstead, J. and L. Wright (2018), 'Empowering nurses to lead interprofessional collaborative practice environments through a nurse leadership institute', *The Journal of Continuing Education in Nursing*, **49** (2), 61–71.

Eriksson, N. and S. Ujvari (2015), 'Fiery spirits in the context of institutional entrepreneurship in Swedish healthcare', *Journal of Health Organization and Management*, **29** (4), 515–31.

Goodyear-Bruch, C., Altman, M. and K. Cox (2017), 'Empowering nurses to innovate at the bedside, then spread their innovations', accessed 29 October 2019 at https://www.healthaffairs.org/do/10.1377/hblog20171121.831571/full/.

Govindarajan, V. and R. Ramamurti (2018), 'Transforming health care from the ground up. Top-down solutions alone can't fix the system', *Harvard Business Review*, **96** (4), 96–104.

Hoholm, T. (2011), *The Contrary Forces of Innovation: An Ethnography of Innovation in the Food Industry*, London: Palgrave Macmillan.

Hoholm, T., La Rocca, A. and M. Aanestad (eds) (2018), *Controversies in Health Care Innovations: Service, Technology and Organization*, London: Palgrave Macmillan.

Kristoffersen, N.J., Nortvedt, F., Skaug, E.-A. and G.H. Grimsbø (2016), *Grunnleggende sykepleie*, Volume 1, Gyldendal Akademisk.

Kunnskapsdepartementet (2018), 'Høring om forslag til nasjonale retningslinjer for helse- og sosialfagutdanninger', 17 April, accessed 17 December 2018 at https://www.regjeringen.no/no/dokumenter/horing-forslag-til-nasjonale-retningslinjer-for-helse--og-sosialfagutdanninger/id2593119/?expand=horingsbrev.

La Rocca, A. (2018), 'Networked innovation in health care: a literature review and research agenda on the interplay of inner and outer contexts of innovation', in T. Hoholm, A. La Rocca and M. Aanestad (eds), *Controversies in Health Care Innovations: Service, Technology and Organization*, London: Palgrave Macmillan, pp. 247–78.

La Rocca, A. and T. Hoholm (2017), 'Coordination between primary and secondary care: the role of ICT-based communication and incentive system', *BMC Health Service Research*, **17** (1), 149.

Leggat, S.G., Bartram, T., Casimir, G. and P. Stanton (2010), 'Nurse perceptions of the quality of patient care: confirming the importance of empowerment and job satisfaction', *Health Care Management Review*, **34**, 355–64.

McCline, R.L., Bhat, S. and P. Baj (2000), 'Opportunity recognition: an exploratory investigation of a component of the entrepreneurial process in the context of the health care industry', *Entrepreneurship Theory and Practice*, **25** (2), 81–94.

Nicolini, D. (2007), 'Stretching out and expanding work practices in time and space: the case of telemedicine', *Human Relations*, **60** (6), 889–920.

NOU 2011:11 (2011), 'Innovasjon i omsorg', Oslo, Norway, accessed 29 October 2019 at https://www.regjeringen.no/contentassets/5fd24706b4474177bec0938582e3964a/no/pdfs/nou201120110011000dddpdfs.pdf.

NTNU (2018a), HSYK3004 – 'Sykepleie 3. år', accessed 12 April 2019 at https://www.ntnu.no/studier/emner/HSYK3004/2018/A#tab=omEmnet.

NTNU (2018b), 'NTNU – Facts and figures', accessed 18 December 2018 at https://www.ntnu.edu/facts.

Orvik, A. (2015), *Organisatorisk kompetanse. Innføring i profesjonskunnskap og klinisk ledelse*, Oslo: Cappelen Damm Akademiske.

Robinson, F. (2008), 'Nurse entrepreneurs', *Practice Nurse*, **36** (5), 11–12.

4. SEMIS (seedlings): sowing the entrepreneurial competences of first-year master's students

Servane Delanoë-Gueguen and Eric Michael Laviolette

DESCRIPTION OF THE INITIATIVE

The *Séminaire d'Initiations Entrepreneuriales* (Entrepreneurial Initiations Seminar; SEMIS) aims to instil entrepreneurial competences among a large cohort of first-year students enrolled in a three-year Master's in Management (MiM) programme. Its pedagogical objective is to enable graduate-level students to master a set of fundamental competences associated with entrepreneurial careers (Kyndt and Baert, 2015; Morris et al., 2013). These competences include persuasive communication, collaborative work and creative problem-solving. They are recognized as important skills for all careers (ManpowerGroup, 2018). Hence, SEMIS targets all students, regardless of whether they envision an entrepreneurial career or wish to pursue other professional paths and seeks to help them develop an entrepreneurial mindset (Robinson et al., 2016). In other words, this initiative takes an entrepreneurial approach to entrepreneurship education, thereby focusing on the 'creative process view' (Steyaert, 2007). Going beyond the traditional 'venture creation' focus, this theoretical approach intends to develop students' entrepreneurial mindset, enabling them to experience transformation potential and further preparing them to rethink the future of organizations and societies as a whole (Kuratko and Morris, 2018).

In practice, the design of SEMIS relies on two pedagogical methodologies of innovation and entrepreneurship that offer practical tools and concepts. First, the architecture of SEMIS was inspired by the design-thinking methodology popularized by IDEO around human-centred design (IDEO.org, 2015). This human and pragmatic methodology to problems and issues is relevant for a one-week intensive seminar. It enables students to tackle complex challenges in a step-by-step fashion, thus resulting in quick prototypical solutions that can be tested. Second, the content of SEMIS brings together selected tools and concepts through a 'practice view of entrepreneurship education'. As proposed by Neck et al. (2014), there are five practices: play, empathy, creation, experimentation and reflection. With a focus on practices as a set of varied activities, this methodology is complementary to design thinking as it is more precise as to the competences that students may acquire and develop, and their evaluation.

Starting up SEMIS

TBS is a French 'grande école', a business school of over 5500 students, that offers bachelor's and master's degrees, as well as executive education. It has been actively involved in entrepreneurship education for years, and its recognition is illustrated by the selection of its incubator as the reference student incubator for the region in 2018. TBS's flagship programme is a three-year MiM for which a new curriculum was released in September 2018. The pedagogical engineering that took place ahead of this release was the perfect opportunity to introduce a new seminar into the students' curriculum. Specifically, the MiM programme committee expressed their interest in a one-week entrepreneurial seminar to raise students' entrepreneurial awareness and instil entrepreneurial competences that could be practised and developed during their curriculum, regardless of their subsequent specialization choices. Having previously been involved in the set-up and running of the school's incubator, the Strategy, Entrepreneurship and Innovation department had built internal legitimacy, which benefited SEMIS and ensured institutional support for the professors involved in designing this new seminar.

The seminar needed to be broad enough to catch the interest of all first-year students, not just those pursuing start-up projects, and narrow enough to be actionable within a week. As professors in entrepreneurship ourselves, we agreed to design and coordinate the seminar in an open and collaborative fashion with all members of our department. Initial discussions resulted in the idea of SEMIS (Seedlings), an entrepreneurial seminar with challenges based on the values of the school that would give students the opportunity to make concrete propositions to their own school, rather than to an external organization or company. Given this orientation, SEMIS was placed in the middle of the second semester, when students would have gained some initial knowledge about their school, given that it is the organization they were going to work on. This timing also enables them to deploy and reinforce the competences developed during the week in their subsequent courses and extracurricular activities.

Framing and Organizing Internal Challenges

Having the students work around their school's values is expected to foster a common sense of belonging to the school. However, for students to come up with actionable propositions, they need to be confronted with specific challenges. These challenges should be specific enough for students to appropriate them and for school collaborators to then act upon the propositions. To win students' commitment (Meyer and Herscovitch, 2001), organizers should make it clear that they, the students, are the primary beneficiaries of the solutions proposed. With this in mind, for each edition of SEMIS, we seek potential sponsors within the institution who are eager to propose such real-life challenges to the students, as illustrated by the 2019 sponsors and their challenges:

1. Boldness (Head of Pedagogical Innovation): 'Transform your student experience with virtual/augmented/extended reality.'
2. Excellence (Deputy Dean): 'Promote the excellence of our students during their studies at TBS: Light on your talents!'
3. Openness (Head of Internal Communication): 'Develop the TBS community by involving all its internal stakeholders.'
4. Responsibility (Head of CSR): 'Dare to implement gender equality in your student life.'

This second edition gathered 364 students who were then divided into 12 sections, each of which were placed under the guidance of a dedicated coach. Furthermore, each section was divided into four groups of students, each working on one specific challenge. Thus, there was a total of 48 teams split into 12 different sections. This setting, whereby groups within each section (and located in the same room) all worked on different challenges, was chosen to foster cooperation within sections while maintaining some emulation across sections.

The students were pre-assigned to the challenges. Allowing groups to choose their challenge might be feasible in smaller settings, but it is easier to prepare assignments in advance for such a large group. This also enables the organizers to ensure consistency across and diversity within the groups in terms of, for example, gender balance or students' original tracks (for example, mixing students from French and English tracks which are usually in separate groups). While this may initially cause some frustration, the initial activities help alleviate this frustration (as we will discuss in the reflection section).

Running the Initiative

In 2019, SEMIS started with a general launch session, during which the four internal sponsors gave a brief overview of their challenges and provided the students with general information about them. The students then attended their classrooms, which had been specifically configured for the seminar: each team had a dedicated space with a round table and a standard creative kit, including post-its, markers, electrostatic paperboard, scissors and so on. Students were informed that, throughout the seminar, they would use their brains, their hands and face-to-face interaction with others rather than usual ICT devices, such as telephones or computers.

As presented above, the design of SEMIS drew on both the design-thinking methodology (IDEO.org, 2015) and a practice view of entrepreneurship education (Neck et al., 2014). The objective was to get students to develop a set of skills related to creativity, opportunity, agility and interaction by working in teams to propose actionable solutions within four days. Throughout the seminar, the teams went through various phases aimed at helping them interpret the challenges, develop innovative ideas, understand their users, gather feedback, develop prototypes and present their ideas via different channels (Figure 4.1).

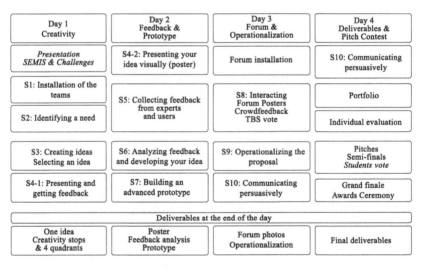

Day 1 Creativity	Day 2 Feedback & Prototype	Day 3 Forum & Operationalization	Day 4 Deliverables & Pitch Contest
Presentation *SEMIS & Challenges*	S4-2: Presenting your idea visually (poster)	Forum installation	S10: Communicating persuasively
S1: Installation of the teams	S5: Collecting feedback from experts and users	S8: Interacting Forum Posters Crowdfeedback TBS vote	Portfolio
S2: Identifying a need			Individual evaluation
S3: Creating ideas Selecting an idea	S6: Analyzing feedback and developing your idea	S9: Operationalizing the proposal	Pitches Semi-finals *Students vote*
S4-1: Presenting and getting feedback	S7: Building an advanced prototype	S10: Communicating persuasively	Grand finale Awards Ceremony
Deliverables at the end of the day			
One idea Creativity stops & 4 quadrants	Poster Feedback analysis Prototype	Forum photos Operationalization	Final deliverables

Figure 4.1   Outline of the seminar

Each day was organized with a precise objective in mind and deliverables to handle. On the first day, the objective was for students to identify an innovative idea and gather initial feedback from the other groups in their section.

The deliverables for this day included pictures of their paperboards used in creativity steps and a visual four-quadrant presentation of their idea.

On the second day, the students gathered feedback from experts and users using a visual prototype (poster), analysed this feedback to improve their proposition and developed an advanced prototype. At the end of the day, they delivered a picture of their poster, a one-page analysis of the feedback they received and a picture of their prototype.

On the third day, the students presented their proposition at a public forum and started operationalizing their propositions. They sent pictures of their forum booth, a retro-planning of their proposition, as well as a simplified budget.

Finally, on the fourth day, the students finalized the formal deliverables (a five-page action plan, a one-page summary and a three-minute pitch), undertook an individual evaluation based on a portfolio of photos of their week and assessed their peers' involvement. This last day culminated in a two-step pitch contest.

During the first day, it was essential to nurture a collaborative team spirit and some routines to facilitate interactions within each team. Coaches acted as facilitators to guide students and help them focus on how to be more empathic and improve their listening and communicating abilities. There were also regular moments when the coach invited the team members to step out of their team to present their work in progress (using storyboards, posters and so on) to other teams within the same section to receive feedback. Given that the teams in each section worked on different challenges, they were eager to share ideas and collaborate.

On the second day, going one step further, students had the opportunity to interact with individuals outside the classroom, an essential aspect of the experiential learning process, especially in entrepreneurship (Blank, 2013). Getting out of one's comfort zone is important to obtain relevant feedback. For this, we organized parallel 'speed-feedback' sessions in four different rooms (one per challenge). In each room, we gathered experts in a large circle. Then, two students from each team presented their initial solution with a poster and collected feedback from each of these experts (a bell rang every ten minutes to indicate that students should move on to the next expert). The experts comprised both insiders from the functional, academic and managing departments of the school, and knowledgeable outsiders (mayors, members of associations and so on). At the end of these feedback sessions, the two students were asked to list their key takeaways and discuss them with their team.

Simultaneously, the other team members collected feedback from potential users of their solution, mainly through face-to-face interviews 'off the street' (in the vicinity of the school). All the school's collaborators were invited to take part in this feedback-giving exercise. They had been informed in advance of the timing of the feedback-gathering session and kindly posted 'Welcome to SEMIS' signs on their doors so that students felt able to contact them. After gathering feedback, students reconvened in their classrooms to revise their propositions under the guidance of their coach. In order to reinforce the iterative nature of the process, they presented the improvements considered to their coach in writing. Having identified improvements to be made to their proposition, they then proceeded to build an advanced prototype to be used to present their idea at the forum the next day.

On the third day, students went for a second round of interaction in a more open fashion. We organized a general forum in the hallway of the school. Each team set up a stand where students presented their ideas with the help of a poster and a prototype. This forum was intended to give the teams the opportunity to show, tell and listen not only to their classmates and coaches but also to all the collaborators of the institution as well as some invited outsiders, such as the experts. A system of cross-challenge voting was implemented. For example, students from the Boldness challenge voted for their favourite Responsibility project and vice versa. Such cross-evaluation was intended to raise students' commitment but also the level of interaction within the seminar beyond their working section. Research in higher education has demonstrated that such peer evaluation helps students achieve learning outcomes that are related to skills such as persuasion and influencing (Faherty, 2015). Our seminar is in line with the view that the assessment of other students enables learning (Race, 2007). In addition, collaborators of the school (over 100 of them attended the forum) could vote on all four challenges. The most voted projects won the Collaborators' Favourite prize (one per challenge).

After the forum, the students went on to operationalize their propositions. This was meant to enable them to show the viability of their propositions by addressing budget and planning considerations, and to be part of their final action plan for their proposition. Once this was done, they started working on the final deliverables designed to communicate in a persuasive manner, which included written presentations of their propositions in the form of a five-page action plan, a one-page summary of their key elements, and a three-minute pitch, all to be delivered on the final day.

Finally, on the last day, after having completed the formal deliverables, the students conducted an individual evaluation. For this, they were first asked to build a photo portfolio of their seminar and then to reflect individually on the experience. They also evaluated their peer contribution to the process. The seminar culminated in a two-step pitch contest. First, as teams worked on different challenges, using a cross-voting system similar to the one described for the forum, students selected the finalist teams that would present to the sponsors (two finalists per challenge). This first selection relied entirely on the students' votes. The finalists then presented their pitches to the sponsors who selected the winners.

Altogether, this succession of activities is in line with the principle of guided mastery (Bandura et al., 1969): students' creative confidence (Kelley and Kelley, 2012) in their ability to do something is raised in a step-by-step fashion, where students experience the concrete implementation of their propositions and thereby engage in an effective learning process. Furthermore, the entrepreneurial experience is framed as an event (Morris et al., 2012), where students experiment with entrepreneurship during a specific intensive period in a specific space with creative resources.

Assessing the Entrepreneurial Competences of Students

The week was compulsory and resulted in the attribution of credits to the students. The grading incorporated a group component, which represented 70 per cent of their final grade, and an individual part for 30 per cent. In addition, the grading system was presented to the students in the introductory session and a detailed document presenting the grading system and each deliverable was made available to them on the school's platform.

For the group evaluation, five equally important criteria were assessed:

1. Persuasive communication: Perceived credibility and attractiveness of visual (posters and plans), material (prototypes), and oral (pitch) forms of communication.
2. Creativity: Degree of novelty and usefulness of the proposed offer or solutions.
3. Opportunity: Degree of desirability (social/market utility) of a solution as well as its feasibility (technical/economic).
4. Group functioning: Ability of the team to mobilize and organize itself to meet the challenge.
5. Organization: Ability of the team to leverage (or even create) available resources and integrate user feedback.

These criteria were assessed in a comprehensive manner (that is avoiding a 'classic' grade-by-deliverable format) by the coaches based on the deliverables presented above. In addition, finalists and winners were granted extra bonus points to their group grade. The individual part of the assessment relied on two items:

1. An individual reflection question (10 per cent of the grade) that was asked just after the students had completed the photo portfolio of their team's seminar. It was conducted online based on the following instructions: 'For this exercise, you will rely on your portfolio. Briefly express your

experience of the week. This reflection is free. The only expectation is your honesty. You can describe what you have experienced, felt, and learned. In addition, you can imagine how you can use this experience elsewhere, for the rest of your journey.'

    In addition, the importance of their involvement in the group activities was made apparent.

2. A peer assessment of the contribution to group work (20 per cent): 'For each member of your group (other than you!), please indicate whether he/ she: Didn't play the game at all; Contributed weakly; Contributed well; Contributed very strongly'. This was converted to points based on the average responses.

Finally, given the importance of attending all activities as each built on the preceding one, a penalty was given for students missing some activities.

REFLECTION ON THE INITIATIVE

It is more and more accepted that entrepreneurship is best taught through experience and practice, whereby students may transform entrepreneurial experiences into knowledge (Costa et al., 2018; Neck et al., 2014). As Neck and Greene (2011: 56) suggest, this leads to considering that 'experience supersedes education'. Hence, a key element for the future of entrepreneurial education will be the ability of educators to make the learning process experiential (Kuratko and Morris, 2018). SEMIS enables us to reflect on this shift in entrepreneurship education from course-related entrepreneurial learning to experiential entrepreneurial learning with so-called co-curricular activities.

Translating Experiences into Competences

As educators, we believe in the value of practical experiences for our students to grasp what entrepreneurship is about. However, it is also essential that such activities enable them to develop competences that they may transfer, adapt and develop beyond the scope of a condensed seminar. We therefore framed our programme around specific activities timed and paced in a sequenced way (as described in Figure 4.1) and related them to activities that entrepreneurs perform: ideation, prototyping, feedback collection and pitching.

    In other words, the activities that students perform are competence-based with the objective of sowing the basic recipes for creating ideas, turning them in prototypes, testing the solutions with users, improving them and finally persuasively communicating with different audiences. For this, we designed the experiences that we wanted our students to live with a set of practices partially borrowed from others (Neck et al., 2014; IDEO.org, 2015). We also enabled students to reflect on their lived experience of practices so as to develop their own portfolios of experience based on their different learning styles (Kuratko and Morris, 2018).

Kolb's (1984) experiential learning theory (ELT) provides a relevant model to reflect on the design of such a sophisticated practice-based view of entrepreneurial learning because its central focus is on learners' experience and their active involvement in transforming it into knowledge. It takes a pragmatic standpoint that shifts the focus to what the learners feel, think, watch and do. As a cognitive and situated theory, ELT is particularly relevant to analysing the learning processes of entrepreneurs (Corbett, 2005) as it suggests that entrepreneurial learning is an ongoing process, where actors build on different concrete experiences that they live or access via other people, and integrate them into their internal worlds and minds after reflective observation, before translating them into real life through experimentation.

Applying Kolb's circle to SEMIS enables us to reflect further on its design. Most of our activities started with concrete experiences that we wanted students to share as users around the four challenges. The activities during Day 1 enabled them to comprehend the problems that they face as users of virtual reality tools or when they face sexism, for example. Then reflecting on the problems they shared, they explored potential solutions that they had to expose within their section. The central movement here went from feeling (experiences) to watching (or observing) in a reflective mode to building knowledge from their experience and the experience of others.

The activities of Day 2 were framed around reflective observation and abstract conceptualization. Building on Day 1 intra-section feedback, students prepared a visual representation of their idea to be presented to outside experts and users. Such exposure was meant to collect feedback that could be conceptualized as observations based on the reactions of potential users and experts when shown the solution. Here, the movement went from watching or observing (reactions) to reflecting (on feedback) so that the students could theorize or conceptualize their solutions.

The activities of Day 3 were structured around abstract conceptualization. Given the different knowledge acquired through concrete experience and reflective observation, students were more confident in their ability to conceptualize a more advanced form of their idea. For them to demonstrate their idea more fully, we asked them to elaborate on a prototype that they had to show in a forum as their 'concept' to people outside. Consequently, the movement here went from thinking about their solution concept to doing by elaborating on their solution in reality for further exposure and tests.

Finally, the activities of Day 4 were meant to engage the students in active experimentation and concrete experience by pitching and selling their ideas to their peers (as potential users) to be selected for the semi-finals, and to the internal sponsors if they were selected for the finals. To some extent, this competitive stage was both a test of their oral persuasive abilities as well as the relevance of their ideas in front of potential users and supporters. Thus, it was an activity of doing that also resulted in feelings as students either felt galvanized or not by the reception of their ideas.

Furthermore, ELT also suggests that individuals may have different learning styles: the 'accommodator' transforms concrete experience into active experimentation, thus feeling into doing; the 'diverger' transforms concrete experience into reflective observation, thus feeling into watching; the 'converger' transforms active experimentation into abstract conceptualization, thus doing into thinking; finally, the 'assimilator' transforms reflective observation into abstract conceptualization, thus watching into thinking. In the design of SEMIS, we did not distinguish students based on their preferred learning style. Rather, our perspective was that the learning process might be more efficient if the learner goes through these different cycles and plays different roles. By temporally structuring the learning cycles, each team member has the opportunity to explore different learning styles. Reflecting on SEMIS through an ELT lens, we can see this seminar as an experiential learning scheme that enables the translation of experience into competences in an intensive and interactive learning environment.

Sustaining the Flow of Entrepreneurship in a Playful and Reflective Style

During the whole process, students discovered entrepreneurship through a set of activities that we formalized in great detail with the coaches, including specific instructions and dedicated time slots. This enabled us to be very clear about the objectives, resources and deadlines throughout the seminar. Time and activity management are indeed essential in such a seminar in order to avoid unexpected delays or interruptions, which could ruin the whole initiative. Furthermore, such formalization leaves time and space for students to express their creativity in an autonomous fashion, as they get the instructions through their coaches.

Still, it should be noted that the 'ramp-up' phase of the week is crucial. In fact, our coaches of the previous SEMIS session all pointed out that the first day of the previous SEMIS session was absolutely critical for students to engage in and commit to the process. Special care and attention must, therefore, be dedicated to the initial activities for them to 'bite in'. For instance, the coaches had to motivate students around the four challenges by asking them to build on their own experience. It was essential to capitalize on what students knew and what they were eager to learn (Schelfhout et al., 2004). Therefore, to frame the problem, each student was asked to share with their group members a story about his or her own experience of the challenge. The coach played a central role as a facilitator that took special care to enable each member to voice and find his or her place within the group, allowing the team to cooperate on learning tasks. All activities were meant to facilitate empathy and group contribution to raise mutual interest and commitment. As students became more and more familiar, enthusiasm rose. In our case, it manifested itself as students invading their creative space, and ideas materializing by words, images and colours, all around the area.

The level of engagement of students is a central aspect of experiential learning for entrepreneurial education (Schindehutte and Morris, 2016). One important dimension to building and maintaining such engagement is the gap between the students' skills and the contextual complexity of the experiential challenge at any point in time (Nakatsu et al., 2005). If the challenge exceeds the skills that the students can potentially have or develop, they will experience positive incongruity that may stimulate them to develop their skills. However, too high levels of positive incongruity may result in high levels of agitation and anxiety. On the other hand, if the students' skills or resource potential exceed those required by the challenge, they might experience negative incongruity that may produce experiences of boredom and ultimately lead to withdrawal. When the challenges and skills are relatively congruent, there is an experience of flow (Csikszentmihalyi, 1997). 'Flow is immersion based on high engagement and energized focus, where emotions are positive and aligned with the task at hand' (Schindehutte and Morris, 2016: 163). For such flow to be achieved, individual skill levels of the students are one dimension to consider.

However, to sustain such enthusiasm, there also needs to be a set of increasingly difficult obstacles that enable students to perceive their shifting from one level of mastery to another (Bandura et al., 1969). In our design, students go through several consecutive steps that are balanced in such a way that there are learning outcomes that relate to each stage. After completing one stage, the students shift to another stage where the learning outcomes are more challenging in terms of complexity and uncertainty. The first learning stages are mostly within-class with guided mastery of the coach and interaction with other peers through visual methods and constructive feedbacks. Then, the intermediate learning stages are both within and outside class to offer a more 'authentic' or 'more realistic' learning environment outside the school context (Schelfhout et al., 2004). The students must gather external feedback by exchanging with real experts and users before coming back to class to improve their ideas creatively and connect them to realistic user profiles. In the final learning stages, the students are mainly outside the class, engaged in more self-regulated learning. For instance, they have to organize their own forum stand to display their solution to a large audience, and for the finals (an oral pitch competition and final documentation), they must organize their team autonomously to deliver on precise deadlines.

Furthermore, achieving flow requires a rational phasing of learning outcomes and activities in terms of complexity of tasks, interactivity between team members and other peers and uncertainty related to openness to a realistic environment outside of class. This rational phasing needs to be carefully calibrated based on the feedback of the different participants. For example, we made some improvements between the first and second edition of the initiative in order to make the iterative process of feedback-improvement loops more apparent to the students. For the second edition, we increased the target amount of user feedback to be collected to 50 within two hours to motivate the students to go out and meet potential users. In addition, the students were invited to formalize the analysis of the feedback collected in writing and the improvements brought to their proposition as a result of this feedback.

Finally, during the first edition, there was a drop in enthusiasm after the public forum that concluded an intense period of creative work. Students may have got the idea that the general forum was the end. Thus, for the second edition, they were asked to develop the operationalization of their idea further after the forum. Managing the rhythm of this seminar with ups and downs is crucial for a better balance between intensive action and reflection. In fact, keeping momentum throughout the seminar is sometimes difficult. To achieve this, one change we made between the first and second edition was to schedule the seminar over four days instead of five. This resulted in a more intense first day, contributing to strong momentum from the start. It also gave a more upbeat pace to the seminar. Beyond the rational phasing of activities in terms of learning outcomes and activities, there is also an emotional dimension that seems crucial to sustaining flow. If emotions are intended to grow from the beginning of the seminar to the end, they are likely to vary between the major phases with ups and downs. The role played by the coach in specific moments when team members are going through emotional highs or lows is crucial.

The following quotation from a participant illustrates how students engaged in the initiative even if the challenge was not on a topic that they were interested in: 'Despite the fact that the theme of virtual reality was not necessarily one of my interests, I finally enjoyed working on it. So, sometimes, you have to learn to get out of your comfort zone and think about subjects on which you are not at first comfortable.'

Escalating Experiential Learning Before, During and After the Week

While we regularly encourage our students to participate in extracurricular entrepreneurial events, we believe that an event-based pedagogical seminar, such as SEMIS, enables an experiential learning experience that is more profound, reflexive and progressive. To pace this experience, we took special care to manage the reactions of the students before, during and after the event.

First, we chose to maintain a certain degree of uncertainty regarding what would be expected from the students during the week (as is the case for many entrepreneurial situations). Students knew that their week was blocked specifically for the seminar but had little information about its actual organization. We sent them a letter two weeks before the beginning of the seminar (thanks to Dr Heidi Neck for sharing this approach) highlighting the philosophy of the course, the engagement that was expected from students and the fact that SEMIS would use their school as its application case. Still, for the first edition, challenges based on internal school issues came as a surprise to most students. While the vast majority mentioned they really enjoyed and engaged in the experience after this first surprise, a few expressed disappointment that they would not be working with outside companies or were not being offered a business game. Managing these expectations is, therefore, important. As a result, for the second edition, we insisted on the fact that although the challenges were designed within the school context, they all represented 'real' issues faced by other organizations. The school was to be used as a privileged environment, one in which the students had direct access to information.

We also chose to favour practice over theory by engaging students in their activities rapidly rather than explaining what design-thinking principles or practice-based entrepreneurship are in advance. In experiential learning systems, a substantial part of the content is delivered through so-called co-curricular learning (Kuratko and Morris, 2018) where interactivity with different actors is central for exposing students to concrete experience either indirectly by interacting with knowledgeable individuals, or by active experimentation (Kolb, 1984) that also relies on interaction with other actors and non-actors (Latour, 2005). While experiential learning activities may be more theory- or practice-oriented (Schindehutte, 2013), we concur with Neck and Greene (2011) that even in practice-oriented challenges, there needs to be a reflective cycle that enables learners to reflect on their practices, on what they have performed in various forms (ideas, prototypes and so on), and relate them to the ostensive aspect of these practices that relate to intended 'methods' (creativity, prototyping, pitching and so on).

Therefore, for the first edition, after each set of activities (such as creativity), we planned short lectures, gathering all students to help them reflect on what they did previously. Thus, we organized lectures to 'theorize' and convey the message that their practices had theoretical foundations that they could expand on. However, the content and structure of these lectures needed to be revised as students evaluated them as being less useful in the seminar. The debriefing that we had envisioned in a large setting did not fit well in the seminar and felt somewhat disconnected from the other activities. As a result, for the second edition, we adopted a different approach by bringing this content back to the individual sections with the coaches. To achieve homogeneity among them, we produced short videos (around three minutes) to illustrate important concepts. These were then shown and discussed by the coaches in their individual sections and later put online. This perspective seems more in line with a fully experiential learning system where action and reflection are better articulated.

One of the important aspects of Kolb's (1984) experiential learning is to allow learners to move from concrete experience and reflective observation to abstract conceptualization and active experimentation. Such movement from feeling and watching to thinking and doing can be enabled through conceptual tools such as creativity tools (brainstorming) or methods (such as design thinking, and so on). In SEMIS, the coaches introduce practical tools to enable such thinking and reinforce the theoretical concepts to push students' abstract conceptualizations further.

Last but not least, to maintain the students' level of satisfaction, and prepare for the subsequent editions, following up on their propositions is also very important. As a result, a session is scheduled in the fall following each edition to present the actions taken by the school following this seminar. There, the internal sponsors present the results to the students. For the second edition, the realizations developed by the first edition were shown during the introductory session. For example, the students were shown pictures of a new innovative teaching room or of the new school app developed following the first edition

UNIQUE ASPECT OF THE INITIATIVE: BUILDING ON INTERNAL CHALLENGES

As entrepreneurship has become increasingly popular, many entrepreneurial initiatives now rely on event-based approaches to sensitize, initiate and train students to venture. The uniqueness of SEMIS is that it is built on internal challenges, and this has strong implications in terms of actionability and community building.

Actionability of an Entrepreneurial Seminar Building on Internal Challenges

Many entrepreneurial challenges rely on sponsors from the outside environment of the schools, such as existing businesses, start-ups or NGOs, for example. For SEMIS, we chose to offer the students the opportunity to work on and make a difference in their own working environment: their school. Our approach is somewhat intrapreneurial, with a willingness to make students realize that the school is an organization in which they are real stakeholders and in which they can act as they will later in their careers, with constraints and opportunities to pursue. Furthermore, working on solutions that they may benefit from later in their curriculum is a key success factor in creativity and innovation management systems. This may spark virtuous circles of participation and creativity as people experience the effects of innovation.

Defining the challenges required some important preparation in collaboration with the sponsors and several iterations. We held a first general meeting with all four sponsors prior to the first edition and had at least three subsequent meetings with each individual sponsor to improve the definition of the challenge and prepare its presentation to the students. It was important for us to involve various departments of the school. In addition, each challenge required the identification of a series of experts, which also necessitated planning ahead of the event.

This choice of internal challenges also gave the students and the school's collaborators a chance to interact in a novel manner. In fact, the expert feedback sessions and the forum provided great opportunities for them to exchange on an open basis and generated very fruitful conversations. The internal challenges revolve around issues that usually concern several stakeholders within the school, such as students, professors, managers and so on. They are complex problems in the sense that they are open-ended. There are different ways to tackle them and, furthermore, their resolution requires the students to (1) sense multiple needs in order to thoroughly understand the problems; (2) cooperate within a team to tackle these problems in a limited period; and (3) convince and engage different stakeholders to resolve them. Given the nature of such complex problems, their resolution develops high levels of empathy, interaction and cooperation.

In line with the human-centred approach of design thinking, SEMIS was thus organized to be a low-tech seminar where artificial interfaces were limited to favour face-to-face interaction. This is also central in the experiential learning process, favouring both rationality and emotion. In fact, some students participating in SEMIS highlighted that this experience had a positive impact on their perception of group work and real interactions. Brainstorming sessions with only paper and pens, prototyping together, or gathering face-to-face feedback highlighted the value of such interactions for them. One student said that it was good to leave 'phones, laptops and all these digital tools aside' to concentrate on 'eye-to-eye' exchanges with other classmates. Furthermore, many students underlined that SEMIS was central for team building, enabling them to get to know one another and establish good teamworking abilities that they could transfer to other activities. The quotation from a student below underlines how this seminar is positively perceived as an activity that enables students to collaborate with new peers in a short period. The realistic dimension of the challenge in relation to the school is also appraised, and the student realizes that the issue is most likely similar to other organizations beyond the business school itself.

> SEMIS is a good exercise. It allowed me to work in groups with people I didn't know. These are certainly busy days, but very interesting insofar as each of us has been able to put our knowledge and imagination to good use in the realization of a common project. This is all the more pleasant because the project carried out can really succeed; it is not just a case study of a typical company. Personally, I am very happy to be able to reflect on the future of the school and propose new ideas. Moreover, by reflecting more precisely on the past week, indirectly and without realizing it, we immersed ourselves in a company case. And it is in these situations that I learn the most. I had already done such a job but for a small structure (the project concerned only about 30 people). Here, we had to think bigger, and the means are also more important.

Building a Learning Community to Develop New Practices

Most entrepreneurial challenges build on experts and professors who come from entrepreneurial and innovation-related fields. Although our approach is based on those fields, we wanted to open the seminar to all professors at our school. Hence, the coaches came not only from strategy or entrepreneurship backgrounds but also from marketing, international business, accounting, law and consulting. Everyone learned during the process and took away some methods that they could use later in their teaching. The coaches involved also appreciated the unique interactions that this seminar enabled with the students. One of the coaches (a professor in business law) underlined:

> One of the specificities of the SEMIS is that it modifies not only the behaviour of students but also professors. . . . We change our posture. Except during the short periods (in SEMIS) when we present the methods, we are [mainly] here to reframe, engage, orient, etc. We only explain when students ask for it. [This is an opportunity] to observe how students [apply] the concepts that they have apprehended. It also creates a direct relationship with students, that a classical course cannot reproduce.

For the coaches, participation was voluntary. Nine months prior to the launch of the first edition, all professors of the school were invited to participate in this new pedagogical adventure. In addition, an external coach (a professional consultant) joined the team. Interested professors from various departments attended a preliminary information session where the general principles were presented. At the time, joining the team required some intrapreneurial spirit as the seminar itself was in its very early design stages. Part of the success of the initiative required the team of coaches to follow a similar schedule and present the same activities to the students. For this, we ran two training sessions for the coaches one month ahead of the seminar. During these sessions, they were taken through the same activities that they later walked the students through, and they provided feedback and suggestions that served to improve the initial design of the seminar. Ultimately, they were also provided with a detailed coaching book including presentational, explanatory and organizational aspects for each activity.

Moreover, during the seminar, we conducted briefing and debriefing sessions with the coaches so that they were clear about the expectations of the upcoming activities, could exchange their experience with the students and, when necessary, get further advice on how to run the activities. These sessions generated strong cohesion within the supervising group and enabled a constant improvement of the seminar design. While SEMIS was also a means to instil a change in the teaching practices of professors, it also benefited from their varied experiences. Our training sessions and the seminar itself thereby led to the formation of a bonded team of professors from various backgrounds driven by a common interest in continuous learning and improvement in pedagogical practices.

Although the coaches are central in this experiential pedagogy, SEMIS is also an inclusive seminar that is meant to engage other internal stakeholders in the learning process. As we underlined in the description, students are engaged in a learning process that encourages them to use their school as a learning environment, everywhere from the classroom to the school as a whole. To be able to engage all these parties in the learning process, there is a need to win and sustain institutional support of the organization. Therefore, one central aspect for such an initiative to be sustained is to communicate frequently in different formal meetings and informal gatherings with different members of the school, whether they be managers, professors, students or other faculty. It is also important to have strong official support from top management. Sustaining and developing such an initiative built around internal challenges is an intrapreneurial endeavour for coordinators.

REFERENCES

Bandura, A., Blanchard, E.B. and B. Ritter (1969), 'Relative efficacy of desensitization and modeling approaches for inducing behavioral, affective, and attitudinal changes', *Journal of Personality and Social Psychology*, **13** (3), 173–99.

Blank, S. (2013), 'Why the lean start-up changes everything', *Harvard Business Review*, **91** (5), 63–72.

Corbett, A.C. (2005), 'Experiential learning within the process of opportunity identification and exploitation', *Entrepreneurship Theory and Practice*, **29** (4), 473–91.

Costa, S.F., Santos, S.C., Wach, D. and A. Caetano (2018), 'Recognizing opportunities across campus: the effects of cognitive training and entrepreneurial passion on the business opportunity prototype', *Journal of Small Business Management*, **56** (1), 51–75.

Csikszentmihalyi, M. (1997), *The Masterminds Series. Finding Flow: The Psychology of Engagement with Everyday Life*, New York: Basic Books.

Faherty, A. (2015), 'Developing enterprise skills through peer-assessed pitch presentations', *Education + Training*, **57** (3), 290–305.

IDEO.org (2015), *The Field Guide to Human-Centered Design*, Canada.

Kelley, T. and D. Kelley (2012), 'Reclaim your creative confidence', *Harvard Business Review*, **90** (12), 115–18.

Kolb, D.A. (1984), *Experiential Learning – Experience as the Source of Learning and Development*, Upper Saddle River, NJ: Prentice Hall.

Kuratko, D.F. and M.H. Morris (2018), 'Examining the future trajectory of entrepreneurship', *Journal of Small Business Management*, **56** (1), 11–23.

Kyndt, E. and H. Baert (2015), 'Entrepreneurial competencies: assessment and predictive value for entrepreneurship', *Journal of Vocational Behavior*, **90**, 13–25.

Latour, B. (2005), *Reassembling the Social: An Introduction to Actor–Network Theory*, Cambridge: Oxford University Press.

ManpowerGroup (2018), 'Révolution des compétences 2.0'.

Meyer, J.P. and L. Herscovitch (2001), 'Commitment in the workplace: toward a general model', *Human Resource Management Review*, **11** (3), 299.

Morris, M.H., Kuratko, D.F., Schindehutte, M. and A.J. Spivack (2012), 'Framing the entrepreneurial experience', *Entrepreneurship Theory and Practice*, **36** (1), 11–40.

Morris, M.H., Webb, J.W., Fu, J. and S. Singhal (2013), 'A competency-based perspective on entrepreneurship education: conceptual and empirical insights', *Journal of Small Business Management*, **51** (3), 352–69.

Nakatsu, R., Rauterberg, M. and P. Vorderer (2005), 'A new framework for entertainment computing: from passive to active experience', in F. Kishino, Y. Kitamura, H. Kato and N. Nagata (eds), *Entertainment Computing – ICEC 2005*, Berlin and Heidelberg: Springer, pp. 1–12.

Neck, H.M. and P.G. Greene (2011), 'Entrepreneurship education: known worlds and new frontiers', *Journal of Small Business Management*, **49** (1), 55–70.

Neck, H.M., Greene, P.G. and C.G. Brush (2014). *Teaching Entrepreneurship: A Practice-Based Approach*. Cheltenham, UK and Northampton, MA, USA: Edward Elgar Publishing.

Race, P. (2007), *The Lecturer's Toolkit*, 3rd edn, London: Routledge.

Robinson, S., Neergaard, H., Tanggaard, L. and N.F. Krueger (2016), 'New horizons in entrepreneurship education: from teacher-led to student-centered learning', *Education + Training*, **58** (7/8), 661–83.

Schelfhout, W., Dochy, F. and S. Janssens (2004), 'The use of self, peer and teacher assessment as a feedback system in a learning environment aimed at fostering skills of cooperation in an entrepreneurial context', *Assessment & Evaluation in Higher Education*, **29** (2), 177–201.

Schindehutte, M. (2013), 'Play to learn and learn to play: an experiential perspective on teaching entrepreneurship', paper presented at the Experiential Classroom, University of Florida, Gainesville, FL.

Schindehutte, M. and M.H. Morris (2016), 'The experiential learning portfolio and entrepreneurship education', in M.H. Morris and E. Liguori (eds), *Annals of Entrepreneurship Education and Pedagogy – 2016*, Cheltenham, UK and Northampton, MA, USA: Edward Elgar Publishing, pp. 161–75.

Steyaert, C. (2007), '"Entrepreneuring" as a conceptual attractor? A review of process theories in 20 years of entrepreneurship studies', *Entrepreneurship & Regional Development*, **19** (6), 453–77.

5. Entrepreneurship and society: providing learners with a social lens on entrepreneurship

Emilee Simmons

Entrepreneurship and Society: Ideas, Opportunities and Value Creation is a short, two-week course or module (here on in) intended to provide a social lens through which to examine and explore entrepreneurship. The module is taught by the Centre for Enterprise and Entrepreneurship Studies (CEES) and developed for non-business undergraduate students who are enrolled in the Leeds University International Summer School (LISS) programme.

HISTORY AND CONTEXT

The Entrepreneurship and Society module is one of over 25 modules for the LISS programme. Similar to other institutions, the LISS programme is administered and managed by the university's central International and Study Abroad Office. In 2013 and 2014, the International Office approached CEES to create a module on entrepreneurship because the business school was yet to be represented in LISS, and business subjects were a growing request amongst incoming students.

LISS offers a holistic approach to short-term study-abroad programmes, whereby international undergraduate students undergo two 2-week modules throughout the month of July. Students can take the programme for fun or for credit; that is, in 2019 students passing both modules could receive up to 20 University of Leeds credits (equivalent to six US credits or 10 ECTS) (University of Leeds, 2019a).

In its entirety, students experience:

1. Academic learning between 9:30 am and 12:30 pm, Monday to Friday;
2. Fieldtrips to various sites (included across all academic learning modules);
3. Cultural and social activities separate from academics from 2:00 pm onwards;
4. Outings to discover the UK and the local region on the weekends.

When developing the module, we wanted to focus on society and social enterprise for several reasons. First, it is a unique selling point, as our competitor research showed that other institutions focussed more on traditional business start-up. Second, we had in-house expertise. This also allowed for experimentation with new approaches and materials. Finally, we designed the module around Post-Generation Y, who are less interested in wealth and want work to have meaning (see Smith and Aaker, 2013). Those in Post-Generation Y are more interested in areas of sustainability, which is driving employers to rethink their ways of working (Ng et al., 2010).

CEES is part of the University of Leeds, which is one of 24 Russell Group universities known for their research and academic achievements. The university provides a full spectrum of undergraduate and postgraduate degrees with an average of 35 000 students each year, representing over 170 different countries and approximately 8700 staff representing at least 91 different countries (University of Leeds, 2019b).

CEES originally stems from the creation of the Centre for Excellence in Teaching and Learning (CETL), funded by the Higher Education Funding Council for England (HEFCE) from 2005 to 2010 (The National Archives, 2008). As part of the 'White Rose Consortium' (2019), the Universities of Leeds, Sheffield and York established the first enterprise CETLs with the aim of embedding enterprise education across each university so that entrepreneurship was not an 'add on', but instead was offered via a full spectrum of activities, from the academic to the practical (White Rose Consortium, 2019).

Originally called the Enterprise Centre, CEES began with a focus on delivering academic modules on enterprise and entrepreneurship across the University of Leeds. In 2015, the Enterprise Centre rebranded as CEES as a way to showcase the new academic direction, which now includes a growing portfolio in research and scholarship. CEES activities run in parallel with the Spark! team, who focus on the 'extracurricular' or practical side of entrepreneurship, that is, running a business incubator, boot-camps and business plan competitions, to name a few. Although two separate entities, both CEES and Spark! collaborate and contribute to enterprise and entrepreneurship across the University (University of Leeds, 2019c).

Today, CEES and Spark! continue to work together in order to provide a holistic, vibrant entrepreneurship ecosystem across the university. We are internationally recognised for excellence, being named Entrepreneurial University of the Year (2015) by Times Higher Education, achieving Small Business Charter Gold status, and being awarded the Duke of York Award for Entrepreneurship (2015) and the Guardian University Award for Enterprise (2016).

THEORETICAL UNDERPINNINGS

In the UK, there is a separation between 'enterprise' and 'entrepreneurship' within education. Under the UK's Higher Education Quality Assurance guidelines, enterprise education builds on learners' 'awareness, mindset and capability . . . in short, having an idea and making it happen' (Quality Assurance Agency, 2018, p. 9), whereas entrepreneurship education builds on learners' enterprising competences that are directly related to being 'self-employed, starting a business or growing an existing business'. Enterprise education is, therefore, a foundational level whereby students learn how to put ideas into action within a 'risk free' environment before moving into entrepreneurship education, which is more action-oriented and 'real' (Quality Assurance Agency, 2018, p. 16). Although we teach both entrepreneurship and enterprise education, the philosophies underpinning CEES as a centre tend to fit within the enterprise education model. However, if we notice a student is inclined to start a new venture, we introduce them to Spark!

For this chapter, the phrase 'entrepreneurship education' will be adopted for the purposes of this book, combining both terms, as other countries around the world do not (normally) make the same distinction.

ABOUT THE COURSE

Entrepreneurship and Society is aimed at undergraduates who are at the mid-point of their degree, with the assumption that they have no previous entrepreneurship knowledge. To date, over 90 per cent of the students who have attended our programme fit this assumption; others had some form of general business knowledge.

The average class size is 25 to 30 students, compared to a typical CEES module, which averages 60. When students join LISS, they can choose any two modules across the programme. All students are international, with five to seven nationalities represented in the module each year (although the majority are from East-Asian countries).

Objectives

The objective of the module is for students to develop an understanding of entrepreneurship and the skills, attributes and abilities of enterprising people, as well as themselves. They should also gain an understanding of how entrepreneurship can be used as a vehicle to bring about social change.

Outline of Activities

Each year various people, all with different expertise and approaches, deliver this module. We therefore meet regularly to discuss our approach, make changes and brainstorm new ideas. Therefore, the outline below is a basic guideline (Table 5.1), and we encourage flexibility for anyone adopting it.

Pre-module learning

Six weeks before the start of the programme, we send a welcome email introducing ourselves and the pre-module learning. Since students are still at their home universities, we provide them with six short (8–10 minutes) introductory videos to introduce foundation topics in business. To support inclusive learning, materials consist of videos, podcasts, cases and reading. All are available online in the module area of our virtual learning environment (VLE).

Days 1–4: Social enterprise and society

The first few days of the course are where most of the knowledge of entrepreneurship in society is delivered. We begin with icebreakers to help break down communication barriers and celebrate cultural differences as a way to examine our own personal lenses of society. Then, as every student is international, we begin with the notion of what enterprise and entrepreneurship are.

In CEES, we take an active learning approach to education. We ask our students to 'learn in entrepreneurial ways' (Rae, 2010, p. 594) through experiential and active learning methods (see Jones and Iredale, 2010), including the notion that 'experience supersedes education' (Neck and Greene, 2011, p. 56). Therefore, in introducing social entrepreneurship (SE), we do not provide them with an 'answer' or lecture. Instead, we provide students with a list of various SE definitions from both academic and non-academic sources. Individually, they are asked to read through and star what is new to them and underline what surprised them. Then they discuss in pairs before a full class discussion, so that they have more confidence in voicing their opinions.

As raised by Pache and Chowdhury (2012), we can no longer teach 'about' social entrepreneurship, but we must educate students 'for' social entrepreneurship. This model of SE requires the blending of theoretical and practical experience of business with third sector and public policy or 'logics' by the authors. Thus, students are able to learn about the full spectrum of complexities around SE, including the fact that key aspects of such a business are different with regard to building an organisation to sustain social value (not just economic), different types of employment (that is, particularly volunteers), idiosyncratic legal status and specific funding patterns. Furthermore,

Table 5.1   Outline of the module

Day/Time	Day 1, Mon. SE	Day 2, Tues. SE	Day 3, Wed. SE	Day 4, Thurs. SE/NVC	Day 5, Fri. NVC	Day 6, Mon. SE/NVC	Day 7, Tues. SE/NVC	Day 8, Wed. NVC	Day 9, Thurs. Assessment
Morning (9:30 am–11:00 am)	Icebreakers About the module and assignments	Fieldtrip: visit local organisation – is this a SE? Cultural Visit: significant landmarks	Teams deliver practice pitch for formative feedback	SE case studies: includes international, opportunities and challenges	Conducting market research and understanding who your target market is	Icebreakers Using networking to build projects	Fieldtrip: visit local businesses, mixture of SE to corporates, start-ups to established businesses	Intro to pricing and costings, and how to insert into the pitch	Deliver team assignment: Dragon's Den-style pitch to a panel of academics, investors and entrepreneurs Module evaluations
Afternoon (11:00 am–12:30pm)	Intro to SE Intro to critical reflective writing	(9:30 am–3:30 pm)	Intro to team assignment and working in teams International Food Day	Intro to creativity: coming up with ideas and spotting opportunities	Time for group work	Intro to stakeholders and stakeholder analysis Time for group work	(9:30 am–3:30 pm)	Group work: support to finalise pitches	

SE includes different uses of resources (for example, subsidies, donations, fundraising, and so on) as well as different methods to assess performance (see Austin et al., 2006; Zahra et al., 2008, 2009; Pache and Chowdhury, 2012; Bacq et al., 2015). By utilising this approach, students gain experience in entrepreneurship through business, social and political lenses.

We educate 'for' social entrepreneurship throughout via our activities, covering a variety of international SEs in order to showcase the complexity of entrepreneurship. We focus on SE, using diverse teaching methods, such as role-play, business simulations and live projects (see Gibb, 2002). For example, we provide interactive case studies about SE, comparing the UK, USA and EU. Then, working in pairs, students conduct further research on the impact of SE in other countries, such as Jordan, Thailand and Columbia. In this way, we again bring society into entrepreneurship by examining the culture, meaning and impact of entrepreneurship in these countries.

In addition to this framework, the CEES ethos is 'learning by doing' (Politis, 2005) and undergoing real-life situations (Hampden-Turner, 2002), although we prefer to minimise the risk for students by employing a hybrid approach, that is, providing live projects like consultancy (Heinonen and Poikkijoki, 2006; also in Chang and Rieple, 2013) or learning through simulations and global classrooms (see Simmons, 2017; Simmons et al., 2017). Thus by Day 3, the students are thrust into the day-to-day of a typical SE through their first group work task (formative).

Students' first task is to visit an organisation and report back on whether or not it is an SE, justifying their answers with primary and secondary research. In the past, we have used a local art gallery that is at least 70 per cent self-funded through various activities, from trading to public funding and philanthropy. More recently, we have used a local charity that could be called an SE. They have a complex organisation that serves several societal needs in a deprived community, from childcare to employment, and healthy eating programmes to meal delivery services for the elderly and school children. There is a plethora of activity, some economic, some social and some working with the local government, thus providing the three 'logics' or lenses to understand social entrepreneurship better (Pache and Chowdhury, 2012).

Days 5–9
By the end of the fourth day, students are introduced to the notion of starting a business, which forms their group assessment, worth 30 per cent of their mark. We also integrate other learnings around developing students' creativity and the significance of stakeholders and networking. We regularly invite entrepreneurs with a variety of demographics and backgrounds to be speakers to humanise the practice of entrepreneurship.

Keeping to the societal lens, we have students use effectuation and social bricolage to build their group's new venture idea. Bricolage is a pattern of behaviour where social entrepreneurs can combine and extract resources 'out of nothing' or 'what is on hand' and apply these to new problems and opportunities (see Baker and Nelson, 2005; Dacin et al., 2010). Effectuation approaches idea creation through the interests of the individual and a set of decisions they make based on the rough notion of a good idea, with no precise product, service or venture per se (Sarasvathy, 2001; Sarasvathy et al., 2003). Entrepreneurs, therefore, use what they have, that is, skills, knowledge and resources available to them and apply this to their new business idea. By approaching students' understanding of entrepreneurship in this way, students gain an orientation to problem-solving and the creative use of resources, especially networks (see Fisher, 2012).

After discussing new business ideas, students are then led through activities to enhance their business knowledge. Areas include external forces (SWOT, PESTLE, competitors), who their target audience is and how to reach them (for example, focus on digital marketing, paying customers), as well as how much things actually cost to make and sell.

The group assignment

On the final day, student teams pitch their new business idea to a type of Dragon's Den (UK) or Shark Tank (USA) panel for their group mark. The panel consists of academics and entrepreneurs.

Students are allowed to create their own teams, consisting of three to four members. For the first task on SE, students are arranged in teams of three by the educators. We do this because the students do not yet know each other at the beginning of the programme, but by the group assignment stage, they should. However, there is a caveat: we show the students research on how diverse teams lead to better creativity and a working environment (Thomas, 1999; Kim et al., 2015) and, therefore, expect them to form teams with a mix of genders, ages, degree programmes and countries, where applicable. We also limit the number of members to four per team for ease of communication and teamwork.

The individual assignment

Instead of a single reflective essay of 2000 words delivered at the end of the module, LISS students complete ten daily 200-word reflections in their online journals. For those wishing to use this method, the journals were designed alongside the principals of Pavlovich (2007).

The first entry occurs prior to Day 1, with specific questions to support students' first reflections, especially for those with no prior reflective writing experience. From there, students are expected to make a new entry each day.

We provide reflective writing exercises throughout the main programme, including a final slide each day with guidance on how to reflect on their learning that day. Furthermore, we offer feedback on every third journal entry.

The benefits of this model are:

1. *Timely feedback:* Students receive feedback within days of writing their entries. For educators, it is a chance to correct any major issues sooner rather than later.
2. *Less stress:* Student feedback suggests that a single, large assignment at the end of a module is very stressful. Therefore, smaller, daily entries help students feel less stressed and focus on their writing, which can better support learners who are not used to reflecting.
3. *Ease in marking:* Instead of reading more than 20 essays, evaluators can break marking into smaller chunks. Marks can also be awarded for learners' growth and development over time, which is more evident in this approach.
4. *Visible engagement:* By breaking down the reflection into separate entries, we encourage students to be more engaged with each entry. This can deepen their understanding of their experiences, skills and engagement in learning.

The final pitch and question answering really inspired me a lot. The reflective writing is also very useful for study. (Student feedback, 2017)

REFLECTION ON THE INITIATIVE

Eye opening experience and module. Enterprising is not what I thought it was! (Student feedback, 2015)

Formal evaluations are conducted by the International Office in line with the university's standard module review scheme. The evaluation is anonymous and consists of two parts: eight questions about the module and four providing a self-assessment on their performance and engagement. Using a 5-point Likert scale, the students rate the module from 'strongly agree' to 'strongly disagree' (average 4.75 out of 5, or 96 per cent); they mark themselves on the same scale. The questions about the module are based on key areas, such as:

- Did it meet the learning outcomes?
- Was it structured so you could understand and follow?
- Was the tutor good at explaining things?
- Were the assessments clear?

However, in the first two years, we often had a lower score (typically 'agree' to 'neither agree/disagree') in an area that entrepreneurship educators may recognise and also struggle with: was the module intellectually stimulating? In the third year of the programme, we interviewed undergraduate students to find out why we scored so low in this regard. Students frequently stated that they associated 'intellectually stimulating' with modules being 'overly challenging' and 'hard to understand', whereas they saw our modules as practical and accessible, hence the lower score.

While we continued to make entrepreneurship accessible, we did use this new knowledge to make some changes. We found that if we took some tasks and 'unpicked' the theories underpinning them, we could highlight the significance and complexity to the students.

> The tutors are really helpful and fun. They designed different activities to help us know what we are learning, as well as helping us to apply. I love the teaching style of them. (Student feedback, 2018)

We also regularly use live cases through our Enterprise Ambassadors: a team of local business leaders and entrepreneurs who volunteer their time with us. We invite them to tell various sides of a case study and how the business has since progressed. In class, students apply theories to unpick the lessons learned, often with the entrepreneur in the room who then tells them about their own research into the topic. Thus, we have not only found a way to apply theories of entrepreneurship, but we have also been able to showcase how research is important beyond an academic pursuit and is essential to business success.

> Overall it is an enjoyable and interesting module as we are always having activities or field trip to enhance what we learn in classes. (Student feedback, 2015)

The four self-assessment questions provide the most diverse results. They are fantastic questions and a real eye-opener for educators. They include:

1. Q9: I attended all/most of the teaching sessions;
2. Q10: I did the module readings;
3. Q11: I participated in seminar discussions;
4. Q12: I found the virtual learning environment (VLE) easy to use.

Questions 9 and 11 are also normally 'agreed' or 'strongly agreed'; However, Questions 10 and 11 may be common or cautionary tales for educators looking to conduct such a programme.

With regard to Question 10, when we first ran the module, we foolishly applied the same reading materials from a normal 11-week module to this intensive nine-day module. We asked students to read the book *Maverick!*

(Semler, 2001) as their pre-learning. It is an autobiography about a young Brazilian's journey from almost bankrupting the family business to turning it around by going against the 'norm' in business management. Although those who read the book found it useful and interesting, students' feedback stated that having to read an entire book before the module was too much. Again, these students are likely to be at their home university and possibly finishing their final exams before joining us in July.

From 2016, we introduced different pre-learning by reusing a set of 'flipped learning' videos that we created for another module on new venture creation for non-business undergraduate students. With each video averaging eight minutes in length, they are more accessible than an entire book. We now ask students to conduct further learning around these videos; this can be based on their own interests and disciplines. This way, students can apply their learning to their own situations and see the value in doing further research.

> The field trips and assessments were extremely interesting and relevant. I really enjoyed this module! (Student feedback 2016)

Question 11 is by far the most variable and the main element outside of our control, as VLE platforms across universities will always be different. Therefore, when you are creating such a course, make sure you keep this in mind. For our module area, we try to make it as simple and well-structured as possible. For example, we use as few folders as possible, with each one clearly marked as Pre-Learning, Learning Resources, Assessment Brief and so on. Within each of these folders, we also make sure subfolders are clearly labelled and that there are as few 'click throughs' as possible since people are no longer as used to clicking through multiple layers online. For more on the impact of learning design on student behaviour, see Rienties and Toetenel (2016).

Due to the small class size, informal evaluations and feedback can occur regularly. Having this connection with the students has also shaped the programme positively. For example, based on student feedback, we now introduce the summative group project earlier on Day 4, where in the past it was often introduced on Day 5 or even Day 6. Also, the costing and pricing sessions were added because students specifically asked for them because they wanted to understand these areas better.

Similarly, the issues with the pre-learning were highlighted by students' informal feedback, with one student stating in 2015, 'I didn't read the required book . . . a shorter reading would have been better for a summer course'. So, that year we discussed as a class what would be more useful. At this point, we showed the students the videos we had made, and together we picked videos we thought would be useful for future students.

WHAT WE'VE LEARNED

I have led and taught this module since it was introduced. Therefore, as a constant in the process, I have seen a lot of the changes over the years and have tried to integrate learnings from each iteration. For example, in the first year, we had a mixture of topics on SE, intrapreneurship and new venture creation. While this provided a diverse lens, it did not tell a coherent story. Thus, we refined the overall programme to first start with SE, which is then interwoven throughout the module to showcase entrepreneurship and society through new venture creation. Although the programme stresses that enterprise is 'more than just start-ups', the direction we have taken is more honed and refined.

Reflecting on the module, we have also come to realise that the administrative work can never start too early. If this is your first time running such a course, below is a basic outline of the main administrative tasks.

1. *Twelve weeks prior:* Send out a 'call for participants' to business contacts. This is for the two fieldtrips as well as live-case participation.
2. *Ten weeks prior:* Finalise teaching on the module and start holding preliminary meetings to discuss the module.
3. *Eight weeks prior:* Make sure all fieldtrips are finalised with any costings. Educators also meet again to discuss the organisations involved this year and any new materials or additional changes needed. Make sure the VLE is ready to go live.
4. *Six weeks prior:* Send the first email to the students, welcoming them to the module and providing instructions on how to use the VLE and start the pre-learning.
5. *Four weeks prior:* Send an email to the students, 'Only four weeks to go', to show how excited you are to meet them. This email also includes additional information about all the educators.
6. *Two weeks prior to starting:* Send an email to the students, letting them know about their individual assignment and providing them with some guidelines for their first reflection (due before the first class).

Also, keeping to a schedule is important. One year, we accidently left the call for entrepreneurs too late, and more entrepreneurs than normal were taking their holiday at that time. Due to this 'perfect storm', we had no entrepreneurs for our main fieldtrip. Being 'entrepreneurial', we contacted our university incubator, and student entrepreneurs came to work with our students.

Inviting students of Leeds who have started their own business was very inspiring. (Student feedback 2018)

Students' visit to the incubator and learning from entrepreneurs their own age played a significant role in boosting their confidence. In observing the students' behaviour with both experienced and student entrepreneurs, we found that our learners were much more relaxed and asked more questions of the student entrepreneurs. However, feedback showed that they also enjoy hearing the 'journey' stories from the experienced entrepreneurs. We have now structured the module so that both groups are represented.

WHAT OTHERS CAN LEARN

Building the Entrepreneurial Mindset

By entrepreneurial mindset, we look to enhance students' 'ability to rapidly sense, act, and mobilise, even under uncertain conditions' (Ireland et al., 2003, pp. 963–89). The time constraint of the module naturally lends itself to supporting this approach. However, we also structure the module to enhance this as well. For example, before the students step foot in the classroom, they are asked to act by reflecting on their decisions and expectations of the course. Then, the first day and all subsequent days are driven by activities that create a sense of urgency and mobilisation.

Our networking activity is a good example of this as students are given a chance to act and mobilise in uncertainty yet with limited to no risk (see Hampden-Turner, 2002; Heinonen and Poikkijoki, 2006; Chang and Rieple, 2013). For this activity, students are placed into five teams, each representing a different SE organisation. Each team is given a one-page brief on their organisation's background, context, motivations and available resources. They are given 15 minutes to read through the text and come up with a strategy to (a) find out who the other businesses are and (b) create and negotiate potential collaborative projects.

Next, we briefly introduce how to network and why it is important. This also sets up the ground rules; that is, students are not allowed to share their information sheets or simply ask, 'what resources do you have?' Instead, they need to treat it like a real networking event, which means shaking hands, introducing themselves and making small talk before discussing business.

Students then have 20 minutes to network before re-joining their group to discuss their findings. This is followed by 20 minutes of brainstorming potential projects with either a combination of some or all of the other organisations. We then interject with a brief introduction to the significance of 'social capital' (see De Carolis and Saparito, 2006) before teams network again to negotiate and discuss their initial project ideas. After another 20 minutes, groups convene again for 30 minutes to illustrate their final project(s) visually and build a three to five-minute pitch. After pitching their projects, students vote on the top projects, that is, which is most creative, most collaborative, and so on.

In the end, students learn that the activity is based on a real case of collaborative projects by the Green Business Network (2018). We unpick the theories behind the various phases of their collaborative projects while highlighting how this collaboration supported the entire network's vision and mission, which led to significant funding and awards along the way.

Supporting an International Cohort

If you have a variety of nationalities or a large number of international students, this needs to be taken into account when designing a module. For us, English is a second if not a fifth language for over 75 per cent of our students. Therefore, we cannot take anything for granted and make sure we explain, in accessible terms, everything we can, removing as many idioms and slang terms as possible. We also provide a variety of materials, that is, visuals, orators, videos, podcasts and reading, to ease students' consumption of learning.

Working in multicultural teams can also be rewarding but frustrating for students. Similar to research in this area, we have found that communication is the primary stumbling block for international teams (see Matveev and Nelson, 2004). However, if managed correctly, multicultural teams can play a positive role in class discussions and group performance (see Taras and Rowney, 2007).

We also make sure our students do not always have to speak in front of the entire class. This is why our activities centre on students first gaining confidence through completing individual tasks before being paired or placed in small teams for discussions. From there, we ask what the subject of the conversation was rather than asking for individual opinions. We find this helps to draw out the shy speakers, allowing them to speak about the task or their team, rather than themselves.

We also want to invite students to join in the conversation and not force our national understanding of business on them. This is why we utilise international examples across our module, but more importantly, we build activities around our students. Where applicable, we ask students to provide examples from their home countries or from research into other nations previously unknown to them. That being said, the students have also elected to join LISS in order to learn more about the UK and Leeds, so, we make sure to weave examples from across the EU, the UK and the Yorkshire region specifically.

Recognition of Timing

It may seem obvious, but the limited time allotted for these initiatives must be considered in all aspects of planning and delivery. For educators, this often means spending more time in the initial planning period to make sure the programme is coherent and achievable.

We have found it useful to create a visual map of learning outcomes, various activities, assessments and evaluations. From a student's point of view, this map should state expectations of when assessments are introduced, how long they have to work on them, and when they are due. From an educator's point of view, it should include the administrative duties around the entire programme, including any processes that need to be completed and when all paperwork is due.

This map also considers the level of participation and external pressures on our students, educators and external stakeholders. With regard to students, we take into account that they may have other responsibilities before, during and after the programme. For educators, the map focuses on efficiency so that processes, especially marking, can be better aligned with the programme, making it faster to complete. With regard to external stakeholders, we make sure they are well briefed and matched with activities they enjoy and feel comfortable with; for example, preferences related to public speaking, working directly or not with students, or providing access to their organisations only.

Involve your Wider Network

For years, we have successfully used these short initiatives to trial new partnerships and collaborations. For example, with the fieldtrips, we always ask a mixture of previously used businesses and new contacts. We also run informal catch-ups for the business leaders. This allows us to run through any logistics and for the previous businesses to share their experience, while the new businesses can share any concerns or questions about participating.

For panellists and guest speakers, we go through a similar procedure; however, individual investors and entrepreneurs may not have the flexibility to meet prior to the module start. For example, we ask panellists to arrive at least one hour before it begins. Again, this allows experienced panellists to share their experiences. We also ask them to stay after the event for an additional 30 minutes (max.) to meet with the learners and provide us with any feedback.

THE UNIQUE ASPECT OF THE INITIATIVE

How the Initiative Promotes Learning for the Faculty

The LISS module allows all educators space to breath, experiment and play. The module itself is not formally workloaded for our educators. Instead, we are given a small nominal fee, and it can form part of our 'citizenship' and collegiate commitments. Thus, it is not mandatory for us to teach, and we are invited by the International Office every year to continue or to rest the module. As a team, we therefore see this as an opportunity to try new approaches and materials alongside a unique cohort of students.

In designing activities, I have been inspired by 'guided play' (Weisberg et al., 2016). Thus, the educator creates activities around particular learning outcomes, but scaffolds in a way that allows for a learner's autonomy or free exploration of learning and discovery (see also, Weisberg et al., 2013). The networking activity previously mentioned is an example of this, as the perimeters are set, yet open to interpretation. The students are then free to explore and come up with new ideas, using the resources and discovery methods they wish. By the end, the reveal of the activity that is based on reality allows us to have a fruitful discussion.

We frame these types of initiatives as high-quality yet informal learning experiences. We openly encourage educators to think of this programme as a fun, innovative way to try out new approaches and materials in a safe environment. This may also include taking current teaching materials in need of updating, reimagining these activities and trialling them. Through this process, we also encourage group brainstorming and co-curricular development, so that best practice and new innovations are shared amongst the team.

We also encourage PhD students and early career academics to work with us on these initiatives, from planning to evaluation. This can give them a year's worth of learning compressed into a few short weeks. We have also found they help question any assumptions we may have made and provide new insights based on their own experiences at other institutions (both good and bad).

One of the other ways we use this course for pedagogical development is to support our PhD students in their teaching training. Calls for teaching assistants go out a few months prior to the start of the module, and we offer positions to all eligible PhDs, regardless of their discipline. We do this because what we cover is multidisciplinary within business, and we want to make sure that different areas of expertise are being fostered across our PhDs. In the end, this allows PhD students to be more employable post-PhD, and, for us as a business school, it means we have a wider pool of PhD students who can help teach.

PhDs are recruited at three functional levels:

1. Assessment and feedback only: Some of our PhD students may be very busy and cannot be on campus often, so they can help support feedback via the online blog and by attending the final day for the group assessment panel. These are often more senior students who have helped teach and mark before and may be near their viva, thus having little time but a desire to be part of the course.
2. Teaching assistants: These are individuals who are in the classroom to assist the educational leader and observe. These are 'green' PhD students who may not have taught yet or who need to build up their confidence before becoming an educational leader.
3. Session leader: These are individuals, typically placed in pairs, who lead the session for a day. These are mid- to final-year PhD students who are confident in the classroom or who have previous experience. No educational leader (full-time academic) is in the room with them.

By recruiting at these various levels, we are able to provide more teaching opportunities within a short time span, outside the normal term time. This allows PhD students to feel less stressed. They can also receive more timely feedback from educational leaders and peers through observation. Furthermore, the average small group size for Leeds University Business School is 50 students; at CEES, we average 65 in the room. Thus, having a group of 25 is much more comfortable an experience for our PhD students to learn how to teach.

REFERENCES

Austin, J., Stevenson, H. and J. Wei-Skillern (2006), 'Social and commercial entrepreneurship: same, different, or both?', *Entrepreneurship Theory and Practice*, **30** (1), 1–22.
Bacq, S., Ofstein, L.F., Kickul, J.R. and L.K. Gundry (2015), 'Bricolage in social entrepreneurship: how creative resource mobilization fosters greater social impact', *The International Journal of Entrepreneurship and Innovation*, **16** (4), 283–89.
Baker, T. and R.E. Nelson (2005), 'Creating something from nothing: resource construction through entrepreneurial bricolage', *Administrative Science Quarterly*, **50** (3), 329–66.
Chang, J. and A. Rieple (2013), 'Assessing students' entrepreneurial skills development in live projects', *Journal of Small Business and Enterprise Development*, **20** (1), 225–41.
Dacin, P.A., Dacin, M.T. and M. Matear (2010), 'Social entrepreneurship: why we don't need a new theory and how we move forward from here', *Academy of Management Perspectives*, **24** (3), 37–57.
De Carolis, D.M. and P. Saparito (2006), 'Social capital, cognition, and entrepreneurial opportunities: a theoretical framework', *Entrepreneurship Theory and Practice*, **30** (1), 41–56.

Fisher, G. (2012), 'Effectuation, causation, and bricolage: a behavioral comparison of emerging theories in entrepreneurship research', *Entrepreneurship Theory and Practice*, **36** (5), 1019–51.

Gibb, A. (2002), 'In pursuit of a new "enterprise" and "entrepreneurship" paradigm for learning: creative destruction, new values, new ways of doing things and new combinations of knowledge', *International Journal of Management Reviews*, **4** (3), 233–69.

Green Business Network (2018), 'About us', accessed 1 September 2019 at https://www.thegbn.co.uk/.

Hampden-Turner, C. (2002), *Learning in the Connected Economy*, Cambridge: University of Cambridge Programme for Industry; Open University.

Heinonen, J. and S.A. Poikkijoki (2006), 'An entrepreneurial-directed approach to entrepreneurship education: mission impossible?', *Journal of Management Development*, **25** (1), 80–94.

Ireland, R.D., Hitt, M.A. and D.G. Sirmon (2003), 'A model of strategic entrepreneurship: the construct and its dimensions', *Journal of Management*, **29**, 963–90.

Jones, B. and N. Iredale (2010), 'Enterprise education as pedagogy', *Education + Training*, **52** (1), 7–19.

Kim, H.K., Lee, U.H. and Y.H. Kim (2015), 'The effect of workplace diversity management in a highly male-dominated culture', *Career Development International*, **20** (3), 259–72.

Matveev, A.V. and P.E. Nelson (2004), 'Cross cultural communication competence and multicultural team performance: perceptions of American and Russian managers', *International Journal of Cross Cultural Management*, **4** (2), 253–70.

National Archives (2008), 'HEFCE: Centres for Excellence in Teaching & Learning', accessed 1 September 2019 at https://webarchive.nationalarchives.gov.uk/20081203000459/http://www.hefce.ac.uk/learning/tinits/cetl/.

Neck, H.M. and P.G. Greene (2011), 'Entrepreneurship education: known worlds and new frontiers', *Journal of Small Business Management*, **49** (1), 55–70.

Ng, E.S., Schweitzer, L. and S.T. Lyons (2010), 'New generation, great expectations: a field study of the millennial generation', *Journal of Business and Psychology*, **25** (2), 281–92.

Pache, A.C. and I. Chowdhury (2012), 'Social entrepreneurs as institutionally embedded entrepreneurs: toward a new model of social entrepreneurship education', *Academy of Management Learning & Education*, **11** (3), 494–510.

Pavlovich, K. (2007), 'The development of reflective practice through student journals', *Higher Education Research & Development*, **26** (3), 281–95.

Politis, D. (2005), 'The process of entrepreneurial learning: a conceptual framework', *Entrepreneurship Theory and Practice*, **29** (4), 399–424.

Quality Assurance Agency (2018), 'Enterprise and entrepreneurship education: guidance for UK higher education providers', accessed 1 September 2019 at https://www.qaa.ac.uk/docs/qaas/enhancement-and-development/enterprise-and-entrpreneurship-education-2018.pdf?sfvrsn=15f1f981_8.

Rae, D. (2010), 'Universities and enterprise education: responding to the challenges of the new era', *Journal of Small Business and Enterprise Development*, **17** (4), 591–606.

Rienties, B. and L. Toetenel (2016), 'The impact of learning design on student behaviour, satisfaction and performance: a cross-institutional comparison across 151 modules', *Computers in Human Behavior*, **60**, 333–41.

Sarasvathy, S.D. (2001), 'Causation and effectuation: toward a theoretical shift from economic inevitability to entrepreneurial contingency', *Academy of Management Review*, **26** (2), 243–63.

Sarasvathy, S.D., Dew, N., Velamuri, S.R. and S. Venkataraman (2003), 'Three views of entrepreneurial opportunity', in Z.J. Acs and D.B. Audretsch (eds), *Handbook of Entrepreneurship Research*, Boston, MA: Springer, pp. 141–60.

Semler, R. (2001), *Maverick!: The Success Story Behind the World's Most Unusual Workplace*, New York: Random House.

Simmons, E.L. (2017), 'Evolution in business simulations: a review of the SimVenture Evolution platform (www. simventure.co.uk), created by Paul and Peter Harrington', *Academy of Management Learning & Education*, **16** (4), 629–32.

Simmons, E.L., D'Angelo, D.C. and J. Cataline (2017), 'Global classrooms: creating international collaborative initiatives', in H.A. Wilder and S.P. Ferris (eds), *Unplugging the Classroom*, Sawston: Chandos Publishing, pp. 187–213.

Smith, E.E. and J.L. Aaker (2013), 'Millennial searchers', *New York Times*, 1 December.

Taras, V. and J. Rowney (2007), 'Effects of cultural diversity on in-class communication and student project team dynamics: creating synergy in the diverse classroom', *International Studies in Educational Administration*, **35** (2).

Thomas, D.C. (1999), 'Cultural diversity and work group effectiveness', *Journal of Cross-Cultural Psychology*, **30** (2), 242–63.

University of Leeds (2019a), 'Leeds International Summer School', accessed 1 September 2019 at https://www.leeds.ac.uk/info/125000/leeds_international _summer_school.

University of Leeds (2019b), 'About us', accessed 1 September 2019 at https://www .leeds.ac.uk/info/5000/about.

University of Leeds (2019c), 'Student enterprise', accessed 1 September 2019 at https:// www.leeds.ac.uk/info/128001/enrichment_opportunities/268/student_enterprise.

Weisberg, D.S., Hirsh-Pasek, K. and R.M. Golinkoff (2013), 'Guided play: where curricular goals meet a playful pedagogy', *Mind, Brain, and Education*, 7, 104–12.

Weisberg, D.S., Hirsh-Pasek, K., Golinkoff, R.M., Kittredge, A.K. and D. Klahr (2016), 'Guided play: principles and practices', *Current Directions in Psychological Science*, **25** (3), 177– 82.

White Rose Consortium (2019), 'Centre for Excellence in Teaching and Learning Enterprise', accessed 1 September 2019 at https://whiterose.ac.uk/projects/centre -for-excellence-in-teaching-and-learning-of-enterprise/.

Zahra, S.A., Gedajlovic, E., Neubaum, D.O. and J.M. Shulman (2009), 'A typology of social entrepreneurs: motives, search processes and ethical challenges', *Journal of Business Venturing*, **24** (5), 519–32.

Zahra, S.A., Rawhouser, H.N., Bhawe, N., Neubaum, D.O. and J.C. Hayton (2008), 'Globalization of social entrepreneurship opportunities', *Strategic Entrepreneurship Journal*, **2** (2), 117–31.

PART II

Start-ups and entrepreneurs from the university

6. SommarMatchen™: a student jump-start into the entrepreneurial life

Arne Jacobsson

SOMMARMATCHEN MATCHES STUDENTS WITH RESEARCH RESULTS FOR INNOVATION

The SommarMatchen is a summer programme started in 2007 for students with an entrepreneurial interest and researchers with commercially potential research results. The SommarMatchen matches one or two students with a researcher. The goal for the student is to verify the researcher's results and move the project one step closer to market as a product or a service.

The length of the programme is five to six weeks, and the first week includes a few crash courses and intensive coaching by experienced coaches from the University Tech Transfer Office. Goals and working methods are established for each project together with the coaches. From the second week on, coaching is more of a follow-up. The final week is dominated by preparing a report and an oral presentation describing the commercial possibilities of the research results. The pre-set programme and approved business ideas and research results, together with planned coaching, provide a jump-start for students' understanding of entrepreneurial life.

INTRODUCTION

SommarMatchen was created at Linköping University, located in the south-east of Sweden. Linköping University has about 4000 employees and 30 000 students and is situated in the region of Östergötland with approximately 450 000 inhabitants in an area of 10 000 km2. Linköping City, with 150 000 citizens, is characterized by a fairly large portion of high-tech companies, usually stemming from the company SAAB, which was founded in Linköping in 1939 and still develops and manufactures advanced aerospace products.

Linköping University's Tech Transfer Office (TTO) is called LiU Innovation and is more of a small venture-company formation organization than a patenting and licensing office. It is, therefore, commonly referred to as an Innovation Office.

But, since the most internationally used term is TTO, it is used in this chapter; hence, what would be tech transfer officers at a TTO are innovation advisers at LiU Innovation.

Since the 1990s, the university has been extensively involved in promoting start-ups and growing firms emanating from the university environment. Good examples of such activities are the ENP programme started in 1994, which aimed to support students and faculty in starting their own firms (Klofsten and Lundmark, 2016). Another programme in the university context is the Growth and Development programme, which started in 1996 with a mission to support firms to take the next step in their business development (Klofsten and Jones-Evans, 2013). These programmes have, over the years, attracted hundreds of entrepreneurs and technology-based firms in the region.

The university has two main tasks: generating knowledge and disseminating knowledge. A lot of knowledge is created that has the potential of creating a start-up company but struggles to find a form. The university also has many students who are eager and curious about entrepreneurship but have not found their way to it. SommarMatchen, therefore, strives to solve this equation and match students and knowledge together.

THE IDEA BEHIND SOMMARMATCHEN

In SommarMatchen, research results are delivered to the students, and the students can begin working on venture-forming questions immediately. In the short summer period, this is found to be efficient and prepares students for their first entrepreneurial journey, whether it is with the appointed SommarMatchen project or a later journey of their own.

The main objectives of SommarMatchen are to create more awareness of alternative carriers for the students; more entrepreneurial knowledge for students, researchers and entrepreneurs in the region; and more researched-based ventures. It also aims to move research results one step closer to market. The three matching components are the researcher, the student and the research results. The TTO manages the programme. The idea is that this matching will enhance the utilization of research results that have not yet found an entrepreneur.

The main results of SommarMatchen are:

1. Research-based ventures have been created;
2. Some of the students have become CEOs for the created ventures or for other ventures;
3. All students have learned more about how ventures are created;
4. Some students have later joined the innovation and entrepreneurial support system;
5. New student groups and new research groups in the university have been reached and have engaged in entrepreneurship.

After 12 years of running this programme, it is notable that young entrepreneurs from earlier SommarMatchen programmes show up in start-ups every now and then. It has also been noted that SommarMatchen has found its way into many corners of the university and is contributing to the entrepreneurial university.

SommarMatchen serves as an important tool to find different entrepreneurial pathways and create an entrepreneurial learning environment for students and staff (Perkmann et al., 2013; Klofsten et al., 2019). The idea of the entrepreneurial university is addressed in SommarMatchen by tying different university parties together, giving them a mutual goal of becoming entrepreneurial and supporting their work to reach that goal. SommarMatchen helps find new categories of researchers and groups of students curious about entrepreneurship. One of the reasons for this is that SommarMatchen is easy to access for beginners of all kinds. Furthermore, it has an easy to explain, pre-set programme and is packaged with broad marketing and a clear focus. It seems that both researchers and students feel a bit safer and more comfortable in the pre-set routines, especially with regard to the support included in the programme. SommarMatchen seems to have an intricate way of finding itself in all corners of the university.

SOMMARMATCHEN: CREATING A 'TURN'

During the programme, students receive coaching and support from innovation advisers at LiU Innovation, which is Linköping University's TTO. Coaching includes business coaching, entrepreneurial coaching and personal coaching. The aim is to give students a real-world experience; since everything is performed with real venture proposals, it is the real thing from day one.

In the first week, many students get confused simply because it is their first real job. For others, it is because they are being asked to perform as an entrepreneur, which requires them to find and create their own job-list and find out what they need to do by themselves. After some time, the students go from feeling lost and strange to feeling somewhat in control of their own situation and start to act more like entrepreneurs. With good coaching from the innovation advisers, this turning point becomes one of the essential student experiences in SommarMatchen.

SommarMatchen works with real projects approved by the TTO that have the potential to become a company at some point. SommarMatchen aims to educate and inform the student about entrepreneurship as one possible career path. The possibility for students to become CEOs of future ventures is encouraged throughout the programme.

Entrepreneurs that are used from outside the idea creation team are sometimes referred to as surrogate entrepreneurs (Lundquist, 2014). However, in many cases, surrogate entrepreneurs are experienced entrepreneurs with many years of experience and not entrepreneurial first timers like most students in SommarMatchen.

The matching of a student with a researcher makes SommarMatchen a unique programme. This process comes with some advantages, which will be discussed in the following section.

HISTORY: HOW IT ALL STARTED

SommarMatchen started in the summer of 2007 with only a few pioneering projects making up the concept. It has since been running every year with approximately 10 to 15 projects and 15 to 20 students per year. Students chosen for the programme originate from almost every major programme at the university, including design, computer science, psychology and mechanical engineering, with a slightly higher representation from economics and business-oriented programmes. Students from master's-level programmes are also more frequently represented than students from the bachelor's level.

In 2006, before the programme was launched, a few issues were identified impeding the start-up scene in the region. First, there was a lack of entrepreneurs in the area; good ideas and projects had a hard time growing due to this fact. Second, almost all students wanted a career in a big company or as a consultant after they finished their degree. They knew nothing or very little about ventures and small company formation. A third issue was identified with regard to university research-based business ideas, which very often slowed down during the summer. Some of them almost stopped for quite some time. On the other hand, it was noted that there were students with lots of energy and general curiosity who might be ready to try something new and different over the summer period.

A lot of planning was conducted before the first SommarMatchen took place in the summer of 2007. The first SommarMatchen started with a small number of students as a pilot project. The pilot went well and was evaluated by the university and regional actors. The idea, planning and execution of the first SommarMatchen were conducted solely by the author of this chapter. The programme was well received and delivered well. It expanded swiftly to include approximately 20 students and 10 to 15 projects per year. It has been running in equivalent size every year since the start and today engages several employees for a few hours a week.

The basic structure of the programme has not changed over the years, although incremental changes have been made almost every year. Sometimes they have been good and progressive and have been adopted into the programme; sometimes they have been less successful, and the programme has been changed back to the original format the following year. Overall,

SommarMatchen has shown to be a sturdy, solid programme with good basic deliverables year after year.

SOMMARMATCHEN PROGRAMME

The yearly SommarMatchen programme starts in December or January with a marketing campaign targeting researchers and then their applications for the programme are received. The TTO evaluates their ongoing projects and new applications. It selects the project to be matched for the summer at the end of February. From February to March, there is a marketing campaign that targets students; the selected projects are presented to students in a short, clear form, and they can apply to a certain project on their wish list. The students do not always get their first choice of project and sometimes not even their second choice. In March (occasionally in April), students are interviewed for their SommarMatchen; and in late April to May, they meet the researcher for the first time. If this meeting goes well, the student and researcher are considered a match, and the involved parties can start signing papers (non-disclosure agreements and employment contracts for the SommarMatchen). SommarMatchen's three-part match – the student, the research results and the researcher – must all 'click'.

In June, there are three to four weeks of work for the students. The first week is intense for both the students and the coaches. This first week of the period is crucial to a successful match. The coaches, TTO innovation advisers, have a delicate task to fulfil in the first week. They are experienced business coaches and practise situational coaching based on each student and project's special needs. This first week's intensive coaching – and a few two- to four-hour crash courses in cold calling, market analysis, sales and patent database searching – are fundamental to students over the course of the programme and in establishing their own true project. This means every project establishes its own goals and own methods of reaching the goals. As an example, almost every project includes market analysis, but the analysis is not performed in the exact same way for all projects; rather, it is performed in a situationally tailored manner for each project.

The student must make the turn, transforming and becoming a person who is in charge of his or her own to-do list. He or she must find the right way to manage arising situations. This turn is crucial for the success of the project, and the student will need support here. All weeks except for the first are similar and are based on the identified need for the project. In most cases, this is market analysis and something more, for example, building a prototype. Some cases have typical decision points in the middle of the programme where the project moves from a more general approach to a more in-depth analysis of an identified topic, for example, a specific branch of a market. In July, the students are released from the programme; they return in August for the final two to three weeks. Most past SommarMatchens have had six weeks of work.

In late August, at the end of the SommarMatchen, the students give an oral presentation and file a report of their work. For the oral presentation, an invitation is sent out to a small, select group of people, usually in the vicinity of the researcher, for example, parts of the research group. In case any confidential material is presented, all listeners must be carefully chosen and signed in under a secrecy agreement. Having a discussion following the presentation is usually very fruitful and reserving an extra hour for such a discussion is recommended.

In summary, the first week of the programme involves intensive coaching and crash courses, then three to four weeks of working according to the set goals. The final week is when things are brought together, including writing a report and preparing for a final oral presentation.

Every year, there is an internal debate as to whether all projects must be delivered by the TTO as early as February. It is always difficult for the TTO to deliver interesting projects in early February when all projects need to be at an 'interesting early start-up-idea-phase' three months later in early June. The TTO would prefer to delay this project selection date for at least one month or preferably two months. However, students find it easier to apply and locate an interesting project as early as possible. They also prefer an application time to tie in with their applications for other summer jobs. So marketing to and targeting students and explaining the content of the SommarMatchen is evidently easier when projects are set in February. This usually results in a couple of late but interesting research results looking for a match in April or even as late as May. Knowing about, matching and planning for this late addition, for example by interviewing a few extra students, makes this disruption easier to deal with, and usually adds a couple of fresh, important projects to the SommarMatchen.

Target Groups

Over the years, many discussions have occurred regarding how to reach different groups of students and researchers, and hence marketing and targeting techniques have changed slightly over the years. It is possible to distinguish a few different phases of students and researchers that did not necessarily change in the same year. Looking back over the years, a phase usually stretches over a period of two to five years.

Target group: researchers
In the first phase, researchers from engineering, electronics and physics were predominant. This was not due to any targeting. It was due to the simple fact that most researchers from this group were asking for SommarMatchens. In

the second phase, broader targeting was applied, and researchers from several areas asked for SommarMatchens.

During the third phase, a conscious choice was made to broaden the targeted researchers and approach all research areas in all faculties. This resulted in a broad spectrum of results and ideas. This conscious choice also broadened the accepted research cases, from 'this case must have a chance of becoming a great company', to 'this case must have a chance to do some good in society'. However, the first case, venture-forming projects, is still dominant.

During this broad third phase, highly influenced by a feeling of 'every project is probably a good project', some drawbacks can be noted. A few projects entering the SommarMatchen have turned out not to be in accordance with the goals of SommarMatchen. Here, we find researchers that, for example, create a 'fictive' problem just to make a case for SommarMatchen, with good intentions from the researcher and others who, for example, want to get basic information and a new platform with which to create their next course. This has little to do with entrepreneurship and, therefore, nothing to do with SommarMatchen. Luckily these projects are few, but there might be an increase in these cases when selecting projects as 'every project is probably a good project'.

Target group: students
In the first phase, master's-level students from engineering and economics were targeted. During the second phase, 'market analysis only', only economics students were targeted; therefore, the SommarMatchen was more streamlined. This was a bit easier to arrange but was found not to be the best for all projects.

During the last phase, 'the broad university phase', more teams of two students were arranged, including a goal to combine students with different majors into small interdisciplinary teams. In the 2018 SommarMatchen, the two-student pairing became a rule, and there were only teams consisting of two students per research project. This was, of course, fruitful for the projects but also incurred a higher cost per project. Even if one single student can deliver a good result, we conclude that it is always advantageous to use a pair of students for a better result in each project rather than a single student.

Future Phase

One prospect for the future could be a student working as an in-house consultant in SommarMatchen, rotating through all, or most of, the projects. This could be one or maybe two students from, for example, communications or business legal, working more as in-house consultants, as many will do in their future jobs. This would become a temporary, extended, cross-functional team and might create a positive shake-up for each project and force the project to reflect on their questions from new and different angles.

Team Building

'Together' is a leading word for SommarMatchen. From the start of a SommarMatchen, all students are placed in one big group. This works very well and makes the students feel comfortable. Conveying the fact that the students are selected from among many applicants and that they are 'this year's selected SommarMatch students' creates a positive atmosphere. Students are also placed in pairs, as they have been from the beginning in 2007. Sometimes they have one project to work on together, and sometimes two different but related projects assigned to two students. In this manner, each student is responsible for his or her own project and also works with a partner on both projects.

Over the years, it has been noticed that students are more creative when they work in pairs. Another way of creating teams that SommarMatchen has tried is to team up three to six students with somewhat similar projects and have them work together for shorter or longer periods. This approach also works well, especially during creative phases, where one or two students are not enough.

A welcome barbeque in the evening of the first day or during the first week, and some subsequent after-work events, are appreciated and start the team building early on. Due to the fact that most students are entrepreneurial beginners, one notable success factor is to kick-start the team building in the first week. Another important factor is that most of the market analysis needs to be done before the holidays in July when it becomes much harder to reach people and get good answers. Strong support from the whole team and the partners helps a lot in this.

REFLECTIONS ON SOMMARMATCHEN

Looking back over the years of SommarMatchen, some lessons are clearer than others; these are essential for a successful result and the reason why SommarMatchen is the long-lasting process it is, delivering results every year. The best projects and the less successful projects have been analysed. A great deal of effort has been put into understanding why some projects deliver less. The reasons and mechanisms behind this have been discussed among the coaches involved, and conclusions have been drawn and organized into the success factors listed in the next sections.

Choosing the Right Students

All student applications are read, and approximately 50 per cent more students than there are places available are interviewed in a regular employment interview. The excess interviews are a must both due to student mobility and in case of new research results being submitted late and in need of a SommarMatchen.

In the interviews, students are selected based on eagerness to learn about entrepreneurship and willingness to engage. If they have these, most things will fall into place during the programme. Previous experience, skills in the entrepreneurial field and skills in the field of the project are also considered along with other regular hiring criteria.

Choosing the Right Cases

The TTO chooses the projects; that is, the research results and the researcher they believe is in need of a SommarMatchen and has the potential to become a venture if the SommarMatchen shows positive results. Researchers from any faculty can apply. The number of projects the TTO can handle in a summer is considered. The students will need coaching from the TTO advisers, and the researcher will also need some support. The chosen timing, the summer period, helps a lot when the students are free and can focus on SommarMatchen only; there is less pressure on both researchers and the TTO.

Criteria for a good research result are, for example, good engagement from the researcher and a fairly easy to understand task for the student. Sometimes the research results are difficult for the student to understand; in these cases, the black box technique is used. If the research results are complicated, it really helps to have an early discussion on how the black box technique will work in the case at hand, before the case is admitted to SommarMatchen.

Marketing of SommarMatchen

SommarMatchen needs to be marketed both to the faculty and researchers and to the students. The TTO is, of course, well connected in both areas, but further marketing is needed. SommarMatchen is marketed via several on- and offline channels, targeting deans, PI and PhD networks, and uses regular research groups or department meetings scheduled by the TTO a few weeks before Christmas.

Coaching of the Students

All students have a coach who is reachable by mail or phone for quick answers. The coach is usually the same person from the TTO who was previously an innovation adviser who coached the researcher in the same project or knew him or her in some way before the programme. There is also a SommarMatchen coordinator appointed every year for the whole group of students, who spends time with students almost every day, answering questions, especially in the first week of the programme. Good coaching from day one is crucial to getting students to start quickly, which is especially good for market analysis and reaching the right people with the right answers before the Swedish nationwide vacation starts in July.

In the past, students have had their place of work close to and on the same floor as the TTO. Hence, it has been easy for the TTO innovation advisers to stop by to coach the students, especially during the first weeks when the students have a lot of questions that could be considered small, but which, in fact, impede their workflow. Of course, it does not take much effort for the students to knock on their coaches' office doors to ask questions, but avoiding these time-consuming interruptions helps students maintain a good speed.

Templates

Even though every case is different, there are a lot of similarities between most cases, and templates for reports, cold calls and other practical jobs can speed up the job a great deal. For many students, it is the first time they have real-life employment, and all supporting templates help them a lot. The templates used are as follows:

1. The need, approach, benefit, competition template (NABC): How to analyse a new idea and start working with it. The NABC template is a method and tool with many underpinnings and is well established in the start-up field. It was developed by Stanford Research Institute in California. In the first days, it helps student to make a quick overview of the opportunities they find, and it also helps them analyse and present reports and give oral presentations. It also gives them a language in which to communicate entrepreneurial questions to their coaches and one another.
2. Cold calls: How to call potential customers for information and leads. Many students have difficulty with cold calling and do not know what to say in these situations.
3. Patent search: How to find information about state-of-the-art ideas and technical solutions and competitors in the field. These competitors could eventually become partners or buy part or all of the project.

Crash Courses

Many students are entrepreneurial beginners, so a few two- to four-hour crash courses are always on the programme in the first week. Subjects for the courses usually include cold calling, market analysis, sales, patents and patent database searching, and go hand in hand with the templates. Some years, a few crash courses have been held as evening classes and sometimes even before the first day of the programme to get a good head-start.

Variations in Content and Execution Over Time

After a couple of years of running SommarMatchen, an attempt to streamline the programme was made. Since there is always a lot of market analysis performed, it was suggested to do market analysis only. This turned out to be good for the recruiting process and made recruiting simpler. However, for the projects and students as a whole, it became too narrow, and the students did not see the aspects of being an entrepreneur. So, after a short period, this attempt was abandoned, and SommarMatchen reverted to its original purpose of supporting the project ideas with what they need to move forward – which is many things but should almost always include market analysis.

In the last two years, there has been a strict stipulation of having two students per project. The students appreciate this, and it also improves the results generally, but it increases the effort required from the TTO substantially, and it is clear that some projects only have need of one student. This two-student stipulation also impedes some projects in the application phase that do not require an employee for a 10- to 12-week job over the summer. This new rule might be discarded in coming years or kept but with a few exceptions.

The length of the SommarMatchen has typically been six weeks, but five weeks have been tested; however, the students seem to need the sixth week to put the work together. The students get four weeks off in July when it is hardest to reach out to perform market analysis and contact the right people via mail or phone. It can be difficult to have a summer engagement divided into two halves like this, but it has turned out to be much easier than anticipated.

Interviews

To evaluate SommarMatchen, interviews are carried out. The persons interviewed come from three categories and have all been involved in SommarMatchen. These are SommarMatchen coordinators, that is, the persons employed by the TTO to take care of a SommarMatchen, researchers and students who participated in the programme. The interviews focus on SommarMatchen and its characteristic of matching students with someone else's idea for commercialization. The interviews ask how this is advantageous for students' development as entrepreneurs and, to some extent, how it raises awareness and commercialization maturity for the researcher.

The overall impression from the interviews is that the programme works, regardless of the participant's relationship to it. The students take the approach of examining the research result quickly and, with newly learned knowledge, move the project forward. On the way, they acquire real entrepreneurial experience in real case training.

In the interviews, the difference between programmes where participants use their own ideas and SommarMatchen's concept (where the idea is matched from someone else) is discussed from various angles. The vast majority of those interviewed speak about advantages, such as a quicker start and more mature view of the entrepreneurships' many aspects. A two-time coordinator for SommarMatchen commented:

> Other programme[s] where the student works with her own idea may provide for the risk where the students work 'only inwards', meaning the student will dig deeper into the idea as such, for example almost only developing some technology functionality. In the SommarMatch, you must start with relating to someone else's idea and maybe more important[ly], to someone else. This means that the students start by 'looking outwards' from the start and look for commercialization possibilities and true needs from customers. This creates new contacts in both the business and the support system. The students learn, and they have [an] easier [time becoming] entrepreneurs if they later chose an entrepreneurial carrier. A student from SommarMatchen who later start[s] a venture . . . is much quicker to get started and to consider all aspects of the entrepreneurship. They know more about what should be done from the beginning and . . . they already have a network. They get started in the right way, and in the right direction and a head up start is good for any start-up adventure.

The researcher side of the discussion includes the new situation of focusing on reframing the research, its goals and its ways of expression into something that fits SommarMatchen's framework. This is sometimes an unusual situation for the researcher and entails new thoughts and sometimes confusion (in a good sense). It must also fit the student. Hence, the researcher is forced into this new situation and new ways of writing regarding the same research but in a new context. At the same time, the researcher must aim for a sometimes new and uncomfortable goal: commercialization. This starts on day one for the researchers in the SommarMatchen application phase.

Another researcher that was interviewed believes a different group of students will be reached compared to those reached if SommarMatchen sought students with their own ideas for development. Students who would apply to such a programme would be more likely to become entrepreneurs anyway at some point. Now new student groups are reached and engaged, thus expanding the group of entrepreneurial students. Students who are given an idea by a researcher to investigate and develop, as in the SommarMatchen format, are given a starting point, instructions and support; therefore, many feel more comfortable applying. The researcher said this group would never apply to a programme using their own idea because they do not have enough confidence in themselves or maybe have never had a start-up idea themselves but are excellent entrepreneurs. This researcher further stated that SommarMatchen provides the evaluation ability and skill set for the students to analyse an idea. In this way, providing the students with support and using researchers' results, SommarMatchen creates entrepreneurs of students that might not ever have become entrepreneurs.

Interviews with the student group reveal more about new learning, new insights and how to make the turn from not knowing where to start, to having a full to-do list in need of prioritizing what is most important. A student who participated in SommarMatchen twice and now works in a start-up company said, 'As a younger person, you don't really know what to work with and you have not yet formulated your own idea. So, participating in the SommarMatchen makes you get going faster'.

A former coordinator from the group of organizers for SommarMatchen characterized the success of SommarMatchen as its size and the established programme. Everything is in place, and all thought through. The 100 student applications received for 20 places results in interested students and good matches.

This group also highlights the higher effect in learning for the students who learn by matching with someone else's idea and how it provides for rational venture-creating thinking. One interviewee, who first came in contact with SommarMatchen as a participating student and has now been a CEO for a start-up company for the past eight years, estimates that approximately 80 per cent of the students in SommarMatchen undergo an entrepreneurial experience.

THE UNIQUE ASPECT OF SOMMARMATCHEN

The actual match itself might be the most obvious unique aspect of SommarMatchen. The aspect of working with someone else's idea in a real case with the aim of starting a real venture is also often mentioned. Looking at the match and its three party criteria – the researcher, the student and the research results or idea – there must be a good unity to make a match. The researcher must have an interest in commercialization and be prepared to participate. Researchers' knowledge of commercialization is not required and can be provided by the TTO, but time to spend in five to eight meetings and answer mail is required.

The student need not understand all the technical details in the research results (this is on the researcher) but should be willing to learn. Over the years, it has also been apparent that some especially difficult to understand, technical research with difficult to embrace market situations can be just too cumbersome for a student. However, most students have surprised both themselves and their SommarMatchen coaches by understanding and grasping the necessary essence of the research results to perform and deliver a good job.

One characteristic of SommarMatchen is the planned and intense introductory week, including the crash courses to quickly reach the turn as described above. A lot of focus and effort is placed on speeding up the student and getting them on the right track from the beginning. If not a unique aspect, this could at least be seen as a solid trademark for SommarMatchen.

Impact on Society

Over the years, students participating in the programme have created a pool of entrepreneurs in the area. There have been some students who have joined start-ups both as CEOs and as partners, and others have started working with start-ups in advisory roles. It should be noted that impact on society is difficult to measure and somewhat anecdotal.

Students over the years who have only heard about the programme and those who apply for the programme but do not get the opportunity will, to a small extent, still become more familiar with entrepreneurship and might see it as an alternative career path. The actual existence of something called entrepreneurship has reached them.

Participating researchers, including some who did not previously see their research results as possible commercial cases, have had their results tested and evaluated and have learned about what is needed to commercialize. Researchers who have never thought about commercialization before have especially gained new experiences after SommarMatchen. Researchers who get a positive result from SommarMatchen are better prepared to continue along the path to commercialization. If the research results are not good enough for a commercial journey, the researchers will at least have gained some entrepreneurial knowledge and knowledge about different results and their possibilities. Hence, they are better prepared for their next commercial endeavour.

Outside University Matching

Most years, SommarMatchen has accepted a few outside matches. These come from the vicinity of the university, including from closely related research institutes or university start-ups. They receive the same programme but with one difference: they have to reimburse the TTO for the costs. At most, there have been three outside projects in one SommarMatchen, but in the past few years, this opportunity has been heavily restricted.

A few larger companies in the area who have heard about SommarMatchen have asked if it would be possible to arrange 10 to 20 matches over the summer for their company alone. Both the university and the TTO have so far said, 'Thanks, but no thanks', due to a lack of resources and a need to prioritize the in-house demand. However, this could be a developmental step for SommarMatchen in the future.

The Teacher's Exemption

For patentable inventions, Sweden has a 'teacher's exemption', meaning that the university cannot lay claim to the patentable inventions of teaching staff within Swedish education. This exemption exists in a handful of countries in Europe. In countries without this exemption, researchers normally get a fair reward originating from a patent and do not have the personal responsibility that the teacher's exemption puts on Swedish patenting teachers.

In my experience, working in an environment without the exemption at the University of California at Berkeley and with the exemption in Sweden, I see no reason why it would not be possible for SommarMatchen to run at a university without the teacher's exemption, maybe in cooperation with the TTO and the Department for Education of Entrepreneurship. If personal ownership increases the eagerness of a teacher or researcher in Sweden to participate in a programme like SommarMatchen, full ownership for the TTO could compensate for that.

CONCLUSIONS

Preparation for the first SommarMatchen took almost a year, and a lot of time was spent on different possible routes. The amount of planning and the number of meetings before the first SommarMatchen paid off from the beginning. The amount of workload per year decreased from the first years, and today there are a lot of pre-made forms, templates and routines to follow. SommarMatchen continues to develop.

All of the involved students and researchers develop their entrepreneurial skills, and the research results move one step closer to their market. One or two projects every year encounter the issue of there being no market or come up against some other serious problem, and the case is closed, which is also considered to be a good result. The researcher and the students both experience new insights and learning outcomes. Some of them even encounter a future they did not plan for in a new start-up. SommarMatchen has contributed to an influx of entrepreneurs in the area.

Using the summer period is advantageous, and the period's lack of other courses increases students' focus; students are, therefore, fully engaged both in time and in mind. They usually work and eat lunch with the other SommarMatchen students, and in this way, they are surrounded by entrepreneurship all the time. Students also sometimes get together in the evenings, for example, attending a barbeque or just socializing.

The students in SommarMatchen gain valued entrepreneurial experience in several ways, including formulating questions, training for cold calls and calling potential customers, but also by reading patents, interacting with researchers and presenting. One of the most important sources of experience is interactions with the coaches and the way they think. Courses, templates and the project stay with students for quite some time.

Another effect of SommarMatchen reported by some students is that they are given an insight into research and the research community. Many students actually spend five years at the university, studying and not seeing the research at all. They do not understand what research is about despite students frequently being in the same hallways and even in the same lab where research is being conducted. Hence, coaching, work-mates, templates, crash courses and someone else's ideas help give students a jump-start in entrepreneurial life.

REFERENCES

Klofsten, M. and D. Jones-Evans (2013), 'Open learning within growing businesses', *European Journal of Training and Development*, **37** (3), 298–312.

Klofsten, M. and E. Lundmark (2016), 'Supporting new spin-off ventures: experiences from a university start-up program', in S.H. De Cleyn and G. Festel (eds), *Academic Spin-offs and Technology Transfer in Europe: Best Practices and Breakthrough Models*, Cheltenham, UK and Northampton, MA, USA: Edward Elgar Publishing, pp. 93–107.

Klofsten, M., Fayolle, A., Guerrero, M., Mian, S., Urbano, D. and M. Wright (2019), 'The entrepreneurial university as driver for economic growth and social change: key strategic challenges', *Technological Forecasting and Social Change*, **141**, 149–58.

Lundquist, M. (2014), 'The importance of surrogate entrepreneurship for incubated Swedish technology ventures', *Technovation*, **34** (2), 93–100.

Perkmann, M., Tartari, V., McKelvey, M., Autio, E., Broström, A., D'Este, P., Fini, R. et al. (2013), 'Academic engagement and commercialisation: a review of the literature on university–industry relations', *Research Policy*, **42** (2), 423–42.

7. Entrepreneurship for research professionals: triggering transformative learning?

Ulla Hytti, Jarna Heinonen and Pekka Stenholm

In this chapter, we investigate a PhD-level course entitled 'Entrepreneurship for Research Professionals' and its elements and participants' reflections through the lenses of transformative learning. The course is targeted at doctoral students at the multi-faculty University of Turku (UTU), but it is open also to post-doctoral researchers with an ambition to work in or collaborate with business life. The course aims to expose the best and brightest in academia to entrepreneurship over a short period of time.

DESCRIPTION OF THE INITIATIVE

Context of the Course

Since its launch in 2013, the Entrepreneurship for Research Professionals course has been offered to all doctoral candidates at the University of Turku (UTU) to familiarize them with entrepreneurship. The aim is to widen their career perspectives from academia to business life. As a public university, UTU has seven faculties and about 20 000 students, including 2000 doctoral students. The role of entrepreneurship at UTU was amplified in 2015 when an entrepreneurial approach was included in the strategy of UTU (University of Turku Strategy 2016–2020) to support the development of an entrepreneurial university (Etzkowitz, 2014; Foss and Gibson, 2015).

The strategy emphasizes multidisciplinary research and education. As an entrepreneurial university, UTU pursues a strong influence and impact in academia and in society nationally and internationally. It has an interest in being a key player in developing businesses and society. By educating a new workforce and developing human capital for the labour market, UTU plays a vital role in the regional entrepreneurship ecosystem (for the entrepreneurial ecosystem, see Isenberg, 2011). However, this takes place in close collaboration with other actors who provide support (for example, start-up counselling, financing services, coaching and an accelerator programme for start-ups) for those engaging in entrepreneurship with an existing initial idea. However, activities that provide exposure to entrepreneurial thinking and behaviour have been missing, and this is the void the Entrepreneurship for Research Professionals course addresses.

Development of the Course over Time

The idea for the course was initiated by the University of Turku Graduate School (UTUGS) working committee, which is in charge of developing joint courses for UTU PhD students. The committee considered it important to provide an opportunity for doctoral students to widen their understanding of and skills in entrepreneurship and business in order to reduce the number of steps involved in entering business life after completing their PhD degrees. Therefore, the Entrepreneurship Unit at the School of Economics was asked to plan and organize a course on entrepreneurship as a part of the 'transferable skills' curricula offered by UTUGS. Besides the course Business Essentials, the Entrepreneurship for Research Professionals course is the only business-related, transferable skills course and the only entrepreneurship course included in UTUGS's curriculum. Naturally, UTU's curriculum has academically oriented PhD courses in entrepreneurship (covering the theories and methodologies of entrepreneurship research) for PhD students in entrepreneurship. However, the course under scrutiny caters to a much wider target group than just business or entrepreneurship students.

The first course was organized in 2013 with the objective of providing students with an introduction to entrepreneurship at the individual, company and societal levels. The course provided a theoretical perspective to entrepreneurship by applying traditional lecturing in a classroom format without a focus on the practical aspects. The course did not include any exercises for iterative business idea generation or experimenting with the entrepreneurial process in action. Passing the course was an academic exercise with learning through lectures, discussions and course readings indicating the participants' learning about the phenomenon of entrepreneurship (Fayolle and Gailly, 2008; Hytti and O'Gorman, 2004; Johnson, 1988). The learning outcomes were demonstrated through reflective individual learning diaries, which were graded as 'fail' or 'pass'.

The students' feedback suggested that they would have expected to learn more about business start-ups and about becoming an entrepreneur during the course. Nevertheless, the participants still reported that the course was interesting and that it opened up a new understanding of entrepreneurship. Therefore, the course was considered valuable by UTUGS, but the format and content needed a revision. In the following versions in 2015 and 2017, the course focused on more practical perspectives to entrepreneurship and start-ups. In the revised and current format, the learning outcomes cover the development of students' competences and understanding of the entrepreneurial process (Bacigalupo et al., 2016).

Additionally, we also took the course outside the university classroom. Currently, the course is run in a shared space (SparkUp Turku), which is located in the campus area and houses several players in the regional entrepreneurship ecosystem. The premises serve as an excellent platform for the course, which aims to familiarize the doctoral candidates with business life. Place is an important element for learning (Levinsohn, 2015), so this course has purposefully been organized outside university classrooms. This chapter focuses on the modified course format and the reflections thereof.

Participants from Different Faculties

The course attracts participants from each faculty of the multidisciplinary UTU, although the majority of the students come from the faculties of Science and Engineering, Medicine and School of Economics (Table 7.1). The course is held biannually, as decided by UTUGS. A total of 40 students have passed the course in recent years. Moreover, about 20 have participated in the course without submitting the final learning diary, which is a requirement for passing the course. The reasons for not submitting are mainly twofold: time constraints because of their PhD projects or having no need of study credits (ECTS) but remaining interested in the topic. The latter includes, for example, post-doctoral researchers and students who want to widen their entrepreneurial skills for their future career.

The highly interactive teamwork format in the current course benefits from the relatively small number of students enrolled in the course (approximately 15 to 20 per cohort). However, the impact of the course is limited due to this small number. Still, the diversity of the participants (coming from different disciplines – such as sociology, biomedicine, law and business – and different cultural contexts) is reflected in team exercises and related learning outcomes as we require teams to have participants from at least two different faculties.

When applying, students have to write a short letter of motivation that includes their reason for attending the course. In practice, all students who are able to justify their motivation are given the opportunity to enrol. Many students highlight their interest in entrepreneurship as they want to pursue entrepreneurial ventures and even business start-ups after obtaining their PhD diploma or at a later stage of their career. However, some of the accepted students do not show up once accepted into the course. Withdrawals usually take place after students receive the final programme and pre-readings. This indicates that these students

Table 7.1   *Students who pass the course*

Faculty/Year	2013	2015	2017	Total
Science and Engineering	8	2	3	13
Medicine	4	1	6	11
School of Economics	2	3	4	9
Education	1	2	–	3
Social Sciences	1	–	–	1
Humanities	–	1	–	1
Law	–	–	1	1
Total	**16**	**9**	**15**	**40**

have weak motivation, experience time constraints or are perhaps unwilling to work intensively during the learning camp. The letters of motivation also help the teachers design a relevant course programme. For instance, if the students have expectations that cannot be met, such as looking for information on how to register a business, or if their expectations are conflicting, this needs to be communicated to them. It is important to share with the students at the beginning of the course how their expectations will or will not be met. Consequently, the students are steered to the correct services offered by the regional entrepreneurial ecosystem.

Intended Learning Outcomes and Modes of Study

The course provides an introduction to entrepreneurial thinking and action, and it enables the participants to assess their own entrepreneurial resources. It aims to enhance students' understanding of what it takes to commit oneself to entrepreneurship and new business creation. Furthermore, the goal is to make the participants assess their own relationship with entrepreneurial thinking and action, which is understood as an idea and opportunity-creation process rather than a purely economic business activity.

The course covers a ten-hour learning camp and a two-hour wrap-up session held three weeks after the camp, as well as related pre-readings. Between the sessions, the participants keep a reflective learning diary of their experiences and readings. Table 7.2 outlines the course design.

The pre-readings provide the participants with conceptual tools that will help them understand the multi-faceted phenomenon of entrepreneurship and its implications at the individual and company levels. The pre-readings consist of selected scholarly articles on lean start-ups (Blank, 2013), entrepreneurial opportunities (Davidsson, 2015; Wood and McKinley, 2010), entrepreneurial behaviour and decision-making (Fisher, 2012) and academic and entrepreneurial identities (Jain

Table 7.2   *Course design*

Modes of Study	Key Points
Ten-hour learning camp	
(The exact exercises should be decided by the facilitators; below is a general approach.)	
Team exercise(s)	During the ten-hour camp, the actions range from
Problem-definition and idea-generation exercises	team building to validating a problem and its
Setting and testing the team's assumptions with	solution, and finally to conducting a demo and
tools, such as Lean Canvas	pitching competition.
Sharing learnings	An important aspect is to set aside the participants'
Demo and trade fair, at which the teams share their	PhD areas of expertise and ask them to focus, for
ideas	instance, on their passion.
Pitching competition	The key is to have a multidisciplinary group of
Reflection of the day	participants.
	During the reflection of the day, identity work is
	introduced to the participants.
Two-hour wrap-up session	
(Two weeks after the ten-hour camp)	
Reflecting on the learnings after two weeks in	The course is built on self-regulated and team-based
a joint group session	learning. These not only give perspectives for
	assessing learning at the individual level but also
	help the participants evaluate their team work.
Learning diary	
The participants are asked to report their personal	The learning diary enables the participants to reflect
learning reflections.	on themselves and their team work, as well as to
They are also asked to utilize at least the pre-reading	discuss their identity as an entrepreneurial person.
material in their reflections and to discuss the course	
topics, such as working in teams.	
The exact form of the diary is decided by the	
participants (the form can range from written to	
video reflections).	

et al., 2009). The content of the articles is not taught during the camp, but students are asked to reflect upon the pre-readings or other relevant literature in their learning diaries.

The underlying idea of the course is to encourage students to immerse themselves in the entrepreneurial process during individual and group exercises. Hence, the course deals with experiential learning simulations (Pittaway and Cope, 2007) that take place during the learning camp (Table 7.3).

The camp starts with a guided but imaginary cocktail party and with team-building exercises during which the participants introduce themselves and share their passion so that they can find individuals with similar interests. After these exercises, the students begin mapping their resources as a team.

Table 7.3   *Learning camp outline*

Rough Schedule	Activity
9:00	Opening
	Warm up at a *cocktail party*
9:30	Team formation
	Problem definition
	Idea generation
10:30	Coffee break
10:45	Idea generation
	Assumption testing
12:30	Lunch
13:30	Learning and sharing
14:00	Problems and solutions
	Lean canvas
15:00	Coffee break
15:15	Demo designing
16:00	Trade fair
17:00	Idea pitching
18:00	Reflections
18:45	Concluding remarks and closing

While doing so, they are asked to put their PhD areas of expertise aside and instead share their passions so they can team up with participants who share these passions.

When teams of (at most) four members have been formed, the participants are asked to discuss their strengths and weaknesses not only as individuals but as a team. This approach enables the students to recognize their team-level diversity and possible void in skills and initiates team cognition, which later supports coherence amongst team members, learning and creativity (de Mol et al., 2015). Thereafter, the participants discuss common themes based on their passions and are asked to consider whether these themes can be translated into something that needs to be solved. This process not only initiates idea generation but also focuses participants' attention away from their PhD expertise areas. In all, the selected structure of team formation and initial idea generation reflects the talent, interests, passions and skills exercise (Hart, 2018).

When moving on to an iterative idea-generation cycle, the participants are required to engage immediately in entrepreneurial thinking and action. By following the lean start-up cycle (Blank, 2013), they turn their ideas into problems, solutions and finally products. Throughout the ten-hour learning camp, the participants are provided with tools for ideation (for example, mind mapping through which participants visually organize the themes, problems and ideas they discuss in their team), crafting a business model (Lean Canvas) and reflections (for example, the Motorola reflection tool, which has participants evaluate the actions they took, what went well and what should be improved next time) to enable team progress in the activities.

The most important phase takes place when the participants are directed out of the classroom to test the viability of their ideas with real target customers when transferring their ideas into a solution for customers. This process follows the lean cycle, as the solutions are evaluated and illustrated through a Lean Canvas tool (Maurya, 2012; Ries, 2011). This process requires participants to conduct interviews with and collect data from potential customers in order to validate the existence of the assumed problems. After returning together, the teams are asked to reflect on and share what they learned from the problem validation exercise. A similar interaction is needed when testing the feasibility of their proposed solutions. Because of the tight schedule involved, the solutions are not validated with potential customers, but instead, the teams' design prototypes, mock-ups or concepts of the solutions. They develop them further based on the comments received during the trade fairs organized between the teams.

Finally, the idea-generation process ends when the teams pitch their ideas to other teams. Accordingly, the ten-hour learning camp addresses the customer search part of the entire customer development framework (Blank and Dorf, 2012). All these activities apply the learning-by-doing approach. The final reflections of the exercises and the lessons learned at the individual and team level are discussed in class at the end of the learning camp and in the wrap-up session. Accordingly, the participants combine both self-regulated learning and group-based learning, which have been shown to support individuals' entrepreneurial learning (Harms, 2015).

The methods and activities used are designed to make participants understand how and when to apply their knowledge, skills, expertise and networks in a real-world context outside of their PhD field. They need to rely on peer students' skills and expertise in the team, emphasizing the social aspect of learning (see, for example, Vosniadou et al., 2001). Often, the most intriguing phase is getting out of the class to validate an idea with real customers and to learn more about it in order to finalize the tasks. Moreover, as this activity is self-managed by the teams, they have psychological ownership of the process (Druskat and Pescosolido, 2002); working together beyond their comfort zone enhances psychological safety within the teams, which, in turn, supports personal risk-taking (Edmondson, 1999). In general, students are initially surprised by the idea that they are being urged to go out and talk to real people (potential customers).

REFLECTION ON THE INITIATIVE

While PhD students who take the course are interested in the idea of starting a venture, only a few of them actually have concrete ideas for a venture. Hence, the course works as a crash course by demonstrating the entrepreneurial process. In this section, results and learning derived from the new course format based on the feedback and assignment, which the students are required to do, are discussed.

First, the students write learning diaries. Then, in the wrap-up session, the facilitators and participants share and discuss their experiences of the course. In the learning diaries, the students reflect on themselves, their teams and what they learned during the process and vis-à-vis the readings they were provided with before the programme. The emphasis is on learning reflections (Hägg, 2017), so only reporting the activities is not enough. The form of the learning diary is open for the participants to decide (the use of photos and colours is encouraged but less used), but the maximum length is ten pages. In analysing the learning diaries, we focus on identifying students' eureka moments and extracting the quotes in which the participants mention facing something or learning something unexpected. Thereafter, the identified quotes are categorized, generating six potential learning outcomes, which are discussed with related suggestions for educators arranging similar courses.

Our analysis indicates how participants have experienced a sense of developing entrepreneurial skills and competences (Bacigalupo et al., 2016; Moberg, 2013). Even if the course did not involve an actual venture creation, past students have described acquiring certain competences that are relevant to new venture creation and being capable of positioning themselves in the process.

Overall, the described learning outcomes vary among participants. While most students are capable of reflecting on the activities and their own behaviour during the learning camp, this is not the case for all. For instance, two former students failed the course because of their shallow reflection in the learning diaries. They just briefly summarized the content of the workshop. Even after being given a second chance, one of the students was not capable of reflecting from the learning perspective and did not pass the course. This implies that university disciplines differ, and not all of them guide and offer resources for students to practise reflection.

In addition, we have identified some differences between students, even during the camp. For instance, on one occasion, one person left the camp without notifying us. This behaviour suggests that this kind of learning method is not for everyone. These differences probably reflect students' different motivations for joining the course and the variation in their existing knowledge and attitudes toward entrepreneurship. Thus, learning is contextualized to the individual learner.

Learning about Entrepreneurship

Some previous participants have expressed that they developed knowledge about entrepreneurship. Despite the short course format, one student reported quite impressive learning, saying, 'I can say that I finished the day with comprehensive, synchronized knowledge regarding forming a start-up'. Thus, the participants have obtained a general sense about the concrete steps required to start a business. However, there have been exceptions: 'Entrepreneurship as a concept is not new to me since I took probably four different entrepreneurship courses during my master's programme, and my thesis was about . . . entrepreneurship; however, facing entrepreneurship as a practice has given me a new perspective'. Even if the participants are in a familiar zone (entrepreneurship studies), the experiential element of the course gives them a new perspective and contributes to their learning. Accordingly, our findings suggest that, in addition to theoretical knowledge, experiential nature should be a core feature in similar short-term courses.

Recognizing Shortfalls and Learning Needs

When students arrive with little or no understanding of entrepreneurship, they are likely to progress quickly and claim to have reached a good understanding of the basics. These students may feel social pressure to exaggerate their learning to pass the course. As facilitators, we need to interpret such manifestations with caution. Accordingly, our second learning outcome deals with enabling students to recognize their own shortfalls and learning needs for the future: '[the] situation put me under lots of pressure [and] ensured that I need to work on my skill of public speaking . . . Even though it's good to have team members who can complement my weaknesses, I prefer to work on my skills'. For their own future (as potential entrepreneurs), students will benefit from recognizing their learning needs. Hence, the finding that the course, even one this short, motivates students to learn more implies that recognition and explication of shortfalls and learning needs are worthy of being emphasized when organizing such courses.

Understanding the Role of Action

The learning-by-doing nature of the course allows students to understand the role of action in entrepreneurship. For example, the learning derived is related to the act of doing, moving forward; as one participant described, it was 'the biggest takeaway of the day, as one has to step outside of one's own comfort zone to actually move forward and do something'. The latter is emphasized by setting strict time constraints during the camp. Since there are only ten hours to use, the scarcity of time is inevitable, and thus, exercises are strictly timed. This forces participants to decide quickly which actions to take (Foss and Klein, 2017). Through this, the learning camp introduces uncertainty in transformative action and interaction between the participants (Berglund and Korsgaard, 2017; Lane and Maxfield, 2005). Succeeding (or failing) under a tight schedule also builds confidence and motivation, and the effects extend beyond the learning camp.

Participants' learning diaries reveal their expectations that entrepreneurship training should have a practical focus, as in the quote below. This might make it difficult to reframe entrepreneurship as an academic discipline with theory-driven input that may be of use.

> After doing the initial readings prior to the event, I wasn't quite sure what to expect anymore, since some of the articles had a decisively academic touch to them and didn't really feel like anything I had heard about the vibrant start-up scene. The seminar, on the other hand, proved to be much different and very interesting—much along the same lines as the article by Steve Blank—uplifting and exciting.

One can argue that there is an expectation that entrepreneurship education should be related to practice (Pittaway and Cope, 2007) and a form of *entre-tainment* (Swail et al., 2014) even at the postgraduate level. While academic articles did not meet this expectation, the learning camp delivered this by being 'uplifting and exciting', 'different and very interesting', as the previous quotation suggests. Thus, we acknowledge the risk that entrepreneurship education be focused only on the activities and practice. Consequently, there is a need to discuss and reflect critically on what the participants learn from the course.

Empowerment from the Team

During the camp, past students have been surprised and even overwhelmed by the fact that the course involved going out of the classroom and approaching potential customers. However, leveraging team resources (networks, peer support) helped teams make the move and approach customers. Accordingly, the fourth learning outcome reflects the role of the team in entrepreneurship, especially team work and team diversity. Teaming up and working with others are entrepreneurial competences (Bacigalupo et al., 2016). The course developed the participants' understanding of entrepreneurship as a team activity: 'I was able to contribute much to team work, which is crucial for starting a new business . . . because a business model requires a lot of expertise. It was a lifetime experience and knowledge'.

The learning camp enabled students to think outside of their own capabilities, contributing their skills for the use of the whole team and learning from one another. They saw the benefits of working in diverse teams to emphasize complementarity: 'I learnt that each person might have different strengths and weaknesses when working in a team; partners can complement one another . . . People from different disciplines have different views on problems and a different understanding of the challenges that might be encountered during a start-up'. Research has evidenced that teams (and, in particular, the resources that become available) positively moderate the relationship between intrinsic motivation and learning outcomes (Hytti et al., 2010). However, the students also experience the challenges of highly diverse teams because learning from others can sometimes be difficult due to varying disciplinary and cultural backgrounds.

Recent research emphasizes that team-based ventures are more successful than solo ones if the teams are diverse and capable of making fast (and sometimes conflicting) decisions and still getting along (Eisenhardt, 2013). Hence, the learning derived on the role of teams is important. 'In my opinion, one of the most important lessons was the necessity of networking. Having great connections with different kinds of people is something that you can't get with money'.

Team work is facilitated with different exercises, such as mapping the team's resources (skills, networks). The team activities contribute to the students' understanding of entrepreneurship as a social and collective process. Furthermore, team experience may also unravel the myth of the heroic entrepreneur (Drakopolou Dodd and Anderson, 2007). Here, we consider ourselves, the facilitators, as a part of the team. One of the past participants wrote, 'It was great and admiring to see the passion that the instructors had towards entrepreneurship'.

While we clearly understand the demanding nature of the problems that the teams work with, we never question or express any doubt that they can be resolved. All the tasks are given in a cheery but self-evident way, contributing to the shared belief that the exercises can be done despite the time restrictions. It is important that educators understand their role as facilitators in creating a positive, relaxed atmosphere – or channelling their passion, as one student suggested – to support entrepreneurial action.

Transforming Problems into Solutions

The approach to creativity during the learning camp focuses on understanding the relevant problems to be solved. Similarly, the students are made to validate the recognized problems and solutions amongst potential customers; how they manoeuvre the validation is up to the team to decide and conduct. This approach suggests that the ability to adapt to change and leverage ambiguity is of greater importance than the ability to predict and plan ahead to decrease uncertainty (Sarasvathy and Venkataraman, 2011). Therefore, a fifth key learning outcome is about understanding how problems can be transformed into solutions when creating new value for others (Lackéus, 2018). This encourages the students, as individuals, to develop their creative skills and practise the skill of acting instead of overthinking. 'The course motivated me to recall my creative self. As a researcher, I've had an understanding of my creative side, but during this course, I identified my innovational abilities as well as limits in creating opportunities as an entrepreneur'. However, as instructors, we need to be careful not to transmit the idea that entrepreneurship is only about doing and acting, and that (critical) thinking has no place.

As researchers, the participants have the advantage of access to the latest knowledge and technology, which they can use to think of problems and solutions for potential customers. However, the participants are not asked to develop just any idea but an idea that they all share. In the past, a mission that collectively covers the participants' passions seemed to function as a mutual goal that they could all work with: 'I believe that grouping people based on their mission was convenient to make the development process less chaotic, in case that's possible. The mission acted as the reconciling element to start something together'. Still, taking away the strict analytical skillset that the participants obtain and replacing it with creativity and actions welcomes uncertainty. This, however, enables the participants to realize that the entrepreneurial process is about taking action towards a goal without knowing whether the action will ever reach that goal (McMullen and Shepherd, 2006).

Reflecting and Doing Identity Work

In this chapter, we employ transformative learning as the theoretical basis for reflection. Transformative learning requires that 'new information be incorporated by the learner into an already well-developed symbolic frame of reference, an active process involving thought, feelings, and disposition' (Mezirow, 1997, p. 10). Learners need support to transform their frame of reference and understand their experience (Mezirow, 1997). We feel the academic readings, the reflective essay and the wrap-up session with participants support transformative learning. For example, the readings on different professional identities and the potential conflicts between academic and entrepreneurial identities are useful (Jain et al., 2009).

In our view, drawing on transformative learning theory (Cope, 2003; Mezirow, 1978), exposure to uncertainty, entrepreneurial thinking, and action are important in guiding the way the students see themselves as entrepreneurial actors and explore their entrepreneurial and academic identity (Jain et al., 2009). We see this as the sixth potential learning outcome. Hence, past students recognized that being an entrepreneurial person could be related to their work in academia:

> In addition to the application of entrepreneurial approaches in running businesses, I found [the methods used during the learning camp] interesting in my research work. They made me wonder how I can exploit them as an academic, [especially] at the present time when academics need to sell their abilities in order to get funding.

Students can also identify their strengths as a researcher if they wish to explore entrepreneurship. Through the readings, they develop an understanding that the roles of a scientist and an entrepreneur can be complementary.

Previous research on entrepreneurship education has emphasized the role of reflection (Lindh, 2017; Hägg, 2017), which we wish to develop further. We do not think that the students, as novice entrepreneurs, would be able to learn from reflection-in-action (Hägg, 2017), particularly as the short learning camp involves fast speed and rapid action. Hence, learning requires reflection-on-action, which is an integral part of the programme through the learning diaries and the wrap-up session. Facilitating identity work is seen as important for entrepreneurship education instead of solely focusing on developing an idea or a venture (Hägg, 2011). Accordingly, entrepreneurship training programmes, even short ones, should be considered as arenas for identity work. The identification of limitations could be turned into learning needs and a transformative agenda: what insights and learning do I need to explore if I want to pursue entrepreneurship?

With regard to similar courses, it is important to allow the students to reflect not only on what they want to become but also on their abilities and current limitations. It seems that PhD students with considerable uncertainty surrounding their career are an appropriate audience for these kinds of entrepreneurial activities and for identity work.

> [T]he uncertainty and insecurity within my academic career have motivated me to study the available options after completing my PhD study, simultaneously with my research work. Therefore, I can identify with the group of academics who are prompted to engage in entrepreneurial activity as a result of their contextual condition and the changes in the broader institutional framework. (Jain et al., 2009)

THE UNIQUE ASPECTS OF THE INITIATIVE

The Entrepreneurship for Research Professionals course is a ten-hour experiential programme delivered in the context of a formal educational programme at the postgraduate level. It connects PhD students from different disciplinary backgrounds in a multi-faculty university. This sets the programme apart from most other courses at the postgraduate level. Additionally, the course target group is different from other initiatives at undergraduate and graduate levels and suggests a certain profile for the participants in an educational context that informs their expectations. The experiential learning approach enables the participants to test the entrepreneurial process and learn through entrepreneurship (Fayolle and Gailly, 2008; Hytti and O'Gorman, 2004; Johnson, 1988). The course offers students a taste of the process that contributes to their understanding of entrepreneurial competences and may later feed into their potential start-up processes.

Reflective Experiential Learning for PhD Students

As PhD students, the participants are not only adult learners but also experts in their own research fields. Pedagogically, the course uses experiential learning (Corbett, 2005; Pittaway and Cope, 2007), that is, learning-by-doing in teams, as explained previously. Because of the discipline-based nature of PhD studies, it may be that students lack opportunities to work and hold discussions in multidisciplinary teams. As all the activities in the learning camp are done in teams, these not only provide a contrast to the participants' PhD projects but also enable them to understand the role of teams. The team exercises help the participants to acknowledge the relevance of the resources that become available through teams and facilitate entrepreneurial action (see de Mol et al., 2015).

At the same time, the course also provides space for identity work (Jain et al., 2009). Identifying the similarities between academic and entrepreneurial work and identities might be the key for eventually making the transition from academia into entrepreneurship. This may be particularly relevant in graduate schools and PhD programmes. Facilitating the processes of identity work with PhD students enables them to explore alternative career options.

Furthermore, experiential learning challenges the scientific and analytical core of university education and emphasizes practice and action. In particular, leaving the classroom to approach potential customers implies going beyond one's comfort zone and thus entering the entrepreneurial process (van Gelderen, 2013). This approach sets our course apart from most of the other PhD modules and necessitates that both instructors and students consider this type of entrepreneurial learning as legitimate even at the postgraduate level. However, experiential learning is increasingly becoming the most common method for entrepreneurship education in lower levels of education, in general (Jones and Iredale, 2010), and sometimes, the experiential learning method is even presented as the preferred method (Pittaway and Cope, 2007) compared with traditional lectures and readings.

On the other hand, the very culture of entrepreneurship – and, in particular, the current start-up culture and the buzz around it (Parkkari and Kohtakangas, 2018) – is transforming the way students, including PhD students, understand entrepreneurship. This understanding informs their expectations, which is evident in our case: none of our past students has questioned the learning camp format, but the academic readings did cause some confusion for the students before the camp started. Yet, in our programme, we specifically assign the students pre-readings to provide the participants with conceptual tools. Participants are asked to use these readings to reflect on their experience in the camp as well as their own career paths and vision for their future. Without proper reflection, the assignments remain decoupled from learning as a form of entre-tainment (Swail et al., 2014). Hence, it is important to provide conceptual tools for participants to make sense of the exercises and practices.

Short Course Can Demystify Entrepreneurial Thinking and Action

Past students acknowledged the role of time and how its scarcity pushed them to act. A clear implication of this is that using active methods and time constraints seems to aid students' understanding of the role of action in entrepreneurship. The experiences from the course suggest that even a short exposure to entrepreneurial thinking and action helps demystify them. Hence, by experiencing the process from idea to business model, the participants started to understand what it takes to start a business. This implies that short exposure to entrepreneurial thinking and action can boost participants' entrepreneurial self-efficacy, but this outcome would require a more detailed analysis. Still, this indicates that the learning-by-doing approach (Piperopoulos and Dimov, 2015; Van Dinther et al., 2011) enhances students' understanding of entrepreneurial thinking and action more than lectures do.

Moreover, the students' reflections of themselves as entrepreneurial actors conceptually transform from external (someone else) to internal (me). Their position towards entrepreneurship changes from passive waiting to see if something is happening to a position in which they can actively move forward (should they so wish). We recognized this change when we developed the programme format from a theoretical approach to a more practical approach. This enabled the students to proceed from a highly abstract view of entrepreneurship to understanding it as concrete behaviour.

In this chapter, we emphasized the short duration of the learning camp, but we have also experimented with conducting this method with even less time (only about three hours). In this experiment, the participants were also academics but come from a broader range – from PhD students to post-doc researchers and even professors. Even with less time, we managed to run the Lean Canvas process with several assignments from identifying a problem to presenting a solution. We concluded that PhD students and academics are highly capable of processing information quickly, adapting to new situations and meeting deadlines in a fast-paced environment, all of which are necessary skills in venture creation.

We feel it is important to highlight the similarities between the capabilities related to the academic and entrepreneurial paths: they are not necessarily two distinct and conflicting career trajectories. Although the lack of time is often presented as a limitation in educational initiatives, we think that the scarcity of time may also strengthen the educational design for experiential education. The time restrictions create a sense of urgency that pushes action as opposed to procrastination (van Gelderen, 2017). Hence, we consider the time element and conscious decision to limit time as necessary for action.

Based on the above, we argue that the learning camp is not only an entertaining experience but also contributes to a transformative learning experience. Kuratko and Hodgetts (2004) propose that the essential components of understanding entrepreneurship include the willingness to take calculated risks, the ability to formulate a team and creatively marshal necessary resources, and the skill to envision opportunities where others see chaos. We believe that at least initial steps towards these components were taken through the camp. Whether these trigger learning and a change in thinking that alters individuals' behaviour in the long run (Clark and Wilson, 1991) remains an important future research topic.

We hope that this chapter encourages readers to experiment with an experiential design with a specific group of PhD students or post-docs even in a short course format. We also emphasize that this is a first step of a process in which students are asked to focus on their passions (rather than their own research); this may help participants understand what is required to create value for others. This kind of ten-hour workshop might be a good icebreaker as the first assignment in a longer process in which participants work with ideas from their own research as a basis for research commercialization. Although the ten-hour camp is all about action, we also emphasize the need for subsequent reflection as a necessary tool for learning. These reflections provide participants with space to think about entrepreneurship as something they may want to pursue in their future careers.

ACKNOWLEDGEMENT

The first author would like to acknowledge the financial support provided by the Academy of Finland (grant #295960), and the second author, the financial support provided by the NordForsk NCoE programme 'NordAqua' (#82845).

REFERENCES

Bacigalupo, M., Kampylis, P., Punie, Y. and L. Van Den Brande (2016), 'EntreComp: the entrepreneurship competence framework', Publications Office of the European Union, doi: 10.2791/593884, accessed 19 October 2018 at https://ec.europa.eu/jrc/en/publication/eur-scientific-and-technical-research-reports/entrecomp-entrepreneurship-competence-framework.

Berglund, H. and S. Korsgaard (2017), 'Opportunities, time and mechanism in entrepreneurship. On the practical irrelevance of propensities', *Academy of Management Review*, **42** (4), 730–33.

Blank, S. (2013), 'Why the lean start-up changes everything', *Harvard Business Review*, **91** (5), 63–72.

Blank, S. and B. Dorf (2012), *The Startup Owner's Manual: The Step-by-Step Guide for Building a Great Company*, Pescadero, CA: K & S Ranch.

Clark, M.C. and A.L. Wilson (1991), 'Context and rationality in Mezirow's theory of transformational learning', *Adult Education Quarterly*, **41** (2), 75–91.

Cope, J. (2003), 'Entrepreneurial learning and critical reflection: discontinuous events as triggers for "higher-level" learning', *Management Learning*, **34** (4), 429–50.

Corbett, A.C. (2005), 'Experiential learning within the process of opportunity identification and exploitation', *Entrepreneurship Theory and Practice*, **29** (4), 473–91.

Davidsson, P. (2015), 'Entrepreneurial opportunities and the entrepreneurship nexus: a re-conceptualization', *Journal of Business Venturing*, **30** (5), 674–95.

de Mol, E., Khapova, S.N. and T. Elfring (2015), 'Entrepreneurial team cognition: a review', *International Journal of Management Reviews*, **17** (2), 232–55.

Drakopoulou Dodd, S. and A.R. Anderson (2007), 'Mumpsimus and the mything of the individualistic entrepreneur', *International Small Business Journal*, **25** (4), 341–60.

Druskat, V.U. and A.T. Pescosolido (2002), 'The content of effective teamwork mental models in self-managing teams: ownership, learning and heedful interrelating', *Human Relations*, **55** (3), 283–314.

Edmondson, A. (1999), 'Psychological safety and learning behavior in work teams', *Administrative Science Quarterly*, **44** (2), 350–83.

Eisenhardt, K.M. (2013), 'Top management teams and the performance of entrepreneurial firms', *Small Business Economics*, **40** (4), 805–16.

Etzkowitz, H. (2014), 'The second academic revolution: the rise of the entrepreneurial university and impetuses to firm foundation', in Thomas J. Allen and Rory P. O'Shea (eds), *Building Technology Transfer within Research Universities: An Entrepreneurial Approach*, Boston, MA: Cambridge University Press, pp. 12–32.

Fayolle, A. and B. Gailly (2008), 'From craft to science: teaching models and learning processes in entrepreneurship education', *Journal of European Industrial Training*, **32** (7), 569–93.

Fisher, G. (2012), 'Effectuation, causation, and bricolage: a behavioral comparison of emerging theories in entrepreneurship research', *Entrepreneurship Theory and Practice*, **36** (5), 1019–51.

Foss, L. and D. Gibson (2015), *The Entrepreneurial University: Case Analysis and Implications*, London: Routledge.

Foss, N.J. and P.G. Klein (2017), 'Entrepreneurial discovery or creation? In search of the middle ground', *Academy of Management Review*, **42** (4), 733–6.

Hägg, O. (2011), 'Yrittäjyysvalmennus ja yrittäjäidentiteetti' [Entrepreneurship training and entrepreneurial identity], PhD thesis, University of Tampere, Finland.

Hägg, G. (2017), 'Experiential entrepreneurship education: reflective thinking as a counterbalance to action for developing entrepreneurial knowledge', PhD thesis, Lund University, Sweden.

Harms, R. (2015), 'Self-regulated learning, team learning and project performance in entrepreneurship education: learning in a lean startup environment', *Technological Forecasting and Social Change*, **100**, 21–8.

Hart, J.D. (2018), *Classroom Exercises for Entrepreneurship: A Cross-Disciplinary Approach*, Cheltenham, UK and Northampton, MA, USA: Edward Elgar Publishing.

Hytti, U. and C. O'Gorman (2004), 'What is "enterprise education"? An analysis of the objectives and methods of enterprise education programmes in four European countries', *Education + Training*, **46** (1), 11–23.

Hytti, U., Stenholm, P., Heinonen, J. and J. Seikkula-Leino (2010), 'Perceived learning outcomes in entrepreneurship education: the impact of student motivation and team behaviour', *Education+Training*, **52** (8/9), 587–606.

Isenberg, D. (2011), 'The entrepreneurship ecosystem strategy as a new paradigm for economy policy: principles for cultivating entrepreneurship', a report of the Babson Entrepreneurship Ecosystem Project, Babson College, Babson Park, MA.

Jain, S., George, G. and M. Maltarich (2009), 'Academics or entrepreneurs? Investigating role identity modification of university scientists involved in commercialization activity', *Research Policy*, **38** (6), 922–35.

Johnson, C. (1988), 'Enterprise education and training', *British Journal of Education and Work*, **2** (1), 61–5.

Jones, B. and N. Iredale (2010), 'Enterprise education as pedagogy', *Education+Training*, **52** (1), 7–19.

Kuratko, D.F. and R.M. Hodgetts (2004), *Entrepreneurship: Theory, Process, Practice*, Mason, OH: South-Western College Publishers.

Lackéus, M. (2018), '"What is value?" A framework for analyzing and facilitating entrepreneurial value creation', *Uniped*, **41** (1), 10–28.

Lane, D.A. and R.R. Maxfield (2005), 'Ontological uncertainty and innovation', *Journal of Evolutionary Economics*, **15** (1), 3–50.

Levinsohn, D. (2015), 'No entrepreneur is an island. An exploration of social entrepreneurial learning in accelerators', *JBS Dissertation Series No. 105*, Jönköping International Business School, Jönköping University.

Lindh, I. (2017), 'An entrepreneurial mindset: self-regulating mechanisms for goal attainment', doctoral dissertation, Luleå University of Technology, Sweden.

Maurya, A. (2012), *Running Lean: Iterate from Plan A to a Plan that Works*, North Sebastopol, CA: O'Reilly Media, Inc.

McMullen, J.S. and D.A. Shepherd (2006), 'Entrepreneurial action and the role of uncertainty in the theory of the entrepreneur', *Academy of Management Review*, **31** (1), 132–52.

Mezirow, J. (1978), 'Perspective transformation', *Adult Education Quarterly*, **28** (2), 100–110.

Mezirow, J. (1997), 'Transformative learning: theory to practice', *New Directions for Adult and Continuing Education*, **1997** (74), 5–12.

Moberg, K. (2013), 'An entrepreneurial self-efficacy scale with a neutral wording', in Alan Fayolle, Paula Kyrö, Tönis Mets and Urve Venesaar (eds), *Conceptual Richness and Methodological Diversity in Entrepreneurship Research*, Cheltenham, UK and Northampton, USA: Edward Elgar Publishing, pp. 67–94.

Parkkari, P. and K. Kohtakangas (2018), '"We're the biggest student movement in Finland since the 1970s!" A practice-based study of student entrepreneurship societies', in

Ulla Hytti, Robert Blackburn and Eddy Laveren (eds), *Entrepreneurship, Innovation and Education: Frontiers in European Entrepreneurship Research*, Cheltenham, UK and Northampton, MA, USA: Edward Elgar Publishing, pp. 146–64.

Piperopoulos, P. and D. Dimov (2015), 'Burst bubbles or build steam? Entrepreneurship education, entrepreneurial self-efficacy, and entrepreneurial intentions', *Journal of Small Business Management*, **53** (4), 970–85.

Pittaway, L. and J. Cope (2007), 'Simulating entrepreneurial learning: integrating experiential and collaborative approaches to learning', *Management Learning*, **38** (2), 211–33.

Ries, E. (2011), *The Lean Startup: How Today's Entrepreneurs use Continuous Innovation to Create Radically Successful Businesses*, New York: Crown Books.

Sarasvathy, S. and S. Venkataraman (2011), 'Entrepreneurship as method: open questions for an entrepreneurial future', *Entrepreneurship Theory and Practice*, **35** (1), 113–35.

Swail, J., Down, S. and T. Kautonen (2014), 'Examining the effect of "entre-tainment" as a cultural influence on entrepreneurial intentions', *International Small Business Journal*, **32** (8), 859–75.

University of Turku (2018), 'University of Turku strategy 2016–2020', accessed 25 October 2018 at https://www.utu.fi/en/university/strategy-and-value.

Van Dinther, M., Dochy, F. and M. Segers (2011), 'Factors affecting students' self-efficacy in higher education', *Educational Research Review*, **6** (2), 95–108.

van Gelderen, M. (2013), 'Giving and taking in networking', accessed 23 March 2019 at www.enterprisingcompetences.com.

van Gelderen, M. (2017), 'Taking action', accessed 23 March 2019 at www.enterprisingcompetencies.com.

Vosniadou, S., Ioannides, C., Dimitrakopoulou, A. and E. Papademetriou (2001), 'Designing learning environments to promote conceptual change in science', *Learning and Instruction*, **11** (4–5), 381–419.

Wood, M.S. and W. McKinley (2010), 'The production of entrepreneurial opportunity: a constructivist perspective', *Strategic Entrepreneurship Journal*, **4** (1), 66–84.

8. VentureLab Weekend: developing entrepreneurial skills from idea to action

Sílvia Costa, Olga Belousova, Aniek Ouendag and Aard Groen

HISTORY, CONTEXT AND THEORETICAL AND PEDAGOGICAL UNDERPINNINGS

What is the VentureLab Weekend?

The VentureLab Weekend is a three-day intensive learning event that gives students a chance to see what entrepreneurship is all about by helping them develop entrepreneurial competences and business ideas into thought-out business models and investor pitches. The weekend is open to students from all faculties and years of education at the University of Groningen. The initiative is organized by the University of Groningen Centre of Entrepreneurship as an extracurricular activity and has taken place every spring and autumn since 2014.

Description of the Initiative

The VentureLab Weekend is a three-day event that gives participants the opportunity to develop their entrepreneurial competences (for example, business planning, idea pitching, and entrepreneurial mindset development) through an intensive training programme, using experiential learning techniques and evidence-based workshops.

During the VentureLab Weekend, participants work in teams to test the viability of their business ideas with peers and experts. This includes developing business ideas, integrating feedback, and actively testing it with potential customers. At the end of the VentureLab Weekend, participants should be able to (1) formulate business ideas within multidisciplinary teams, (2) identify the target audience for their business idea, (3) explain the business model of their idea, and (4) pitch their idea convincingly to a group of experts and investors. The three best teams are selected and awarded a monetary prize; the team receiving the first prize is also granted entrance to the VentureLab North Accelerator programme, a one-year programme to support business development.

The VentureLab Weekend takes place twice in the academic year and is open to students from all study backgrounds. Because the VentureLab Weekend is an extracurricular activity, it is organized at a time of the year when it does not interfere with regular course work and fits students' schedules. Thus, the ideal timing for the VentureLab Weekend is at the end of class periods (before exams), allowing for the knowledge obtained during the entrepreneurship curricular courses to be refreshed and reinforced.

The VentureLab Weekend is open to and usually attracts a diverse audience from different backgrounds. Students taking part in the VentureLab Weekend come equally from bachelor, master and PhD programmes, represent varying faculties (slightly dominated by business, engineering and medical students), and are very diverse in terms of national backgrounds (30 per cent of students at the University of Groningen are international). Over the years, the number of participants has fluctuated between 21 (the very first edition) and 61 participants; our experience has shown that a group of 35 to 40 participants is ideal for such an educational event with regular active moments (such as pitching), feedback moments, and team and coaching work.

History and Context of the VentureLab Weekend

The University of Groningen, established in 1614, is a research university with a global outlook, deeply rooted in Groningen, in the northern part of the Netherlands. Its 31 000 students receive high-quality education and conduct research in a broad range of disciplines. The university distinguishes itself in the international market through a close link between education and research, and by focusing on three key societal challenges: energy transition, healthy ageing and creating a sustainable society.

The VentureLab Weekend is an initiative developed by the University of Groningen Centre of Entrepreneurship (UGCE). The UGCE was founded by the board of the University of Groningen, with the goal of stimulating a more entrepreneurial climate at the university. The UGCE mission is based on three important pillars: engaged education, excellent research, and active business development support.

In order to achieve the goal of engaged education, the UGCE offers a wide range of educational activities to different faculties of the university. The main goal of these activities is to provide students with an evidence-based education in entrepreneurship, which helps them develop their entrepreneurial skills, which can be applied in a large spectrum of contexts throughout their academic and professional careers.

The VentureLab Weekend is one of the core educational activities of UGCE. It was first created in 2014 as a follow-up to The Extracurricular

Course in Entrepreneurship (see figure 8.1) in order to provide a next step towards disseminating entrepreneurship across the university and developing the students' entrepreneurial competences in an applied setting. A graphical overview of UGCE educational activities is represented in Figure 8.1.

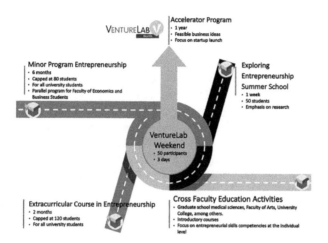

Figure 8.1   Positioning the VentureLab Weekend in the landscape of entrepreneurship education offered at the University of Groningen

As displayed in Figure 8.1, the educational activities offered by UGCE can be compared to a funnel. It starts with a wide range of entrepreneurship awareness creation courses (such as the extracurricular course in entrepreneurship, which is open to students from all faculties; summer schools, and introductory curricular courses for social sciences, engineering and medicine students). The participants from these educational activities who want to develop their ideas and entrepreneurial skills further with a hands-on approach are welcome to join the VentureLab Weekend. The funnel culminates in the year-long VentureLab North Accelerator programme, where participants who are interested in further developing the ideas they generated and preliminarily tested during the VentureLab Weekend can benefit from a one-year business development trajectory.

As an intermediary stage between the introductory educational activities (curricular and extracurricular courses) and a serious business development trajectory (acceleration programme), the VentureLab Weekend provides an opportunity for individuals to experiment with entrepreneurship and test whether developing a business is something that interests them. At the same time, as the programme focuses on competence development, participants can apply these in other contexts of their lives even if they choose not to go further in their entrepreneurial endeavours. Thus, the VentureLab Weekend is valuable as a stand-alone activity and an important gate for students to proceed from basic knowledge and awareness about entrepreneurship, gained through the introduction courses, to the advanced business development support of the VentureLab North Accelerator.

Local and International Partnerships

The VentureLab Weekend is strongly embedded in the local and European entrepreneurial ecosystems. Over the years it has leveraged support from a number of partners, who come together to share resources, knowledge, and their network. For example, another local university, the Hanze University of Applied Sciences, often sends participants and coaches to the VentureLab Weekend. The VentureLab North Accelerator supports the VentureLab Weekend with the main prize (participation in the acceleration programme) and a coaching network.

Other local specialized partners are EnTranCe (a facility for applied sciences focusing on the issue of energy transition) and the University Medical Center Groningen (the academic hospital associated with the university). They provide expertise for the thematic weekends through coaches and jury members in their respective areas (energy and health), thus enabling the VentureLab Weekend participants to access specialized knowledge as they work on their business ideas throughout the programme.

The VentureLab Weekend also counts on European partners, such as European Union programmes that provide financial support, and outreach to international partnerships. For example, students from other European universities participating in the European Institute of Innovation and Technology (EIT) Health network can gain access to the VentureLab Weekend. The network covers travel expenses, and registration is free for these participants. This way, the thematic Health VentureLab Weekend regularly attracts applications from EIT Health partners from Germany, France, and Sweden.

At the same time, these partnerships have brought the VentureLab Weekend programme to other countries, such as Sweden (Uppsala University), Hungary (in partnership with General Electric), and India (Thapar University). This enables participants of the VentureLab Weekend to easily access a broad network if they choose to pursue their business idea beyond the duration of the programme. These international partnerships also serve as an additional source of participants from these universities for the Groningen edition as well. An example of such an agreement is the International Master in Innovative Medicine dual degree programme with Uppsala University and Heidelberg University. Within this partnership, six to ten students from Uppsala University can join the Health VentureLab Weekend in Groningen. We plan to increase such partnerships and agreements, with the aim of gaining a broader and more international audience for future VentureLab Weekends.

Theoretical and Pedagogical Underpinnings of the VentureLab Weekend

The educational programme of the VentureLab Weekend builds on three important pillars that guide our understanding of the content, context, and process of entrepreneurship. We use the social systems theory applied to entrepreneurship (Groen, 2005) to convey the basic content, or functions, required to run a viable business. Specifically, the social systems theory for entrepreneurship (Parsons, 1964; Groen, 2005) suggests that, to be viable, a venture needs to develop several forms of capital to at least a minimum level: strategic capital (the ability to go from idea to action), economic capital (financial means and ambition to scale), cultural and human capital (patterns of organization and maintenance of an organization) and social capital (the network of the entrepreneur). The training programme of the VentureLab Weekend covers the basic aspects of these four capitals. Each day of the programme is, furthermore, concluded by a networking session, helping participants develop their social capital, which can compensate for the lack of other capitals (Groen, 2005; Groen et al., 2008).

We further follow the effectuation approach (Sarasvathy, 2001; 2008) as an overarching principle for the whole course in order to stimulate understanding the role of uncertainty in the entrepreneurship context. This means that we designed the programme to be control-based: by enabling participants to develop the abovementioned critical capitals, we empower them to control their entrepreneurial endeavour by developing these skills and dealing with uncertainty (Sarasvathy, 2001; 2008; Pittaway and Cope, 2007).

Finally, to help students learn about the process of entrepreneurship, we rely on the experiential learning pedagogy by simulating an entrepreneurial learning context throughout the weekend (Pittaway and Cope, 2007). This includes enabling a context where participants engage in an entrepreneurial activity through experiential methods (Pittaway and Cope, 2007), while engaging in four learning processes: concrete experience (feeling), reflective observation (watching), abstract conceptualization (thinking), and active experimentation (doing) (Kolb, 1984; Kolb and Kolb, 2005).

By creating the conditions for participants to use these learning processes, the programme helps them develop knowledge through particular individual-centred styles: convergent, assimilative, divergent or accommodative, depending on their preference to reflect upon their experiences (intentions vs extension, and comprehension vs apprehension). These learning processes are central for opportunity identification and exploitation processes (Corbett, 2005) as well as building the experiential activities in solid theoretical foundations (Costa et al., 2018). Furthermore, we make sure that an atmosphere of trust and collaboration is maintained among all participants and guests, as active and safe experimentation contributes to better learning experiences (Edmondson, 1999; 2004; Politis, 2005).

The VentureLab Weekend programme was designed so that each activity (1) stimulates the different experiential learning processes as well as moments for reflection (pedagogical underpinnings) and (2) promotes the development of the critical entrepreneurial capitals (theoretical underpinnings). Figure 8.2 shows how each activity of the VentureLab Weekend combines the theoretical and pedagogical underpinnings of the programme (indicated under each moment). The figure also depicts the chronological component of the programme (Day 1, Day 2, Day 3), and the arrows represent the interaction between learning moments and how the skills developed in certain moments are applied on the next. The expression 'moments' here depicts an opportunity for interaction and work, and can last more than an hour at a time. There are different types of moments experienced throughout the weekend:

1. The *workshop moments* are a means to assure that participants understand what is expected from them in terms of entrepreneurial behaviour and knowledge during the weekend, which is crucial when simulating entrepreneurial learning settings (Pittaway and Cope, 2007).
2. The *action moments* allow participants to experiment actively throughout the learning process and apply the knowledge gained during the workshop moments. The action moments focus on one of the key aspects of simulating entrepreneurial learning: forcing participants to step out of normal educational processes and adopt more innovative ways of acquiring the competences they need to achieve the learning outcomes (Pittaway and Cope, 2007).
3. The *coaching moments* are of utmost importance in the VentureLab Weekend programme. Coaches are not assigned to a specific team, which means that one team may receive (solicited or unsolicited) feedback from multiple coaches, which also creates uncertainty and ambiguity as a key element in the process (Pittaway and Cope, 2007).
4. The *working with peers moments* are moments when team members reflect on what they have experienced in the other learning moments and apply this to the development of their business idea. This is essential to simulate an entrepreneurial learning context as it means students are taken out of the normal educational process, and their emotional exposure is heightened (Pittaway and Cope, 2007).
5. The *feedback moments* foster feedback from peers, coaches, and jury members, which is then used in the reflection moments to reflect critically

on the process and experiences individuals go through (Holman, 2000; Rasmussen and Sørheim, 2006; Hägg and Kurczewska, 2016).

6. The *social moments* are created to enable participants to reach out to other participants outside of their teams and eventually share resources and create commitments, which can be beneficial for several teams.

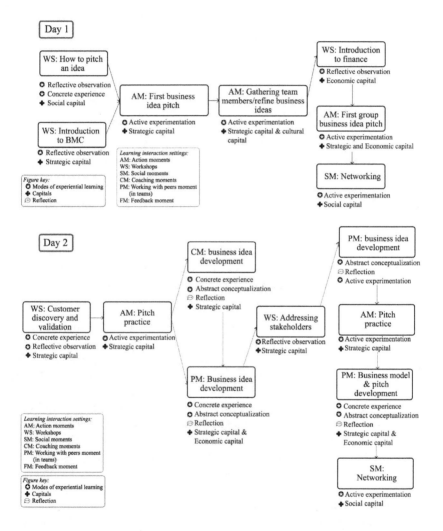

Figure 8.2   Overview of activities developed within the VentureLab Weekend programme and their relation to theoretical and pedagogical underpinnings

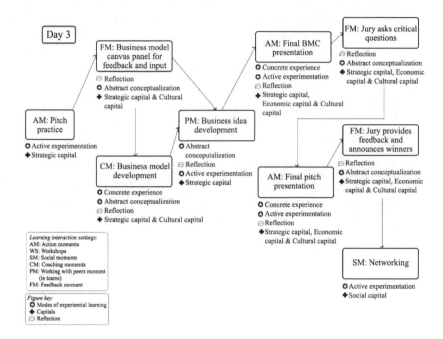

Figure 8.2   *Overview of activities developed within the VentureLab*
(continued)   *Weekend programme and their relation to theoretical and*
                   pedagogical underpinnings

We describe each day of the programme in Figure 8.2 and illustrate how, on each day, the theoretical and pedagogical underpinnings are considered.

On Day 1, participants start out by having two workshop moments: one focusing on how to pitch an idea and the other introducing the Business Model Canvas (BMC). These workshops focus on different entrepreneurial capitals, such as social capital during the workshop about pitching (since this workshop is focused on how to communicate a business idea to the other participants rather than on how to develop the idea at that stage). Strategic capital is addressed in the workshop on how to work with the BMC and customer discovery and validation. Economic capital is addressed in the workshop about finance.

The workshops trigger mostly reflective observation (watching) and concrete experience (feeling) processes. The competences developed in these workshops are typically applied in the next action moment. Specifically, the first action moment is focused on pitching – where participants practise pitching, developing their notion of strategic capital so they can develop an action plan for their idea to become a reality – and through active experimentation (doing). In the second action moment, participants pitch the ideas they bring to the VentureLab Weekend and gather a team around them and their idea, using both the techniques they have just learned about pitching and some preliminary concepts of the BMC (for example, value proposition). This action moment enables participants to gain both strategic and cultural capital, as they communicate their idea and gather interest around it through active experimentation.

Using the principles underlying the effectuation approach, we decided not to form teams before the event, but let the teams form naturally during this action moment based on the passions and ideas available among the participants (the 'means' principle) and the leaders or ideas that team members believe in the most (the 'self-selected stakeholders' principle).

Later on in Day 1, there is another workshop moment on introduction to finance, focusing on the development of financial capital through reflective observation (watching). Immediately after, participants are once again led into an action moment (another pitching moment), where they are encouraged to include this new information. In this way, the strategic and economic capital contents are again developed through active experimentation (doing).

The day ends with a social moment, which creates an opportunity for participants to develop their social capital through active experimentation in an informal networking event.

The same logic is present on Day 2 when participants have a workshop moment about customer discovery and validation. At this moment, they gather knowledge on how to shape their idea into reality (strategic capital). Afterwards, participants have an action moment to pitch their idea and experiment actively with the knowledge gathered during the workshop.

On Day 2, the coaching moments are introduced. At this point, participants feel the need to seek advice and guidance beyond their initial business idea. Thus, coaching moments provide an opportunity for feedback and reflection, which then are integrated into the working with peers moments to develop the business idea further. Following the effectuation principles, we decided not to assign a coach to a specific team. This means that a team must actively solicit feedback from a coach, and one team may receive different feedback from different coaches (the 'pilot in the plane' principle).

Thus, after a coaching moment, participants have a working with peers moment, where these new learnings need to be integrated into the business idea as well. The working with peers moments are meant to trigger reflection, thinking, and feeling within the team about the knowledge gained during the workshops, action moments, and coaching moments about the strategic and economic capital of their idea. The working with peers moments are opportunities to pause and think as a team about how to transform the business idea into a sound business model, integrating the feedback received. During some of these moments, participants are also encouraged to 'go out of the building' and conduct preliminary market research about their idea with individuals external to the VentureLab Weekend.

On Day 3, there are no more workshop moments, as it is time to refine the business idea and prepare for the final presentations. Therefore, the day starts with an action moment to refine the pitch and a feedback moment on the teams' BMC, followed by working with coaches. Thus, the day starts with a focus on strategic capital and active experimentation. All the activities lead to the last two action moments of the day: presenting the BMC to a panel of jury members (which may include investors) and pitching to this panel. During the BMC moment, the participants have the opportunity to elaborate on the details of their business idea (focusing on their strategic, economic and cultural capitals). Afterwards, there is a discussion between the participants and the jury. During the final pitch presentation, participants present their idea in a three-minute pitch. After each of these moments, the jury provides feedback on the business idea and the pitching skills, triggering an opportunity for reflection and abstract conceptualization (thinking). The jury then convenes to decide on the winning teams, and this is announced at the end of the day with a small ceremony.

At the end of each day, there is time dedicated to socializing. The overall programme of the VentureLab Weekend is designed to create communal work through group dynamics, which is central to simulating entrepreneurial learning settings (Pittaway and Cope, 2007). Thus, it is important that participants also have moments to connect with one another. These social moments may occur informally, as well as during the designated networking time at the end of each day.

REFLECTING ABOUT THE VENTURELAB WEEKEND: EVOLUTION, EVALUATION, RESULTS, AND LESSONS LEARNED

Between 2014 and 2019, we organized 11 editions of the VentureLab Weekend: six general weekends, two weekends focusing on energy transition ideas, and three weekends focusing on health-oriented ideas (we further reflect on the different themes ahead). This provides ample opportunity to discuss the evolution of the VentureLab Weekend from the point of view of educators, organizers, and students. To reflect on the different editions of the VentureLab Weekend, we follow Fayolle et al. (2006) and focus on the analysis of four points: (1) audience and event's dynamics; (2) the type of programme and objectives; (3) contents, teaching approaches and methods; and (4) the success factors of the VentureLab Weekend. Additionally, we have included participants' feedback to illustrate some of the changes we have performed over time.

Audience and Event's Dynamics

The general VentureLab Weekends are very diverse in terms of faculties rep-resented, while the thematic weekends attract a more homogeneous audience (for example, more medical sciences students attend the Health VentureLab Weekend). Although diversity has been shown to stimulate team creativity and innovative performance (West, 2002; Kirkman et al., 2013), in such an intense weekend, having a more common background allows participants to converge on the nature of the idea and start taking steps to develop it faster, which seems to be beneficial for their progress.

As the core purpose of the VentureLab Weekend is to develop students' entrepreneurial competences, we do not attempt to limit or manipulate the profile of participants. We also do not limit the number of applicants with ideas and do not form teams before the event. Even though forming teams during the weekend may affect the group dynamics (relationships within the group, its ability to find a way to work cohesively), we consider this as an important element in students' learning. The downside of this approach relates to idea providers who do not succeed in forming a team around their ideas and do not find another team to join. If there are many such participants, they have to form a team and develop an idea on the spot. Such a 'forced' team (as compared to the teams that get together because they are interested in a specific idea) is a high-risk situation: there is a risk that the participants will not agree on a direction, will not commit to the development of the idea or may even quit. However, in most cases, the team dynamics are still positive, and such a 'forced' team can even win the VentureLab Weekend.

In the event that the teams come into the weekend as a pre-formed team, they can still recruit new members, and formation may change throughout the programme. Although they enjoy the benefit of having the idea shaped prior to the weekend, as well as the commitment of the team members to the idea, these teams still learn how to recruit team members, network with other participants, and get mentors and experts to work with them. In sum, all participants go through the entrepreneurial learning environment that the weekend promotes.

Lastly, the number of participants is a factor that seriously impacts the dynamics, cohesiveness, and outcomes of the VentureLab Weekend. Over the years, the number of participants has fluctuated between 21 (the very first edition) and 61 participants. With about 20 participants, active engagement is required of everyone and is vital – every person is very visible and can change the atmosphere of the event. On the other hand, with 50 or more participants, it becomes increasingly difficult to pay attention to every individual, form a reasonable number of teams or provide substantial feedback during the pitch sessions. This is why, over the editions of the VentureLab Weekend, we have found that a group of 35 to 40 participants is ideal for the programme. Thus, we have set the cap for the maximum number of participants to 50, and numbers are monitored during the application period. If more than 40 participants sign up, we approach extra coaches. Furthermore, usually a few applicants drop off before the start; this way the number of applicants remains under control.

Type of Programme and Objectives

Over the years, we have debated the double formal objectives of the VentureLab Weekend: (1) help develop and test business ideas (using the BMC), and (2) teach students to be able to present ideas clearly to the interested audiences (pitching). This appeared to be a challenge, as we would see teams with great business ideas, but poor delivery technique; teams who learned and developed during the weekend beyond expectations but lacked either a great idea or a great pitch; and teams who could present themselves exceptionally well, but had obvious issues with their business model. Balancing the contribution of theoretical learning and execution, the quality of the business ideas, and the ability to present them was further complicated by the diversity of the ideas and the jury's inability to judge all of them simultaneously.

Additionally, while no grades are given in the VentureLab Weekend, the top three teams are selected, and cash prizes are awarded: 500 euros for first place and direct entrance into the VentureLab North Accelerator programme, 250 euros for second place, and 100 euros for third place. Thus, to assess the learning goals and outcomes and select the top three teams, we have experimented with different modes and moments of evaluation. For instance, in the last three editions, the evaluation of the knowledge developed by the participants during the weekend happens on the third day during two action moments: one where participants present their business idea and business model, and another where participants present their idea in a pitch format. Here, the first moment is focused on explaining the business concept in detail, while the second focuses on the communication and presentation skills of participants, thus providing the balance between the two learning goals of the weekend.

Furthermore, we have developed two instruments to assist the jury members in rating the presentations of the canvas and pitch. The first instrument is a form for assessing the BMC. It focuses on the quality of the business idea and asks for a value judgement on the separate aspects of the BMC. The second instrument is a form to assess the quality of the pitch, based on the pitch guidelines used throughout the weekend. Both forms use Likert scales to assess different components of the BMC and of the pitch. Thus, both forms are processed immediately after being completed by the jury, so that when the jury convenes to discuss their impressions and decide on the winners, they can count the objective scores of their evaluations to help them make an informed and objective decision, eliminating the abovementioned ambiguities in judging.

Contents, Teaching Approaches, and Methods

The content of the weekend has also been assessed based on feedback from participants,[1] coaches and staff, and thus further developed. We have strived to identify a balance between the workshop moments, and the working with peers moments. For example, since the first edition of the VentureLab Weekend, the balance of workshop moments, pitching and feedback sessions, and working with peers and coaches has shifted significantly (see Figure 8.3). The weekend used to start on Friday at noon with an extensive introduction to the tools employed during the weekend, with lecturing throughout the weekend up to 2 pm on Sunday, with the aim of equipping students with the theoretical tools necessary for their business idea development. This did not allow the teams to reflect and apply the knowledge they had gathered during the lectures of the weekend. Additionally, the time to work together with peers and get feedback from coaches proved to be quite limited. This reflection among the team members led to subsequent changes in the following editions of the VentureLab Weekend.

The current balance allows for a better reflection of the non-linear and non-sequential nature of the entrepreneurial process (Bhave, 1994). While participants sometimes still note that even more work time would be desired (for example, 'Some more time to work on the first pitch would be helpful because we had to write that after the programme for Day 1 was completed'. Participant feedback, VLW, November 2017), we believe this would take away too much from the workshops, which are central to assure the strong theoretical foundations of the practice moments.

We have addressed the timing and content of the workshops: in our early editions, we scheduled the working with peer moments for after each workshop moment, aiming to provide an 'exercise' opportunity. However, it became clear to us that the theoretical input needed to be introduced earlier, equipping participants with necessary tools and letting them utilize these tools as ideas develop, reflecting the uncertain and iterative nature of the entrepreneurial process ('Short free time to discuss'. Participant feedback, VLW, November 2017). Starting with the second edition, all of the workshop moments had to be delivered by the end of Saturday; Sunday was used for the working with peers moments and working with coaches moments, and feedback sessions on both business model and pitch.

Besides balancing the workshop and action moments, we opted to take out some workshops that covered topics that were more likely to be useful at a later

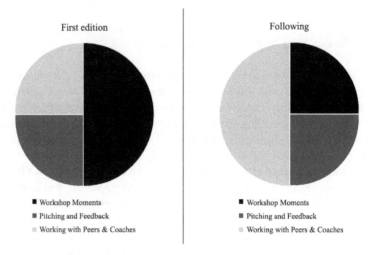

Figure 8.3   The two editions of the VentureLab Weekend programme

stage of the process (for example, prototype building). We further changed the organization of certain activities based on our own reflection and availability of technology: we used to have a so-called 'video panel', aiming to provide extensive feedback on the presentation skills of the teams in an individual setting with a panel of reviewers. This session would be video recorded, and the recording would be immediately shared with the teams. With the development of the mobile phone possibilities (allowing easy and efficient recording of the video without compromising phone memory) and the development of our coaching pool (more coaches are now present and ready to give feedback during the pitching sessions; some coaches specialize in presentation skills), this session became redundant. We currently use this time to give extensive individual reviews of the BMC.

Third, as some editions of the VentureLab Weekend are themed, focusing on specific challenges that can be addressed through entrepreneurship (for example, Health VentureLab Weekend, where participants are encouraged to come up with business solutions related to the health sector), some workshops in these themed editions were adapted to match the specific context of the business ideas (for example, discussing 'stakeholders in healthcare' instead of a general 'selling your idea' workshop). For these occasions, a coaching pool specific to energy or healthcare issues is called to participate in order to provide more expert support and knowledge for developing business ideas

('The panels and coaching are the most useful in the course'. Participant feedback, VLW, November 2017).

Finally, we introduced more informal review moments to keep the energy going ('[The VentureLab Weekend should start with] activities to increase energy'. Participant feedback, VLW, March 2018). For example, over the past editions, a mid-weekend award moment was developed: the 'VentureLabbie Awards'. While the awards serve no official purpose and are not based on official evaluation, they serve as a tool to increase morale and energy midway through the weekend, highlighting the importance of learning and pivoting (one of the prizes) independent of the initial starting point and idea quality, as well as to stimulate group cohesion among the participants.

Success Factors of the VentureLab Weekend

There are a few aspects that are central to the success of the VentureLab Weekend as highlighted by participants and organizers. From the student perspective, this is the learning experience from peers, workshops, and coaches. From the organizer's point of view, it is the flexibility and modularity of the format, the support ecosystem developed throughout the years by the UGCE team, and the availability of the next steps for the ideas generated during the weekend.

First, for students, it is important that the competences developed during the programme last beyond the duration of the weekend and are applicable to other entrepreneurial endeavours participants would like to pursue. For example, participants have the chance to work in teams and develop their team competences. There are examples of participants who came to the VentureLab Weekend to work on someone else's idea (even though they already had their own start-up in progress) in order to further their business modelling and presentation skills, and to learn to work as a team member under someone else's leadership. Furthermore, although not everyone will start a business on their own, they might become business developers in established organizations. There are several cases of participants who now work in large companies and recognize that the competences acquired during the weekend were essential for their career as business developers ('It helped me a lot to think about how to adapt my idea to the market need'. Participant feedback, VLW, March 2019).

Next, the programme offers a unique combination of solid theoretical foundation and real-life experience across a number of educational, coaching, and networking moments. We consider it important to have a training programme based on solid theoretical foundations and a systematic pedagogical approach. This means that the VentureLab Weekend goes beyond an approach that only motivates individuals to experiment with the process of developing an entrepreneurial idea, as it also provides a space for reflection and transformation of these experiences into knowledge.

In addition to evidence-based training, the VentureLab Weekend also provides coaches who are experts in entrepreneurship. It was very clear from the beginning that this resource is valued by participants. The coaches, whose expertise stems from being actual entrepreneurs, business developers, and investors, provide a first-person account of entrepreneurial experiences from which participants can learn and make sense of their own experiences ('The openness of the coaches is great and really helps with the progress'. Participant feedback, VLW, November 2018).

Finally, the VentureLab Weekend has a strong focus on trust, communication, and sharing knowledge among participants. Participants are encouraged to learn from one another: they rehearse pitching their ideas in front of the whole group and share feedback on one another's ideas and presentations. While the programme has a competitive element to it, it also promotes community and collaboration values from which participants benefit. The coaching group plays a very important role in this. Over the years, the group became an active co-player and stakeholder in the VentureLab Weekend: most of the coaches stay beyond the hours they are contracted for and even try to join for a part of the event if they cannot attend the full weekend. Additionally, they bring in new potential coaches from their own networks, thus co-developing, extending, and renewing the coaching pool. This has led to a great atmosphere of trust and collaboration among coaches and among organizers, which continues to develop and transcends the interactions between the participants during the weekend, contributing to active and safe experimentation and learning (Edmondson, 1999; 2004).

> Continue with the welcoming feeling that the staff gives. The last thing you'd want in a weekend where creativity is important, is the feeling that you cannot express your opinion and ideas. A large part of this can be your group members, but also they are influenced by the example that you give us. I would really like to thank you for this weekend! (Participant feedback, VLW, March 2018)

From the organizer's point of view, a great aspect of the programme is its flexibility and modular nature. Over the years, we have applied the concept to general as well as specialized contexts by integrating special workshops, and adjusting the coaching pool expertise and focus. Such adjustments can easily be incorporated in the existing organization: preparation and delivery of the weekend; making the flow smooth and familiar for organizing, facilitating and coaching teams; and allowing better scalability and faster adjustment. This flow has been a key factor in bringing the model of the VentureLab

Weekend to other locations, such as Uppsala (Sweden), Budapest (Hungary), and Patiala (India). We first invite the partners to observe the VentureLab Weekend locally in the Netherlands and then adjust it to the needs and themes at the destination.

Another crucial aspect of the success of a programme like the VentureLab Weekend is its integration with the local ecosystem. A very obvious argument lies in the consistency between the interests and ideas of participants (and a theme of the weekend, if it has a thematic focus) and the local human capital (such as the expertise and coaching pool, for example). Health and energy orientations are in the main focus areas of the University of Groningen, suggesting there is a lot of interest from the students and local players in energy and health ideas, which makes it easier to attract coaches and establish the follow-up steps for seriously motivated teams.

Furthermore, as much as it can be developed in a weekend event, the resulting project is just a start for a serious and long-term development, which is impossible (if not damaging) without supportive infrastructure to assist in the follow-up stages. The VentureLab North Accelerator programme is a next step for the ideas developed during the VentureLab Weekend in Groningen. In the Accelerator, teams can work on their individual and team competences, business capabilities and functions, and future strategy for scaling up. Across the locations where the VentureLab Weekend is offered, other accelerator programmes similar to the VentureLab North exist or are in development, allowing the ideas developed during the VentureLab Weekend to flourish.

THE UNIQUE ASPECTS OF THE VENTURELAB WEEKEND: A PARTICIPANT-CENTRED APPROACH TO DEVELOPING ENTREPRENEURIAL SKILLS

An avid entrepreneurship educator will probably note that pitch competition events are not uncommon in the modern practice of teaching entrepreneurship, especially with the rise of franchised events around business idea competitions, gaining more and more visibility. Nevertheless, the fact that the VentureLab Weekend is participant centred in several ways makes it unique.

First, being participant centred, rather than idea centred, means that we do not pre-select idea-owners and teams based on their business ideas and readiness or potential demonstrated (such as in, for example, bootcamps and hackathons), but rather focus on the skills and competence development of participants willing to invest their time in learning about entrepreneurship. This means that if, for instance, a philosophy student without an idea for a business signs up for the programme, we will work on developing his or her skills and competences in business modelling and pitching. Furthermore, most of the participants create the teams at the beginning of the event, allowing participants with very early stage entrepreneurial ideas a chance to partner with other participants who can help them develop those ideas further, utilizing experiential and curiosity-based learning strategies (Robinson et al., 2016). This open, student-centred policy reaches a much broader community of students than regular courses (which would not be offered at, for example, a regular faculty of philosophy), thus creating a larger impact on the student community and differentiating the VentureLab Weekend from other similar activities (for example, other initiatives across Europe, such as the StartUp Weekend franchise).

Second, the VentureLab Weekend is positioned in the niche between courses and modules integrated in regular university programmes (such as minors on entrepreneurship and other courses that integrate the regular curriculum) and other more advanced, hands-on and specialized trainings that focus on business development (the VentureLab North Accelerator programme at the University of Groningen and other similar programmes in the country). By combining the hands-on initiative and several workshops focused on the important theoretical foundations of entrepreneurship, the VentureLab Weekend is an educational activity that creates unique value for the participants by developing their business and presentation competences simultaneously. Thus, our programme provides an opportunity for participants to explore their knowledge from other courses from a practical perspective and further enhances their entrepreneurial skills.

Third, although the VentureLab Weekend positions itself at a very early stage of the entrepreneurial process and is open to participants without prior exposure to entrepreneurship, it aims at providing a real-life experience and prepares participants for the next step of business creation. To do this, we bring together experienced coaches from a variety of businesses and expertise backgrounds (for example, law, marketing, finance, and start-up expertise) who work with the participants and share their practical experience.

Furthermore, participants are aware that if they are serious about business development, they can be eligible to enter the year-long VentureLab North Accelerator programme. It also helps that the team organizing the VentureLab Weekend is the same team that runs the VentureLab North Accelerator programme. They can answer any questions about the programme and, at the same time, scout promising participants for the programme.

Respect and shared attitudes towards the activity are among the core aspects of an efficient classroom (Kenworthy-U'Ren et al., 2005; Sorenson and Milbrandt, 2015). Thus, participants know they are in a community of like-minded people who are serious about the topic and are not attending for the sake of the activity only. There is a real, possible next step that motivates participants to engage with the event and promotes their intrinsic motivation. These elements – focus on the participant, skill, and knowledge development in an experiential way, and commitment to the next step – make the programme comprehensive and evidence-based and allow participants to apply theoretical content in practice with a focus on their personal entrepreneurial development.

The VentureLab Weekend has become an event that the student community looks forward to at the university and excites everyone who is involved, from the organization team to jury members and coaches. By providing an intensive training programme with solid theoretical grounds and an experiential pedagogical approach, the VentureLab Weekend programme is a relevant event that enables participants to develop certain entrepreneurial competences, which they can apply to a wide range of contexts in their lives. As a participant-centred programme, we have taken feedback from participants seriously over the years and reflected within the organization team on how to move forward with the initiative. The feedback has prompted changes (such as the ones described in the reflection section), and it has mostly motivated the organization team to keep developing the VentureLab Weekend as a main activity at our centre.

> Keep it as it is, keep pushing future generations as hard as us and show them—like you did with us—how much is possible in a weekend. We came with vague ideas and shaped them into workable businesses, that is fantastic! (Participant feedback. VLW, March 2019).

NOTE

1. After the first editions of the VentureLab Weekend, we conducted informal reviews of the VentureLab Weekend with participants in our network. Since 2017, we have put a participant evaluation questionnaire of the VentureLab Weekend in place, which focuses on the following questions: 'Thinking about this weekend and all its activities, can you indicate three things that you would like us to: (a) Start, (b) Stop, and (c) Continue.'

REFERENCES

Bhave, M.P. (1994), 'A process model of entrepreneurial venture creation', *Journal of Business Venturing*, **8**, 223–42.
Corbett, A.C. (2005), 'Experiential learning within the process of opportunity identification and exploitation', *Entrepreneurship Theory and Practice*, **29** (4), 473–91.

Costa, S.F., Santos, S.C., Wach, D. and A. Caetano (2018), 'Recognizing opportunities across campus: the effects of cognitive training and entrepreneurial passion on the business opportunity prototype', *Journal of Small Business Management*, **56** (1), 51–75.

Edmondson, A. (1999), 'Psychological safety and learning behavior in work teams', *Administrative Science Quarterly*, **44**, 350–83.

Edmondson, A. (2004), 'Psychological safety, trust and learning: a group-level lens', in R. Kramer and K. Cook (eds), *Trust and Distrust in Organizations: Dilemmas and Approaches*, New York: Russell Sage, pp. 239–72.

Fayolle, A., Gailly, B. and N. Lassas-Clerc (2006), 'Assessing the impact of entrepreneurship education programmes: a new methodology', *Journal of European Industrial Training*, **30** (9), 701–20.

Groen, A.J. (2005), 'Knowledge intensive entrepreneurship in networks: towards a multi-level/multi-dimensional approach', *Journal of Enterprising Culture*, **13** (1), 69–88.

Groen, A.J., Wakkee, I.A.M. and P.C. de Weerd-Nederhof (2008), 'Managing tensions in a high-tech start-up: an innovation journey in social system perspective', *International Small Business Journal*, **26** (1), 57–81.

Hägg, G. and A. Kurczewska (2016), 'Connecting the dots: a discussion on key concepts in contemporary entrepreneurship education', *Education and Training*, **58** (7–8), 700–714.

Holman, D. (2000), 'Contemporary models of management education in the UK', *Management Learning*, **31** (2), 197–217.

Kenworthy-U'Ren, A., Zlotkowski, E. and A.H. Van de Ven (2005), 'Toward a scholarship of engagement: a dialogue between Andy Van de Ven and Edward Zlotkowski', *Academy of Management Learning & Education*, **4** (3), 355–62.

Kirkman, B.L., Cordery, J.L., Mathieu, J., Rosen, B. and M. Kukenberger (2013), 'Global organizational communities of practice: the effects of nationality diversity, psychological safety, and media richness on community performance', *Human Relations*, **66** (3), 333–62.

Kolb, A.Y. and D.A. Kolb (2005), 'Learning styles and learning spaces: enhancing experiential learning in higher education', *Academy of Management Learning & Education*, **4** (2), 193–212.

Kolb, D.A. (1984), *Experiential Learning: Experience as the Source of Learning and Development*, Englewood Cliffs, NJ: Prentice Hall.

Parsons, T. (1964), *The Social System*, New York: The Free Press.

Pittaway, L. and J. Cope (2007), 'Entrepreneurship education: a systematic review of the evidence', *International Small Business Journal*, **25** (5), 479–510.

Politis, D. (2005), 'The process of entrepreneurial learning: a conceptual framework', *Entrepreneurship Theory and Practice*, **29** (4), 399–424.

Rasmussen, E. and R. Sørheim (2006), 'Action-based entrepreneurship education', *Technovation*, **26** (2), 185–94.

Robinson, S., Neergaard, H., Tanggaard, L. and N.F. Krueger (2016), 'New horizons in entrepreneurship education: from teacher-led to student-centered learning', *Education + Training*, **58** (7/8), 661–83.

Sarasvathy, S.D. (2001), 'Causation and effectuation: toward a theoretical shift from economic inevitability to entrepreneurial contingency', *Academy of Management Review*, **26** (2), 243–63.

Sarasvathy, S.D. (2008), *Effectuation: Elements of Entrepreneurial Expertise*, Cheltenham, UK and Northampton, MA, USA: Edward Elgar Publishing.

Sorenson, R.L. and J.M. Milbrandt (2015), 'A family affair – teaching families versus individuals: insights gained from 24 years of family business education', *Academy of Management Learning & Education*, **14** (3), 366–84.

West, M.A. (2002), 'Sparkling fountains or stagnant ponds: an integrative model of creativity and innovation implementation in work groups', *Applied Psychology: An International Journal*, **51**, 355–424.

9. Training entrepreneurial competences involving key stakeholders

Patricia P. Iglesias-Sánchez, Carmina Jambrino Maldonado and Carlos de las Heras-Pedrosa

DESCRIPTION OF THE INITIATIVE

The short entrepreneurship education initiative at Malaga University trained entrepreneurial competences through a hackathon, role playing, team building and a practical case with an entrepreneur. The week-long initiative targeted Malaga University students in any degree course. What is highlighted in this chapter is the involvement of lecturers, students and entrepreneurs in the design, implementation and evaluation of activities. Our initiative shows that their participation improves predisposition to learn and motivation in an educational environment. The ultimate goal is to test whether the acquisition of entrepreneurial competences can improve graduates' employability and increase entrepreneurial intention (EI).

Context

The University of Malaga (UMA) is a public institution in southern Spain that promotes outstanding research and teaching within the European Higher Education Area with a university community of just over 40 000 people. Currently, UMA offers an extensive catalogue of specialized teaching and postgraduate study and all kinds of scientific and cultural activities for better and more complete university training.

UMA has been striving to showcase entrepreneurship as a professional development opportunity for several years. Its efforts to become an entrepreneurial university can be seen in several consolidated and recent initiatives. It is worth recognizing the importance of the annual spin-off contest, a trail-blazer in Spain, which has now been held over 23 times and enjoys the support of several business development programmes and business incubation services.

Additionally, UMA has formed Link, an incubator and a place for meeting and motivating entrepreneurial spirit with a comprehensive annual activities programme. Moreover, it is considered a way to improve relationships between the academic institution and the production framework and even a good formula to increase the transfer of technology and knowledge. As a result of this, UMA offers a complete ecosystem of programmes to enhance entrepreneurial spirit, incubators, accelerators, contests of business creation, challenges with enterprise participation, events and forums, mentoring programmes and so on.

Despite extensive experience in entrepreneurial activities, UMA currently promotes entrepreneurship and employment programmes separately. The first programme focuses on business creation and transfer of technology – specially focusing on spin-offs and start-ups, as well as activities to disseminate and raise entrepreneurial spirit. The second programme is designed to teach graduates how to know and adapt themselves better to the marketplace. In this regard, it should be emphasized that the job guidance and intermediation service has a unit on professional practices during and after graduation and has its own employment agency.

Origin of the Initiative

Educational innovation has been a strategic element for UMA in recent years in order to provide a range of educational offerings geared to the needs of current society. A call for proposals is, therefore, published annually, and lecturers can design activities aimed at achieving higher quality in student learning, overcoming the traditional paradigm at the university. 'It implies transcending academic knowledge and passing from the student's passive learning to a conception where learning is interaction and it is built among all' (UNESCO, 2016: 3). There is no dispute regarding students' need for opportunities to practise what they are learning and experience the kind of tasks they will be expected to demonstrate competence in during their professional life. This context was the starting point for the initiative to train entrepreneurial competences.

The project was entitled 'Empowerment of entrepreneurship as cross-curricular competence for employability and enterprise creation in university students and the setting-up of good practice environment for designing entrepreneurial education programmes in higher education' (PIE 17-088). The pilot scheme with training activities was run over a week in the 2017–2018 academic year, although the design and evaluation, even the focus group, lasted longer.

Focus

Entrepreneurship is considered to be a transversal competence that aims to increase employability and adaptability to the job market (Brockmann et al.,

2011). In recent years, policy makers have focused fully on this issue (Eurostat, 2017) since the solution to youth unemployment requires a shift to active employment policies, training and access to the labour market. The dimension of the youth unemployment problem is not the same in all European countries, but it is a shared challenge for governments. Greece, Spain, Italy and Portugal have the highest rates: in Spain, specifically, the youth unemployment rate was 31.7 per cent in 2019 (Eurostat, 2019). In this regard, involvement of multiple stakeholders, including the university, is needed (Machin and McNally, 2007).

Higher levels of employment and effective policies in business creation are a priority that cannot be left solely up to governments. Universities can play a fundamental role in keeping their social commitment. The solution involves developing competences according to labour market requirements (Brockmann et al., 2011), and universities that ensure graduates' employability. Consequently, the challenge is to go beyond the knowledge component to combine curricular changes based on competences with innovative learning methods. Heijde and Van der Heijden (2006) and Jackson (2014) have conducted some of the most relevant research on this topic. They focus on how competences have an impact on the improvement of employability. However, present day connection between entrepreneurial competences and employability remains widely under-researched (Machin and McNally, 2007; Morris et al., 2013) precisely because of a deep conviction that entrepreneurship is primarily related to business creation only. Challenging this traditional approach was the core of the initiative.

Purpose and Description of the Initiative

The aim of the project was to train competences, specifically those related to entrepreneurship, as a differentiating factor to be more competitive in the labour market. Currently, theoretical knowledge is not the most demanded aptitude by companies; they prefer young university graduates with specific skills rather than extra qualifications without a competence profile of well-established practice (Evers et al., 1998). Employability is not dependent upon literacy or numeracy skills; it is the result of a balanced set of communication, teamwork, problem-solving, self-management, planning and organizing, technology, lifelong learning, and initiative and enterprise skills. All of these are easily associated with being an entrepreneur. Furthermore, the association between entrepreneurial competences and outcomes in labour development made by RezaeiZadeh et al. (2017) endorses the approach adopted in this proposal.

For the initiative, 329 students were divided into groups and participated in a role-playing game, team building, real case studies with an entrepreneur as problem-solving exercises, and finally in a hackathon. Participation was completely voluntary. Nevertheless, we tried to achieve a fair distribution

Table 9.1   Demographic factors

		Frequency	%
Gender	Male	153	46.5
	Female	176	53.5
University degree	Computer Engineering	19	5.2
	Industrial Engineering	18	4.9
	Sciences	35	9.6
	Tourism	72	19.8
	Business Management	137	37.6
	Communication Sciences	34	9.3
	Social and Labour Sciences	3	0.8
	Law	11	3.0
Knowledge area	Business Management	137	42.0
	Non-business Management	192	58.0

Source: Iglesias-Sánchez et al., 2019.

between students in each kind of activity; consequently, 80 students participated in team building, 80 in the hackathon, 84 in case studies and 85 in the role-playing game.

Students came from various degrees and different centres belonging to UMA (Table 9.1). The criterion for choosing students was that they be enrolled in university degrees that included specific courses on business creation. Nevertheless, participation in this programme was open, and the invitation clearly sought to train entrepreneurial competences, not to create businesses specifically.

Gender distribution and area of knowledge are two considerations that were always kept in mind. On the one hand, both genders were well represented in the study (46.5 per cent men and 53.5 per cent women), which was in line with the gender balance at UMA. On the other hand, the students were equally distributed between business and management programmes and non-business and management programmes precisely so that the research could overcome a gap in the literature, which mainly focuses on students participating in business and management faculties and economic and business sciences faculties. In this initiative, the sample, disaggregated by areas, correlates with 42 per cent of students pursuing non-business degrees compared to 58 per cent pursuing business ones. This question should be stressed because the trend in the previous literature is to select a sample of students from business (Susanj et al., 2015), or to a lesser extent, engineering (Morales-Alonso et al., 2015), but the two groups are compared in very few instances (Maresch et al., 2016; Solesvik, 2013). Degrees of humanities and some social sciences, as included in this project, have been considered to a far lower extent.

Regarding lecturers' involvement, it should be emphasized that they belonged to different knowledge areas, and those who taught business creation did not necessarily take part. The same gender distribution and area of knowledge criteria were applied.

After thoroughly reviewing the literature of entrepreneurship education, the methodological learning tools to promote capacity development over short periods were chosen. However, given the large number of described activities in the literature, the choice was supported by common agreement of lecturers and students. Both groups reflected their vision of different types of activities. First, they agreed on specific skills and competences related to each activity, and immediately after, they discussed what content and focus would be more attractive and inspiring to learn about, but above all, what would be best to improve the discussed competences. This discussion was first held on the virtual campus over two days. Afterwards, the main conclusions were presented and discussed with a small group of volunteers (lecturers and students) in a two-hour session. This debate served to choose the following activities: a hackathon, team-building activities, a case study with an entrepreneur, and a role-playing game.

A more detailed explanation and the technical details of each activity are described below and in Table 9.2 in order to understand the underpinning concept of the initiative.

1. *Hackathon*: An activity focused on solving practical problems that continues for a long time and requires a great deal of energy, patience and determination. It combines participants with different profiles who generally do not meet one another beforehand.
2. *Team building*: The action or process of causing a group of people to work together effectively as a team, especially by means of activities and events designed to increase motivation and promote cooperation focusing in a common challenge. There is competition between groups.
3. *Practical case study with an entrepreneur*: A case study is a learning method that involves an up-close, in-depth and detailed examination of a case subject and its related contextual conditions. Participants must work together to search for proposals to the case study problem before the real solution and consequences are revealed.
4. *Role playing*: A technique that allows students to explore realistic situations by interacting with others in a managed way in order to develop experience and test different strategies in a supported environment. It is a way of working through a situation, a scenario or a problem by assuming roles and practising what to say and do in a safe setting.

Each of these activities involved the lecturers' collaboration. They managed the development of the activity, even in practical cases with entrepreneurs. Role playing and practical cases with entrepreneurs were organized in conventional classes. However, the hackathon and team building were two activities organized outside the university, taking advantage of attractive events for undergraduates such as entrepreneurship forums. All the activities described took place once only, and their organization required dividing the students into small groups to ensure better management and learning outcomes of the experience. In a sense, competition between participants was necessary to provide a wider collection of proposals and ways of solving the same problems.

Furthermore, the organization of groups enabled us to examine how the training activities had an impact on the improvement of employability and to evaluate which questions were more valuable from the point of view of the students, lecturers and entrepreneurs. Therefore, the questions are, in a way, the result of a shared discussion between key stakeholders in educational programmes. In Table 9.3 and Table 9.4, the details of each focus group are provided. The focus groups were held one week after the training activities.

The contrast between the results of quantitative measurement of EI, entrepreneurial competences before and after the programme and the discussions related to the focus groups provides a better understanding of which entrepreneurial-related competence-training activities were more attractive and effective for undergraduates and lecturers for future labour integration.

Theoretical Framework and Assessment

As mentioned above, measuring and comparing the results derived from each learning tool are barely covered in previous research or similar experiments. The theory of planned behaviour (TPB) (Ajzen, 1991) and identification of entrepreneurial competences were used to overcome this aspect and to meet the set objectives. In line with our objectives, the effect on competence profile, highlighted entrepreneurial skills and the measurement of EI are the indicators for assessing the outcomes of the initiative (Table 9.5). From a broader perspective, entrepreneurship is always understood as a particular way of making decisions and facing certain situations in personal and professional life (with or without one's own business).

On the one hand, Ajzen's TPB model (1991) supports the initial EI measurements in university students. Additionally, the most mentioned entrepreneurial competences in the literature are the basis for designing different training tools and, consequently, they are the focus of the final analysis (Mitchelmore and Rowley, 2010; RezaeiZadeh et al., 2017). First, the application of the TPB is justified because it is the most solid model that can be used to explain the predisposition and intention to set up a business (Armitage and Conner,

Table 9.2   *Technical details of training activities*

Hackathon: Plan and design for the next entrepreneurs fair, and work in a dossier for attracting sponsors.

Participants	Duration	Space	Groups	Technical orientation	Human resources
80	The entire day	Outside the university in entrepreneurs fair	8	The groups compete against one another with a common challenge. There was an award for motivation.	Four lecturers, two coaches (two external collaborators)

Team building: Two different team-building activities were developed.
The barter puzzle and **building a bridge**.
1. Groups must complete a puzzle, but the pieces are mixed. All groups have the pieces needed for the other groups to finish the activity. So they have to strategize, assign roles and barter with other teams to get the pieces for their puzzle.
2. The groups are re-organized into larger ones. Each group has the same material for building a bridge (dry noodles, Lego, popsicle sticks and so on). The goal is to construct two bridges as identical as possible. The group cannot see what the other team is doing, but they are allowed to communicate verbally.

Participants	Duration	Space	Groups	Technical orientation	Human resources
80	Four hours	Outside the university in entrepreneurs fair	4	The students are engaged in different tasks that can be solved together. The students are involved in large group team building and small-group team building. First, students are placed in set groups that are together for the entire activity. After, at the end of the activity, all groups work together in a community challenge.	Three lecturers and two external collaborators specialized in business events

Hackathon: Plan and design for the next entrepreneurs fair, and work in a dossier for attracting sponsors.

Practical case: Three different entrepreneurs present a real case of their companies. Students must solve problems by making choices as in real life and thinking about resources, communication and consequences. After, each group presents their solution. In the final part, there is a discussion regarding all proposed scenarios and decisions. Finally, the entrepreneurs explain their decision made and the results of performance.

Participants	Duration	Space	Groups	Technical orientation	Human resources
84	Two hours	Conventional classes	14	Lecturers work with entrepreneurs to identify real problems or situations in their companies for a practical case according to the case study method.	Three entrepreneurs and three lecturers

Role playing: There are cards with the description of a fictional business venture and cards corresponding to investors. These are distributed among participants randomly. Each student has to perform the role that they have. They have 60 minutes to prepare their speech. After this, they should present their business with the goal of achieving funds from their classmates. The ventures are presented almost exactly as they would be presented in a real-life situation: a three-minute elevator pitch followed by an investor summary and financials.

Participants	Duration	Space	Groups	Technical orientation	Human resources
85	Two hours	Conventional classes	Participants divided into five large groups. In each group, the participants are organized in pairs.	Participants work in pairs. Role playing is developed in practical classes in which the number of students is less numerous.	Six lecturers

Source: Iglesias-Sánchez et al., 2019.

2001), especially if the focus is on pedagogical processes and learning contexts (Aloulou, 2016; Fayolle et al., 2006; Krueger et al., 2000). In any event, we insist on the idea that EI could be useful in other areas beyond business creation. For example, EI may also reflect a greater ability to face complex situations as a selection process.

On the other hand, according to Krueger et al. (2000) and based on Shapero's and Sokol's model (1982) and Ajzen's model (1991), internal traits

Table 9.3   *Participants in focus groups*

Focus Group 1 – Students A

1. Student participant in the hackathon pursuing a Business and Management degree (F)
2. Student participant in team building pursuing a Business and Management degree (M)
3. Student participant in the case training activity with a collaborator entrepreneur pursuing a Business and Management degree (F)
4. Student participant in role playing pursuing a Business and Management degree (M)
5. Student participant in the hackathon pursuing a Non-business and Management degree (F)
6. Student participant in role playing pursuing a Non-business and Management degree (M)
7. Student non-participant degree in the first year of a Business and Management degree (F)
8. Student non-participant in the final year of a Non-business and Management degree (F)

Focus Group 2 – Students B

1. Student participant in the hackathon pursuing a Non-business and Management degree (M)
2. Student participant in team building pursuing a Non-business and Management degree (F)
3. Student participant in the case training activity with a collaborator entrepreneur pursuing a Non-business and Management degree (M)
4. Student participant in role playing pursuing a Business and Management degree (F)
5. Student participant in team building pursuing a Business and Management degree (M)
6. Student participant in the case training activity with a collaborator entrepreneur pursuing a Business and Management degree (F)
7. Student non-participant in the first year of a Non-business and Management degree (M)
8. Student non-participant in the final year of a Business and Management degree (M)

Focus Group 3 – Lecturers

1. Lecturer involved in the hackathon and in role play (F)
2. Lecturer involved in team building and in the case training activity with a collaborator entrepreneur (F)
3. Lecturer responsible for business creation subject but non-participant in the pilot training activities (M)
4. Collaborator entrepreneur in the case training activity (M)
5. Lecturer involved in the hackathon and case training activity (M)
6. Lecturer involved in team building and role playing (F)
7. Lecturer responsible for business creation subject and participant in all the training activities (F)
8. Lecturer non-participant in the pilot training activities, not related to business creation programmes but with some involvement in work experience programmes (M)

Source: Iglesias-Sánchez et al., 2019.

and external aspects (sociocultural factors) could be moderated by the learning process, and entrepreneurial competences could be improved as a consequence of this (RezaeiZadeh et al., 2017). There is a wide focus in the literature on entrepreneurial personal traits and skills, but consensus regarding a certain core of shared characteristics is emerging out of this intensive discussion: creativity, risk-taking and proactivity.

These three entrepreneurial competences are shared in each training activity, but common ideas from students and lecturers about other valuable competences are also linked with the chosen activities. Curiously, the additional

Table 9.4   *Demographic factors of focus group participants*

Gender	Male	10	42.0%
	Female	14	58.0%
Knowledge area	Business and management	12	50.0%
	Non-business and management	12	50.0%
Kind of activity	Hackathon	4	16.6%
	Cases	6	25.0%
	Role play	6	25.0%
	Team building	4	16.6%
	Any activity	4	16.6%
Role	Students	12	66.0%
	Lecturers	7	30.0%
	Collaborators	1	4.0%

Source: Iglesias-Sánchez et al., 2019.

competences are in line with the sets of skills and abilities detailed previously in this chapter. Mitchelmore and Rowley (2010) emphasized the relevance of establishing an agenda for future research and experiments in relation to entrepreneurial competences and their implications in economic and social development. So far, the influence of the aforementioned entrepreneurial competences on entrepreneurship has been shown in several research papers (Liñán, 2008; RezaeiZadeh et al., 2017; Sarri et al., 2010; Uy et al., 2015; Veciana and Urbano, 2008). Additionally, Bowman (2010) and Brockmann et al. (2011) stress that entrepreneurial competences are better adapted to the labour market.

The questionnaire used to evaluate the initiative is divided into five blocks. The first three, creativity, risk-taking and proactivity, correspond to the entrepreneur internal dimension (Liñán, 2008; Sarri et al., 2010; Uy et al., 2015). Regarding the external dimension, entrepreneurial image is the main item (Veciana and Urbano, 2008). A 7-point Likert scale, with 1 expressing strongest disagreement and 7 the highest level of agreement, was used to analyse all the aforementioned items.

The approach should be based on a holistic and comparative view so EI from the TPB model and entrepreneurial competences are measured among the same students before and after participation in the activities (Tables 9.5 and 9.6). In a traditional way, this initiative measures the impact of entrepreneurial activities in higher education through EI, and entrepreneurial-related skills are complementarily included as an outcome. There is a connection between these two concepts but beyond the improvement in competency profile, the contribution in graduates' employability can be highlighted.

Table 9.5   *Average EI and entrepreneurial competences before and
after participation in activities*

	Before Training Activities	After Training Activities
Entrepreneurial intention	4.4	4.7
Creativity	4.9	5.4
Risk-taking	3.7	5.2
Proactivity	4.9	5.1
Entrepreneurship image	3.1	5.2
Entrepreneurial competences (sum of the averages)	4.2	5.2

Source: Iglesias-Sánchez et al., 2019.

REFLECTION ON THE INITIATIVE

The core of this research work is analysing entrepreneurial competences and EI as an indicator of being better prepared to face labour market and professional development. Our reflections are based on our qualitative and quantitative assessment of the initiative. In line with the main objective pursued, the focus is to test the effectiveness of a set of tools designed to improve entrepreneurial competences and to compare their results. Fayolle (2013: 696) points out that few studies set out to compare the effectiveness and efficiency of different teaching methods.

Based on the results, we emphasize that the training activities carried out during the initiative show that EI increases 0.3 per cent (Table 9.5) with respect to the initial measurement made before participation. Despite a general improvement in EI, students' intention to start a business was moderate. Although this seems to have little relevance in quantitative terms, the qualitative results provide an interesting explanation of these values. They show that setting up one's own business is an attractive but long-term goal.

The average of each skill was counted separately for each training activity (Table 9.5), and the sum of the averages of internal dimensions was calculated in order to provide a general value of entrepreneurial competences before and after participation (Table 9.5). It should be emphasized that all training activities had a positive effect on the chosen skills. Overall, entrepreneurial competences improved by one percentage point from 4.2 per cent to 5.2 per cent. Likewise, the improvement took place separately in each activity. However, the most striking difference was in risk-taking. Participation in any of the training activities showed an improvement in students' entrepreneurial competences. The case

Table 9.6   *EI and competences classified by type of training activity*

	EI	Creativity	Risk-taking	Pro-activity	Entrepreneur image	Σ Entrepreneurial competences	Additional outstanding competences mentioned in focus groups
Hackathon	4.8	6	5.3	4.4	5.8	5.3	Teamwork, communication skills
Team building	4.9	5.7	5.2	5	4	5	Teamwork, negotiation skills
Case with an entrepreneur	5	5	5.6	5.2	6.3	5.5	Problem-solving skills, self-management
Role play	4.2	4.9	4.7	5.3	4.5	4.8	Communication skills, employability

Source: Iglesias-Sánchez et al., 2019

with an entrepreneur had the best overall results, followed by the hackathon, team building and finally role playing, which placed lowest in the ranking.

Additionally, this study found a significant correlation between EI and training activities. However, the main point was to find out which tools can improve entrepreneurial competences. The development of measurement tools to test the real impact of entrepreneurial competences has been referred to in previous literature (Schelfhout et al., 2016), and this initiative focused precisely on this issue. Table 9.6 shows the impact of each training activity on EI. The discussions derived from the focus groups reinforce the results of the quantitative analysis, providing extra details about this quantitative approach. The engagement with each activity agrees with the aforementioned values.

Nevertheless, some training activities contributed to additional competences. For example, the hackathon was the training activity that allows the participants to develop creativity; risk-taking was taught through the case with an entrepreneur. Meanwhile, role playing was shown as the best tool for improving empathy and negotiation skills, and team building was positively valued for acquiring communication skills. Therefore, the pedagogical method that highlights active problem-solving in real-life situations is inspiring and enhances skills. The students gained self-confidence because they learned how to organize the resources at their disposal in a natural way. They felt that they were able to solve problems and were aware that competences are valuable to themselves and companies. Therefore, acquisition of entrepreneurial competences influenced students' competence profile, and this experiential learning contributed to gaining these kinds of skills.

In fact, students need a set of skills to join the employment market and act entrepreneurially in different contexts beyond starting a business. As a result of this, educational institutions should assume that learning involves the active participation of the main stakeholders. Their role is crucial to the construction of new understanding and the achievement of desirable rates of graduate employment. Regarding the reflections of the qualitative analysis, we would like to point out that all participants sensed that improvement in their competences would make their integration into the labour market easier. Moreover, they were aware that competences are not just useful in starting up companies but are also becoming a requirement in selection processes.

Furthermore, there is a consensus as to how innovative and practical methods have a positive effect on the learning, motivation and predisposition of students. Curiously, both lecturers and students indicated their desire to participate in these kinds of practices, but it is difficult to make this possible, usually due to a lack of tools or as result of the relative rigidity of education programmes in higher education. Lecturers also assume the need to be trained, advised, equipped and supported for this challenge, and curricula need to be modernized, coinciding with the research by Peltonen (2015). It should also be noted that the participants agreed that a balance between knowledge and competences might be established in order to achieve quality higher education and ensure a better match between academic requests and labour market demands, even in their daily lives. Moreover, the training activities developed are linked to other additional competences that match the conclusions of RezaeiZadeh et al.'s research work (2017).

To summarize, the initiative has succeeded in providing entrepreneurship as a way to improve the level of enterprise creation and employability in higher education. In this way, students and graduates understand how their skills could be improved and adapted successfully to labour market requirements through different teaching and training competence programmes.

All these reflections prompted us to propose that university graduates would have their different competences certified with a standardized and common mechanism on their academic record and an official document. For this purpose, training competence activities and an evaluation system of their acquisition would be necessary. Thus, the recruitment processes would be easier and faster and would benefit from the university guarantee regarding valuable competences in job performance. Additionally, this would allow us to evaluate the efficiency of effort made and to demonstrate the potential of designing educational programmes with the competence-based approach.

Additionally, the enhancement of relationships with key stakeholders is seen as a challenge in any field, but specifically in higher education. The involvement of students, lecturers and companies is the starting point for building a collaborative model. As demonstrated by this pilot experience, the implementation of spaces for participation, dialogue and reflection increases self-empowerment, allowing all the stakeholders to generate confidence in themselves and participate actively in the continuous improvement of the quality of higher education. Perhaps this is the main value of the initiative. As a result of this, it encourages us to undertake similar initiatives and learn from them.

Finally, the following can be highlighted regarding the lessons learned from this experiment:

1. Having institutional support is essential. The involvement of different faculties adds complexity to the logistics of activities for training entrepreneurial competences. Communication and engagement should be shown at all levels.
2. Entrepreneurs are a key element because students and even lecturers realize that entrepreneurship is an attitude and a philosophy to solve problems and face life with or without being self-employed.
3. Designing a collaborative model involving lecturers, students and entrepreneurs means accepting a dynamic process. It should be associated with criteria merely to support the implementation and evaluation system to enable the model.
4. Finally, another lesson learned is that participation in this initiative did not simultaneously contribute to engaging and training competences step-by-step and allowing students to test their progress and outcomes better. Moreover, a more reliable comparison would be possible as each group of students participated in a different training activity in this experiment. The individual traits are linked to EI and involve a level of development for each competence; consequently, only a joint measure would reflect the impact over time.

THE UNIQUE ASPECT OF THE INITIATIVE

The most innovative aspect of our initiative is the perspective regarding being an entrepreneur. It seems that, generally speaking, students link entrepreneurship with business creation, and they do not think about it as an attitude toward life. Generally speaking, university students do not rely on entrepreneurship as a career opportunity. The initiative breaks away from the limitation that the positive effect that entrepreneurial education has on business creation, and it provides participants (lecturers and students) with a global vision of the contribution of entrepreneurial competences to personal and professional development. As a result, the training activities have generated improvements in traditional entrepreneur vision. This is especially noticeable among those who participated in solving a practical case with an entrepreneur.

Furthermore, undergraduates were very much in favour of the idea of becoming an entrepreneur after participating in this project. The initial reticence regarding setting up a business was a recurring theme in the focus groups with students. The downside of the current methods of teaching business creation is that they seem boring or scarcely credible. Most students do not see preparing a business plan as a motivating activity to awaken their entrepreneurial spirit. In any event, this question is consistent with the opinions expressed in favour of innovative and practical learning methods.

This initiative shows that learning methods that focus on experiential learning with a competence-based approach are more efficient than the dissemination of knowledge. Using active participation to find solutions to problems in real-life situations as a teaching method creates more engagement with students. It should be emphasized that collaborations with entrepreneurs and using scenarios and places outside the university increase students' attention and motivation, as they are seen by students as a chance to keep in touch with the real world.

As a result, motivation and a lasting impact occur. Likewise, lecturers are receptive and interested in applying this pedagogy to their lessons whenever they have the support and recognition of their practical implementation. Finally, companies – through real entrepreneurial vision – welcome the existence of programmes that prepare students for entry into employment. Furthermore, lecturers and entrepreneurs agree that a special effort should be made in this direction to fulfil company expectations and implement the university's commitment to society.

Learning provided by this initiative highlights that this method allows competences to be naturally developed in a more efficient and sustainable way as they are not considered compulsory knowledge. Entrepreneurial education programmes usually focus more on knowledge than on competences. Too much attention is given to transferring learning methods and not enough to individual small-group learning methods, such as individual counselling, workshops, project teams and so on.

The short entrepreneurial-competence training activities function properly, but they should underpin the whole curriculum. Furthermore, the mainstreaming advantages and the effects on employability should be emphasized. Entrepreneurial competences could have a multiplying effect on students' professional and personal profiles. In conclusion, the authors propose a new framework to analyse tools to train competences and, specifically, the potential of entrepreneurial competences for integration into the labour market. Moreover, new tools or ground-breaking initiatives promote entrepreneurship from a different and global perspective. At present, this pilot experience only tests the improvement of entrepreneurial competences from a student's point of view but an evaluation of their performance in the labour market is needed.

Despite the many positive elements related to these kinds of initiatives, it should be recognized that as they are not part of a global university strategy, the impact is not nearly as great as that of comparable, entrepreneurial training improvement programmes. Entrepreneurship as transversal competence implies an additional effort of communication and coordination because it is not involved solely in a specific knowledge area or degree.

Additionally, the support necessary for academic staff and the strengthening of ties between the university and companies should be developed. Consequently, the main issue that has been raised concerns the available tools and specific workshops aimed at lecturers in order to enhance the application of these innovative learning methods. Regardless of their personal motivation, lecturers need institutional support to develop and implement these measures effectively. However, strengthening the relationship between the university and companies is essential. According to the comments gathered, only dedicated collaboration between both would provide an enabling environment for improved employability. Additionally, this coordination between the academic and business world could be the next step for suitable assessment of competence profiles.

This latter question is a point that is of particular interest because it remains a great challenge in higher education to achieve the desirable scenario proposed by the triple helix model (Etzkowitz and Leydesdorff, 2000). Therefore, this effort seems to confer a benefit to university image in terms of traditional entrepreneurial education programmes and provides a global and more open vision of entrepreneurship and entrepreneurs. The whole university community appreciates the university's firm commitment to increasing the availability of training resources and tools over the coming years for these kinds of proposals.

The designing of training programmes, tools and learning methods in higher education is usually the responsibility of the education system, but universities maintain a degree of autonomy. This small freedom makes a difference in what each institution does and how. This framework is an opportunity to change the traditional image of the university and move closer to society's new requirements. However, the above inspiring scenario requires additional efforts and adaptation to implement it properly.

In general, the initiative provides insights about pedagogy and quality of dynamics for training competences, with a clear distinction between process and content-based approaches. In the short term, a growing number of universities could be involved in engaging and experimenting with experiential and participative practices for the purpose of improving entrepreneurial competences for employability improvement, marketing and branding, as well as the potential for developing new revenue streams. However, even today, further efforts are needed on stakeholders' involvement in the educational environment.

This initiative shows that motivation for students to contribute is varied. Regarding lecturers, they want to keep motivated in the context of the learning environment and strike a balance between knowledge associated with higher education and labour market requirements. Other potential entrepreneurial education programmes can be developed with the capacity to come together to solve the unemployment problem and the effective connection between the productive sector and universities. This potential should be highlighted as the main innovative aspect of the design and development of this initiative.

REFERENCES

Ajzen, I. (1991), 'The theory of planned behavior', *Organizational Behavior and Human Decision Processes*, **50** (2), 179–211.

Aloulou, W.J. (2016), 'Predicting entrepreneurial intentions of final year Saudi university business students by applying the theory of planned behavior', *Journal of Small Business and Enterprise Development*, **23** (4), 1142–64.

Armitage, C.J. and M. Conner (2001), 'Efficacy of the theory of planned behavior: a meta-analytic review', *British Journal of Social Psychology*, **40** (4), 471–99.

Bowman, K. (2010), 'Background paper for the AQF Council on generic skills', Australian Canberra: Qualification Framework Council.

Brockmann, M., Clarke, L. and C. Winch (2011), *Knowledge, Skills and Competence in the European Labour Market: What's in a Vocational Qualification?* Abingdon: Routledge.

Etzkowitz, H. and L. Leydesdorff (2000), 'The dynamics of innovation: from National Systems and "Mode 2" to a Triple Helix of university–industry–government relations', *Research Policy*, **29** (2), 10–123.

Eurostat (2017), *Quality Report of the European Union Labour Force Survey 2015*, Luxembourg: Publications Office of the European Union.

Eurostat (2019), 'Youth unemployment rate in EU countries', available at https://www.statista.com/statistics/266228/youth-unemployment-rate-in-eu-countries/.

Evers, F.T., Rush, J.C. and I. Berdrow (1998), *The Bases of Competence. Skills for Lifelong Learning and Employability*, San Francisco, CA: Jossey-Bass Publishers.

Fayolle, A. (2013), 'Personal views on the future of entrepreneurship education', *Entrepreneurship & Regional Development*, **25** (7–8), 692–701.

Fayolle, A., Benoît, G. and N. Lassas-Clerc (2006), 'Assessing the impact of entrepreneurship education programs: a new methodology', *Journal of European Industrial Training*, **39** (9), 701–20.

Heijde, C.M. Van der and B.I. Van der Heijden (2006), 'A competence-based and multidimensional operationalization and measurement of employability', *Human Resource Management*, **45** (3), 449–76.

Iglesias-Sánchez, P.P., Jambrino-Maldonado, C. and C. de las Heras-Pedrosa (2019), 'Training Entrepreneurial Competences with Open Innovation Paradigm in Higher Education', *Sustainability*, **11** (17), 4689.

Jackson, D. (2014), 'Testing a model of undergraduate competence in employability skills and its implications for stakeholders', *Journal of Education and Work*, **27** (2), 220–42.

Krueger Jr, N.F., Reilly, M.D. and A.L. Carsrud (2000), 'Competing models of entrepreneurial intentions', *Journal of Business Venturing*, **15** (5–6), 411–32.

Liñán, F. (2008), 'Skill and value perceptions: how do they affect entrepreneurial intentions?' *International Entrepreneurship and Management Journal*, **4** (3), 257–72.

Machin, S. and S. McNally (2007), 'Tertiary education systems and labour markets', Education and Training Policy Division, OECD, **6**.

Maresch, D., Harms, R., Kailer, N. and B. Wimmer-Wurm (2016), 'The impact of entrepreneurship education on the entrepreneurial intention of students in science and engineering versus business studies university programs', *Technological Forecasting & Social Change*, **104**, 172–9.

Mitchelmore, S. and J. Rowley (2010), 'Entrepreneurial competencies: a literature review and development agenda', *International Journal of Entrepreneurial Behaviour & Research*, **16** (2), 92–111.

Morales-Alonso, G., Pablo-Lerchundi, I. and M.C. Núñez-Del-Río (2015), 'Entrepreneurial intention of engineering students and associated influence of contextual factors', *Revista de Psicología Social*, **31** (1), 75–108.

Morris, M.H., Webb, J.W., Fu, J. and S. Singhal (2013), 'A competency-based perspective on entrepreneurship education: conceptual and empirical insights', *Journal of Small Business Management*, **51** (3), 352–69.

Peltonen, K. (2015), 'How can teachers' competences be developed? A collaborative learning perspective', *Education & Training*, **57** (5), 492–511.

RezaeiZadeh, M., Hogan, M., O'Reilly, J., Cunningham, J. and E. Murphy (2017), 'Core entrepreneurial competencies and their interdependencies: insights from a study of Irish and Iranian entrepreneurs, university students and academics', *International Entrepreneurship and Management Journal*, **13** (1), 35–73.

Sarri, K.K., Bakouros, I.L. and E. Petridou (2010), 'Entrepreneur training for creativity and innovation', *Journal of European Industrial Training*, **34** (3), 270–88.

Schelfhout, W., Bruggeman, K. and S. De Maeyer (2016), 'Evaluation of entrepreneurial competence through scaled behavioural indicators: validation of an instrument', *Studies in Educational Evaluation*, **51**, 29–41.

Shapero, A. and L. Sokol (1982), 'The social dimensions of entrepreneurship', in C. Kent, D. Sexton and K.H. Vesper (eds), *Encyclopedia of Entrepreneurship*, Englewood Cliffs, NJ: Prentice Hall, pp. 72–90.

Solesvik, M.Z. (2013), 'Entrepreneurial motivations and intentions: investigating the role of education major', *Education & Training*, **55** (3), 253–71.

Susanj, Z., Jakopec, A. and I.M. Krecar (2015), 'Verifying the model of predicting entrepreneurial intention among students of business and non-business orientation', *Management: Journal of Contemporary Management Issues*, **20** (2), 49–69.

UNESCO (2016), *Education for the Twenty-First Century*, Bangkok: UNESCO.

Uy, M.A., Chan, K.Y., Sam, Y.L., Ho, M.H.R. and O.S. Chernyshenko (2015), 'Proactivity, adaptability and boundaryless career attitudes: the mediating role of entrepreneurial alertness', *Journal of Vocational Behavior*, **86**, 115–23.

Veciana, J.M. and D. Urbano (2008), 'The institutional approach to entrepreneurship research: introduction', *International Entrepreneurship and Management Journal*, **4** (4), 365–79.

PART III

Entrepreneurial citizens

10. Pursuing Entrepreneurship: a blended approach to teaching entrepreneurship in two weeks

Vegar Lein Ausrød and Jeppe Guldager

Pursuing Entrepreneurship (PE) is an extracurricular course at Aarhus University (AU) that targets a broad range of university and college students who are attracted to entrepreneurship. The objective is to inspire and invite everyone to try entrepreneurship and to dismantle the notion that entrepreneurship is an elite activity for the few who have a brilliant idea. The purpose of PE is twofold: first, to inspire and invite the broader masses of students to try entrepreneurship, and second, to attract more students to the university incubator. PE includes a mix of on- and offline activities (which is referred to as blended learning). Two one-day workshops are connected by an intervening two-week period in which students perform course activities on- and offline. The short-term success criterion is whether participants pursue entrepreneurship, while the long-term success criterion is whether more students find their way to the university incubator.

DESCRIPTION OF THE COURSE

Background

Pursuing Entrepreneurship (PE) was developed within the project Entrepreneurship in Education (EiE). EiE has run for 3.5 years (from 2017 to 2020) and is funded by the European Social Fund and Region Midt (one of five Danish regions). The goal is to promote entrepreneurship within the educational sector. In order to accomplish this, the institutions participating in EiE are committed to the following three objectives. First, 7000 students receive extracurricular entrepreneurship education. Second, 2500 students sign an incubator contract. A contract is signed and registered when a student is officially enrolled in the incubator after attending an introductory programme. Third, 350 of these students start an officially registered venture. These goals are proportionally distributed between three participating institutions: Aarhus University (AU), VIA University College and Aarhus Business Academy.

Aarhus University Incubator (AUI) has been in charge of developing PE. Attendance in PE contributes to EiE's goal of 7000 students (AUI is accountable for 1500) receiving extracurricular entrepreneurship education. AUI is the largest incubator at AU, and it serves students from all four faculties: Arts, Science and Technology, Business and Social Science, and Health. There are 38 000 students enrolled and 8000 employees at AU. AUI is open to all students who have a specific idea they would like to pursue. Approximately 45 start-ups are enrolled at any time, and they vary broadly in terms of industries and stages of development. Some are initial ideas on a piece of paper, while others have developed into businesses with a considerable annual revenue. The incubator seeks to offer a resource-rich environment for entrepreneurs, which includes, but is not limited to, sparring with internal advisers and external expert mentors, talks, networking events and access to a lawyer and accountant. In addition, AUI offers short (20 hours) extracurricular introductory entrepreneurship courses, which are all ungraded. PE is one of these courses.

Given the ambitious objective in terms of the number of students receiving 20 hours of extracurricular entrepreneurship education (7000 in total; 1500 for AUI), PE targets the broad masses of students who are attracted to entrepreneurship but have not acted upon it yet. However, in a time where successful entrepreneurs attract significant media attention, students may be discouraged from embarking on entrepreneurial projects, due to unrealistic perceptions of the entrepreneurial process. We tend to forget that successful entrepreneurs also started with nothing but an unproven idea. Therefore, PE seeks to bring down the barriers for students who are curious about entrepreneurship and invites them to pursue entrepreneurship despite the inherent uncertainty in the entrepreneurial process (McMullen and Shepherd, 2006).

Uncertainty, in contrast to risk, cannot be calculated in advance (Knight, 2012) and to act under such conditions is difficult because events and outcomes cannot be predictable in advance. PE invites students to be means-driven and apply an effectual logic (Sarasvathy, 2001). The effectual logic principle 'the crazy quilt' is central in PE. This principle is about inviting known people (for example, family and friends) and unknown people (for example, partners and customers) to contribute to an idea. As these people add new perspectives, resources and ideas to the original idea, it develops – into a crazy quilt.

Just as the crazy quilt is a guiding metaphor, the following three learning objectives serve as cornerstones in the course: first, that students are able to formulate an idea (pitch) after participating in PE; second, that they are able to apply lean start-up tools; and third, that they can thereby understand that ideas develop because people are invited to contribute to the idea (crazy quilt).

Activities

Before going more into detail about how the learning objectives translate into course activities, let us turn to learning theory in an entrepreneurial setting. As noted by Robinson et al. (2016), taking different learning theories into account when designing entrepreneurship courses can be advantageous. Robinson et al. categorize four learning theories that often, implicitly or explicitly, guide entrepreneurship teachers: behaviourism, social learning, situated learning and existential learning.

1. *Behaviourism* relates to getting to know about entrepreneurship, for instance, in a one-size-fits-all lecture setting where knowledge is more or less passively transmitted from teacher to students.
2. *Social learning theory* stresses that human beings are inherently social and that other people's experiences are valuable. This can be achieved through interaction with the teacher or by inviting experienced entrepreneurs into the classroom.
3. *Situated learning* regards learning as an apprenticeship, where mastery in a community of practice gradually improves. The learner starts out as a novice observing other people's actions and over time develops into an expert him- or herself. According to Robinson et al. (2016), entrepreneurship settings, such as incubators and hackathons, rest on a situated learning logic.
4. *Existential learning* concerns the individual's values and beliefs. In order for existential learning to take place, the learning process has to be meaningful for the future existence of the individual. Existential learning may occur when individuals experience something that is utterly different from what they are used to. Reflection is important in this regard when the student evaluates an experience or a course and its content: how is this relevant and meaningful to me and my life?

These four learning theories have guided the course activities in PE. In addition to this, the course is blended by design. According to Garrison and Kanuka, blended learning is a 'thoughtful integration of classroom face-to-face learning experiences with online learning experiences' (2004: 96). The two weeks of PE begin with a workshop (Kickoff) and end with a workshop (Launch). In the intervening two-week period (Workzone), students receive instructional videos that serve as a launch pad for performing course-related activities. Below is a course overview of PE.

Table 10.1   Overview of Pursuing Entrepreneurship

	Kickoff	Workzone			Launch
Format	Workshop	Videos	Videos	Videos	Workshop
Time	Day 1	Day 1–2	Day 3–4	Day 7–9	Day 14
Content	- Ideation - Keynote - Introduction to Workzone	Track 1: Commit to an idea	Track 2: Why and how to pitch	Track 3: Understand customers	- Reflection - Keynote - Next steps
Activities	Identify ideas; commit to an idea; describe the idea by applying the NABC framework.	Describe the idea by applying the NABC framework.	Formulate, perform and record a pitch.	Formulate and conduct hypothesis test on potential customers; record a pitch.	Reflect on experiences gained throughout Workzone.

Kickoff

A key ambition of PE is to bring down the perceived barriers to entrepreneurship, such as 'I need to have a brilliant idea and an investor in order to pursue entrepreneurship'. At Kickoff, the purpose is to create a safe atmosphere and urge the participants to take initial steps of action, such as daring to tell others about an idea they have thought about. The keynote speaker is carefully selected among the student entrepreneurs in AUI in order not to create too much distance from the students. Having a realistic and relatable role model is key to social learning (Robinson et al., 2016); thus, the content and style of the keynote must be authentic, sympathetic and nuanced. The keynote speaker is invited to talk about their initial considerations and uncertainties to highlight that it is impossible to know everything in advance.

Participants ideate prior to and after the keynote. They further develop one another's ideas in group sessions with Post-It notes, and they present their ideas in pairs. Again, barriers, such as 'my idea is not good enough', are moderated as teachers emphasize that at this point the idea in itself is not important – it will develop. Students are invited to engage actively in developing and committing to an idea. They discuss the idea with peers and teachers, while at the same time comparing their own process with that of the more mature entrepreneur. These activities revolve around social and situated learning.

The NABC model is introduced as a tool for assisting students and helping structure their initial idea. *Need* refers to what need or problem is being addressed. *Approach* refers to how the need or problem is solved for the user or customer. *Benefit* refers to what kind of benefits the user or customer of the idea experiences; and finally, *competition* refers to which existing solutions compete with the idea. Reflecting on these aspects and adding structure is a way to get started with pitching the idea. Returning to the crazy quilt metaphor, the NABC model serves as the initial step towards creating the quilt. Later, during Workzone, other people are invited to contribute to it. Therefore, it is crucial that students commit to an idea before leaving Kickoff; otherwise, the activities in Workzone will be irrelevant.

Workzone

Workzone is the two-week period between Kickoff and Launch, where students are expected to continue pursuing and developing their idea. We ask students to pitch their idea to strong social ties, such as friends and family (Granovetter, 1973). Students are also expected to contact potential partners and customers related to their idea in order to confirm or disprove their hypotheses. Hypothesis testing is central in lean start-up logic (Ries, 2011), and feedback from potential partners and customers is expected to add to the crazy quilt. These activities are especially related to PE's second and third learning objectives: applying lean start-up tools and experiencing that ideas develop continuously.

In order to support students in accomplishing these learning objectives, we send them text messages (SMS) three times during Workzone (see Table 10.1 for an overview of the three tracks). The text messages encourage them to keep exploring their ideas. They also include a link to a YouTube playlist with five consecutive videos. Below is an example of a text message that students receive during Workzone. The text message below is related to Track 2 when students have committed to an idea:

> Hi [first name]. We hope your idea still keeps you energized. Now it's time to get ready to talk about your idea, so you can get some valuable feedback. You might think; how to get started? Well, we have prepared a little kit for you to guide you in the process. Enjoy the videos: [short link to YouTube playlist with five videos]. Best regards from your hosts [hosts' names].

Each playlist follows the same structure: setting the frame (video 1 and 2), introducing a tool (video 3), applying the tool to a start-up (video 4), and finally presenting reflections from the founders of the startups (video 5). The same start-up is used as an example throughout all three tracks.

In Track 1, the first video is about putting vanity aside. This is done to lower the perceived barrier of the need to have a brilliant idea. The second video is about daring to commit to an idea despite unclear conditions associated with it. The third video introduces and explains a tool. In Track 1, this is the NABC model. The fourth video exemplifies the tool by applying the NABC model to a local start-up. Finally, in the fifth video, the founder of the local start-up reflects on how he got the idea and his considerations regarding pursuing the idea further.

Track 2 relates to pitching and the importance of talking to people about the idea in order to acquire resources and get feedback on the idea that adds to the crazy quilt.

Track 3 relates to lean start-up logic, testing assumptions related to customer needs, and the importance of entering into dialogue with people that have a potential stake in your idea.

A call to action is presented in the text message and not in the videos because if we need to change the action, it is easier to rephrase the wording in a text message than remake a video. In Track 1, the call to action is to commit to an idea. In Track 2, the participants create a pitch and talk to family and friends about the idea. In Track 3, we encourage participants to identify some of their own assumptions regarding the idea and to test them on potential customers.

There are clear elements of behaviourism in Workzone in so far as the purpose of the videos is to transmit knowledge. As an attempt to incorporate social and situated learning, the videos are not confined to transmitting theoretical knowledge but also feature a local and more experienced start-up and reflections on the matter at hand.

Launch

Two weeks after Kickoff, all participants reconvene at Launch. At Launch, there is a new keynote, and students are invited to reflect on experiences throughout Workzone and consider potential next steps. In contrast to Kickoff, they now have practical experience acting on an idea, and they have experienced the frustrations as well as the benefits associated with exposing an idea to other people. This is also an opportunity to address existential learning: is entrepreneurship meaningful to me and my life?

At the end of Launch, students reflect on two topics: engagement in Workzone and the next steps in the entrepreneurial process. Students are given five minutes to fill in a short questionnaire for each of the two themes with room for additional comments. Subsequently, the written content is discussed in two groups, each facilitated by a teacher. The teacher asks openly if anyone wants to share his or her reflections and makes sure that everyone gets to voice their opinion. Ten minutes are allocated for each of the two topics.

REFLECTION ON THE INITIATIVE

Compared to traditional classroom teaching, PE's blend of on- and offline activities provides a unique opportunity to analyse students' engagement with course content and compare it with qualitative reflections from students and teachers. The analyses and reflections below are based on two editions of PE held in the spring and autumn of 2018.

Engagement during Workzone

By using YouTube, we gain access to the data crunching part of the service: YouTube Analytics. This makes it possible to achieve a more detailed analysis of students' engagement with videos during Workzone. As a proxy for engagement, we analyse views and retention. A view refers to when someone starts watching a video. Retention refers to how long students stick to the content – how much of the videos they watch. If a video is two minutes long and students watch one minute on average, retention is 50 per cent. Strictly speaking, we cannot tell if students have their attention directed towards their screens or elsewhere when videos are playing. There is a chance that videos are running without being watched. However, if the student loses interest in the video, we assume that he or she stops the video.

Figure 10.1 displays number of views and retention for all 15 videos that are distributed to students during Workzone.

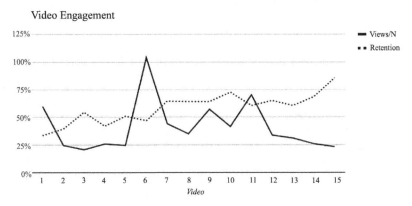

Note: The x-axis displays video number; y-axis displays retention rate and number of views as proportion of participants registered at Kickoff. The graph constitutes the aggregated numbers from the first and second edition of PE, which had similar patterns.

Figure 10.1   Overview of video engagement

There are peaks in the number of views for videos 1, 6 and 11. This is natural as these videos are the first in a series of five. Video 6 has been viewed more than 100 per cent, which indicates that some students viewed it multiple times.

There is a significant drop in the number of views for videos 2 to 5. These videos had already been shown at Kickoff to expose and accustom students to the content and style of Workzone. We interpret this as a sign that most students had a limited need for repetition, although 25 per cent of the students did watch the videos over again.

Video 6 is the first video students receive that they have not seen before. The number of views peaks in this video. We interpret this to reflect curiosity and interest in the video and the SMS/video format. From video 6 onwards, there is an overall decline in the number of views. At the same time, the dotted line reveals that retention increases. While the amount of views decreases throughout Workzone, retention increases. Mirrored in the analysis of video engagement, a decreasing number of students watch the videos; however, those who do, watch more of the content. One group of students opens the video, watches limited parts of it (low retention) and loses interest in the video and the course. When they receive subsequent videos, they do not bother to open them, and there is a mental dropout from the course. There is also a physical dropout as they do not attend Launch. We denote this group of students, 'the dropouts'. We denote the other group, 'the responsive group'. They are the ones that stick to the course, open the videos and watch larger parts of them (high retention).

According to Guo et al. (2014), video engagement in extracurricular online courses is at its highest if videos are kept between zero and three minutes. We were aware of this during the development of the course and kept videos to less than three minutes in length. However, we tried to bypass the findings in Guo et al. by distributing videos in batches of five (a YouTube playlist containing five consecutive videos with a total duration of approximately ten minutes). It did not quite work as intended, as we noticed a quick decline in the number of views of each batch of videos. If the intention is that students watch the videos on the go during other daily activities, a better way would probably be to distribute one short video every day instead of batches of five videos every five days. This remains to be tested, and YouTube Analytics will reveal whether this changes student interaction and engagement in Workzone.

Students' Reflections

In the first edition of PE, 22 students (out of 44) completed the course. All of these said they would recommend the course to others, and many of these activated themselves throughout Workzone. 75 per cent of the students who completed the course spent more than one hour on course-related activities during Workzone, and nearly 20 per cent spent more than 6 hours. In other words, the majority of students were active to a certain extent during Workzone. We intentionally designed Kickoff to create a safe atmosphere and a sense of community before the bar was raised, and students were challenged to 'get out there' and try entrepreneurial principles in real-life settings. Students reported that it felt safe to pitch their idea in a safe, pedagogical environment in front of fellow and like-minded participants and receive feedback at Kickoff before testing their idea during Workzone: 'I don't think it [presenting an idea] has been challenging. I am glad it has been done in small groups and pair wise instead of in front of a whole group. That way one gets more comfortable talking/pitching it' (Student A).

On the question concerning the challenges of pitching ideas and the value of getting feedback from other people, the vast majority of students (close to 90 per cent) reported that feedback from other people on one's idea is rewarding and stimulating and leads to development and improvement of the idea: 'It was challenging at the beginning, because I didn't believe in my idea. After some time when I talked to others and did research about it, I fell in love with it' (Student B).

Others brought an idea to the course that again spurred reflection and reiterations of the concept: 'It has been challenging because I already had worked with the idea/defined it before coming here. It was more or less a concrete idea, which was nowhere near launch. But talking about it made me start to re-think the idea and concept' (Student C).

However, a large number of the respondents also highlighted the challenges of presenting an immature idea: 'A little hard to talk about my ideas as they were new and I had a hard time fully explaining them' (Student D).

Despite expressing doubts and challenges, many of the students got to the point where they presented their idea to people outside of the course context, which added new perspectives and nuances to the original idea. This indicates that social learning had taken place as they activated themselves and discussed their ideas with peers and people outside the course context (Robinson et al., 2016). However, very few got to the point where they tested their assumption on potential partners or customers, which was the objective of Track 3. Despite not reaching this stage, several participants indicated that PE had introduced them to another way of working and thinking compared to traditional university lecturing and that it had been mind-opening for them. Robinson et al. (2016) suggest that existential learning takes place when students reinterpret themselves as entrepreneurs. We do not claim that this full transformation took place over the course of PE, but statements such as 'it has been mind-opening', point to an experience that is radically different from what they have experienced before. That is why we suggest that PE can serve as an entry point to existential learning.

Reflection is important in all sorts of learning and vital in existential learning due to the depth of it. Thus, we prioritized time for individual and group reflection at the end of Launch. While our intention was to facilitate the students' own reflection, a couple of students unexpectedly suggested that the reflections served an important purpose in themselves: the students felt that they were taken seriously. When students raised their voices, the teachers would ask follow-up questions to make sure they understood the perspective, without necessarily providing an answer or counterargument. Reflection seemed to contribute positively to the self-understanding of the students. The teachers also enjoyed the positive energy associated with the reflection sessions. Despite the positive feedback from students who completed the course, the teachers had more conflicting reflections.

Teachers' Reflections

Teachers' reflections were mixed after the first course. On the one hand, students who belonged to the responsive group were satisfied. They had interacted with the course material, which YouTube Analytics confirmed, and the qualitative feedback indicated that the learning objectives had been met at least partially. On the other hand, we were also somewhat disappointed by the rather large dropout rate.

PE was developed to contribute to AUI meeting its share of students who receive extracurricular entrepreneurship training: 1500 students over 3.5 years. PE is certainly not the only initiative that contributes to the fulfilment of this goal; however, with its blended and scalable set-up, it has the potential to reach numerous students. According to a review of 221 extracurricular courses held entirely online, there is a huge variation in completion rates, with a median of 12.6 per cent (Jordan, 2015). Although PE is held partly – not entirely – online, there are still similarities to Jordan's data as the courses are extracurricular. Consequently, students may commit less as opposed to if it had been curricular. The completion rate in PE is 50 per cent, which, in comparison to Jordan's data (2015), is rather high. Nonetheless, we felt that there was untapped potential, so we made a couple of changes to improve the completion rate.

Lack of confidence in an idea was mentioned as a possible factor for dropping out. Several students indicated that committing to an idea during Kickoff was hard and that ideas perceived as poor may have caused students to quit the course. In the first version of the course, we allocated limited time for ideation as we assumed that students being somewhat interested in entrepreneurship would have already thought about an idea. PE could then be a place where this potentially small idea could receive its first attention and action. Sarasvathy also has students commit to mundane venture ideas in the first or second day of her classes: 'I usually have to reassure them in many ways about not waiting for the truly novel or the compellingly high-potential new venture idea' (2009: 231–2). However, we concluded that leaving students at Kickoff facing Workzone and working on their own with a (perceived) weak idea was too precarious. Consequently, we increased the time spent on ideation from around

20 minutes in the first edition of PE to around 70 minutes in the second edition. The rationale for this was that ideation over a longer period of time would increase student confidence in the idea, which again would lead to more confidence and commitment to the course throughout Workzone. Despite actions taken, almost identical results appeared in the second edition of the course: views and retention followed the same patterns, the dropout rate repeated itself, and the student group split in two: the dropout and the responsive group.

One conclusion could be that a blended entrepreneurship course, with a similar set-up as PE, is more suitable for students who start the course with an idea to pursue. We do believe there is some rationale in this, and it would be interesting to arrange PE in the wake of a case challenge or a hackathon where numerous ideas are worked on. However, limiting PE to students with an idea automatically reduces the target group significantly, and the original purpose of the course – inviting everyone to pursue entrepreneurship – is compromised. Instead, we would propose the following, more self-critical thought: PE has not revealed its full potential as a blended format due to the lack of teacher interaction throughout Workzone. We will look into this in the following section.

UNIQUE ASPECT: A BLENDED APPROACH TO TEACHING ENTREPRENEURSHIP

Sticking to the definition provided by Garrison and Kanuka (2004), blended learning is a mix of classroom and internet-based activities. Furthermore, these authors note that 'a defining characteristic of blended learning is the ability of the Internet to provide an interactive learning experience to large numbers of students' (p. 100). As mentioned at the beginning of this chapter, AUI is responsible for reaching 1500 students who receive short (20 hours) extra-curricular courses in entrepreneurship. In order to reach this goal, a scalable solution was preferred, and a blended set-up seemed attractive.

Another important consideration when designing PE was that we did not want to restrain ourselves to teaching entrepreneurship theoretically. We wanted the students to experience how the initial phases of an entrepreneurial process could unfold by integrating experiential activities. A flexible set-up, which included blended learning, that students could bring along in their daily lives seemed to match our needs and ambitions as organizers. In the remainder of this chapter we focus on technology and teaching in a blended entrepreneurship course. The explicit focus on technology is because technology is a vital part of conducting blended learning. In its broadest sense, technology refers to the making and using of artefacts (Mitcham, 1994). This definition, however, encompasses more or less all things that surround us, which makes it hard to operationalize. In the context at hand, we apply an ostensive definition of technology and mainly focus on smartphones and the digital world they connect to.

Pervasive and Persuasive Technology

In the wake of digital technologies covering multiple aspects of daily life, such as communication, social media, news, entertainment, dating and so on, a battle for users' attention becomes apparent. Mere observations in the public sphere reveal that smartphones are good at absorbing people's attention. Technology also plays a crucial role on a more subtle level and is invisible to the naked eye, for instance in regard to the huge amounts of data that tech companies collect from users who use their products. The analysis of video engagement in the previous section is an example of this. In short, technology seems to be everywhere: it is pervasive. How do you approach this when designing a product, or in this case, a blended course on entrepreneurship?

According to Fogg (2009), the answer is through persuasion. Persuasion can be achieved when three factors are present: motivation, ability and a trigger. Put simply, if one is sufficiently motivated and has the ability to do something, one can easily be persuaded into doing it when encountering a trigger, which is an invitation to act. In PE, this trigger is the text message notification received throughout Workzone. The notification itself serves as a trigger that urges action by clicking the message icon to view its content. Using widespread technology, such as SMS and YouTube, which are used by billions of people every day, we assume that students' abilities are adequate. We also assume that students are sufficiently motivated to do course-related activities since they voluntarily signed up for PE in the first place.

Our choice of technology was deliberate as students are accustomed to it, or, in behaviouristic terms, conditioned to it. We could have chosen email or a conventional learning management system as a delivery method for the videos, but we considered SMS to be the most powerful trigger. When sending out text messages, we expected that students would open them, click the link and watch the video playlist on YouTube as a result of persuasion.

However, as touched upon in the previous section, not all students opened the videos. This is most likely not due to a lack of ability (students all know how to open an SMS and click the attached link); rather, it is a lack of motivation. The dropouts were obviously not motivated but, more interestingly, students in the responsive group also experienced motivational variations during the day. This perspective is supported and nuanced by one of the students who evaluated the course. On a question regarding content delivery, she stated: 'I opened the SMS but didn't click the link as I intended to do this later on a more suitable time of the day' (Student E). The student may have been motivated to watch the videos, but she did not receive it at a suitable time of the day, and, therefore, postponed watching it. She was not motivated enough to prioritize PE over whatever she was doing at the time of opening the text message.

As mentioned earlier, distributing one short video every day instead of batches of five videos every five days could potentially lead more participants to watch the video while on the go and not postpone it and potentially forget about it. The majority of the students applauded the videos and SMS as a distribution channel: '[The text messages and videos] were a good reminder, easy to access and more exciting than reading a text' (Student F).

Despite positive feedback on the SMS and video format, comparing the two statements from Student E and Student F above reveals a potential tension between persuasive and pervasive technology, which is a challenge when designing and running a blended extracurricular course. Student E noticed that she received a text message, but she postponed further action. This indicates that she is structured enough to know that there is a better time of the day to proceed with it, and she has enough mental surplus to reflect over the choice at hand. Student F indicated that PE succeeded in creating a compelling and persuasive technological product as he emphasized the easy access and persuasive power of watching a video instead of reading a text. Student F did not suggest that the SMS was pervasive, but she pointed to the fact that it did not suit her to proceed by clicking the link at that specific time of the day.

PE is in a battlefield, competing with other persuasive technologies, such as social media, Netflix, Blockbuster and of course non-digital everyday activities as well. This incentivizes course designers to create a persuasive course that draws attention, but it also leaves course designers with an ethical responsibility of not being pervasive. Just because students sign up for a course on entrepreneurship does not mean we can intrude or persuade them with text messages as often as we want to during the course. Not only would this be intrusive, but it would potentially cause frustrated students to drop out of the course as a result. On the other hand, the supportive environment that was created at Kickoff could be nurtured during Workzone with continuous online interaction. Striking the right balance between persuasion and interaction without becoming pervasive is a challenge.

Technological Aspects of Entrepreneurship as a Social Practice

As mentioned earlier, a key ambition of Kickoff was to create a safe atmosphere, to bring down barriers and to foster social and situated learning. In order to continue the sense of community that we sought to cultivate during Kickoff, a communal Facebook group with students and teachers was created with the intention of continuing the social practice (discussions and reflections) during Workzone.

Most students joined the group and teachers posted keynote slides, reminders of course activities and links to events and talks at AUI that could be of interest to the students. However, there was little to no interaction (likes or comments) with these posts, so communication was formal and mainly one way from teacher to student. In fact, it was everything we tried to avoid at Kickoff.

Reflecting on our own practice during Workzone, we unconsciously faced a barrier in interacting with and supporting the students online. Reduced interaction by the teachers throughout Workzone could be an expression of polite and reserved teachers who sought to strike the right balance between being persuasive and pervasive. It could also be an expression of teachers lacking sufficient online interaction skills when using technology in relation to teaching.

The prefix in technology – techne – means *art* or *skill*, and conducting pedagogy can be viewed as *pedagogical techne*. As teachers, we certainly felt that our pedagogical techne was being challenged during Workzone because we were inexperienced in using technology in a blended pedagogical setting. Thus, our use of technology in PE is more accurately described in the lens of behaviourism rather than social or situated learning.

We also do not consider ourselves technologically unskilled or digitally illiterate. What is at stake here, however, can be illuminated by applying a sociocultural perspective: '"skills" and "techniques" take on very different forms when embedded in different social practices involving different purposes and where different kinds of meaning are at stake' (Knobel and Lankshear, 2006: 16). This points towards the unconscious barrier we felt when not interacting with our students. Despite using social media in our private lives, the situation at hand was entirely different.

We believe that teachers' skilful online interaction could have prolonged the safe atmosphere and social interaction from Kickoff into Workzone, for instance, as a forum to highlight and unfold central points in the videos. In this way, social and situated learning could have been brought into the online sphere. The videos featuring a local student start-up could potentially be a beneficial point of departure for online interaction because the participants could identify with them as fellow students. Reflection questions linked to these videos with subsequent online discussions with teachers, peers and potentially the entrepreneurs could help. Those with a perceived poor-quality idea stick to the course; those with perceived better ideas could potentially develop their ideas even further, and the responsive group could be even more responsive.

Skilful online interaction with large groups of students will require time and attention from teachers, both prior to and during the course. Consequently, the attractive efficiency (the large number of students that can be reached with limited resources) in blended courses must be revised, or at least nuanced, because teachers have to take time out of their daily routines to interact skilfully online. In addition to this, practice and sociocultural awareness of skills are situationally bound.

Garrison and Kanuka (2004) stress the importance of being thoughtful when designing blended learning. Despite the importance of being thoughtful when designing a course, there are limits to how much teachers can grasp and know in advance when making design decisions (Simon, 1972). Videos are recorded in advance, which can lead to a dilemma. We hired a professional company to ensure videos of high quality that included background music and pop-up icons. However, because it is impossible to know everything in advance, you may end up in a sunk cost issue and refrain from making needed changes to the videos because of the considerable amount invested in the video production. A more flexible alternative is to make the videos yourself using your private phone and additional editing programmes. This obviously results in lower quality compared to professionally produced video, but there is not much difference in terms of student engagement between more and less professionally made instructional videos (Guo et al., 2014), and this allows more room for changing video content and style between course editions.

Keep in mind that the videos in themselves are only one part of the technical solution embedded in a blended course. A decision to go for a low-cost solution, producing video content on your own, should also involve considerations regarding all the other technical issues in a blended set-up. Organizing a YouTube channel, adding captions and handling an SMS distribution system are among the skills required to develop and run PE smoothly. These are all things that need to be taken into account when designing a blended course that involves SMS and video elements.

ACKNOWLEDGEMENT

The development of Pursuing Entrepreneurship was financially supported by the project 'Entrepreneurship in Education' and its funding providers The European Regional Development Fund and Central Denmark Region. The Danish Foundation for Entrepreneurship also provided financial support. The authors are very grateful to the funding institutions.

REFERENCES

Fogg, B.J. (2009), 'A behavior model for persuasive design', in *Proceedings of the 4th International Conference on Persuasive Technology*, ACM, p. 40.

Garrison, D.R. and H. Kanuka (2004), 'Blended learning: uncovering its transformative potential in higher education', *The Internet and Higher Education*, 7 (2), 95–105.

Granovetter, M.S. (1973), 'The strength of weak ties', *The American Journal of Sociology*, **78** (6), 1360–80.

Guo, P.J., Kim, J. and R. Rubin (2014), 'How video production affects student engagement: an empirical study of MOOC videos', in *Proceedings of the First ACM Conference on Learning@ Scale Conference*, ACM, pp. 41–50.

Jordan, K. (2015), 'Massive open online course completion rates revisited: assessment, length and attrition', *The International Review of Research in Open and Distributed Learning*, **16** (3).

Knight, F.H. (2012), *Risk, Uncertainty and Profit*, North Chelmsford: Courier Corporation.

Knobel, M. and C. Lankshear (2006), 'Digital literacy and digital literacies: policy, pedagogy and research considerations for education', *Nordic Journal of Digital Literacy*, **1** (01), 12–24.

McMullen, J.S. and D.A. Shepherd (2006), 'Entrepreneurial action and the role of uncertainty in the theory of the entrepreneur', *Academy of Management Review*, **31** (1), 132–52.

Mitcham, C. (1994), *Thinking Through Technology: The Path Between Engineering and Philosophy*, Chicago, IL: University of Chicago Press.

Ries, E. (2011), *The Lean Startup: How Today's Entrepreneurs Use Continuous Innovation to Create Radically Successful Businesses*, New York: Crown Business.

Robinson, S., Neergaard, H., Tanggaard, L. and N.F. Krueger (2016), 'New horizons in entrepreneurship education: from teacher-led to student-centered learning', *Education Training*, **58** (7/8), 661–83.

Sarasvathy, S.D. (2001), 'Causation and effectuation: toward a theoretical shift from economic inevitability to entrepreneurial contingency', *Academy of Management Review*, **26** (2), 243–63.

Sarasvathy, S.D. (2009), *Effectuation: Elements of Entrepreneurial Expertise*, Cheltenham, UK and Northampton, MA, USA: Edward Elgar Publishing.

Simon, H.A. (1972), 'Theories of bounded rationality', *Decision and Organization*, **1** (1), 161–76.

11. 5UCV-E2: fitting your business proposal in seven sessions

María Ripollés, Andreu Blesa and Laura Martínez

The 5UCV-E2 programme seeks to coach students in entrepreneurship while nurturing their adaptive capabilities. The 5UCV-E2 training programme was designed around the tradition of situated and social learning and recognizes student–entrepreneur teams as units of learning. It is also intended to facilitate the interaction between knowledge from the university and practice from the business world, in which the participation of selected entrepreneurs was a key element.

5UCV-E2 INTRODUCTION

Because entrepreneurial capabilities have been shown to be important, several efforts have been made by Spanish universities to foster them among their students to improve their employability. The five Valencian public universities are no exception and, in their strategic plans, fostering entrepreneurial values has been considered an important goal. The public university system in the Valencian community consists of the Universidad de Alicante, Universitat Jaume I de Castelló, Universidad Miguel Hernández de Elche, Universitat Politècnica de València and Universitat de València. In the academic year 2017–2018, these five universities had a combined total of 100 666 undergraduate students, 16 061 master's degree students and 8509 PhD students, and offered a total of 197 bachelor's and 379 master's degrees.

With this aim in mind, in 2013, a collaboration called *Campus del Emprendimiento Innovador* (Innovative Entrepreneurship Campus, hereafter IEC), was set up by these universities and the *Dirección General de Economía, Emprendimiento y Cooperativismo* of the Valencian regional government. The IEC gave priority to analysing the actions that were being carried out independently at each of the five universities; establishing possible synergies through coordinated actions among them, both in the design and implementation of new entrepreneurial actions; and fostering learning about the university entrepreneurial context. Therefore, the IEC was set up to enhance the role of the five universities as key agents in the entrepreneurial ecosystem of the Valencian community. As a very powerful instrument, the IEC makes it easier for the five Valencian public universities to fulfil their objectives concerning student entrepreneurship.

The 5UCV-E2 programme is one of the IEC activities that are carried out simultaneously at each of the five universities with the help of the Santander International Entrepreneurship Centre (CISE). This centre, with its Student × Entrepreneur programme, is a leader in Spain in the design of entrepreneurship programmes in which entrepreneurs are actively involved in the student training process. What distinguishes the 5UCV-E2 is its design, which is focused on cultivating undergraduate students' adaptive capabilities – an important competence conducive to entrepreneurial success (Krueger, 2007; Tseng, 2013). Additionally, other learning outputs are expected to be accomplished through this programme, such as acquiring specific knowledge related to entrepreneurship, increasing participants' entrepreneurial intentions and improving the perceived feasibility of their ideas (Nabi et al., 2017).

5UCV-E2 TEAM BUILDING

The 5UCV-E2 programme sees student–entrepreneur teams as the main vehicle to enhance entrepreneurial learning and considers setting up multidisciplinary (bearing in mind students' backgrounds) and cross-cutting teams (given the combined participation of business people and students in the same team) to be an important feature of 5UCV-E2 that inspires the selection process. The teams have to have two types of participating students. First, there is the student-tutor, who assumes the role of leader. She or he has to create a good team environment, manage the project development, interact with the team and communicate the requirements of the programme (deadlines, improvements, challenges and so on). The second type consists of the rest of the students in the team, who are expected to be predisposed to working as a group and to carrying out the project under the leadership of another student.

In the registration process, students must choose between playing the role of student-tutor or being just a member of the team. In addition, a CV highlighting the student's involvement in entrepreneurship-related activities and a motivation letter must be attached to their online registration form.

Accordingly, in the selection process, represented visually in Figure 11.1, two types of students need to be identified: student-tutors and student team members.

Applicants' CVs, motivation letters and the result of the group interview are studied in order to select the student-tutors. The group interview seeks to find out how candidates interact with one another in order to analyse whether they could lead teams. The entrepreneurial specialists from each university are

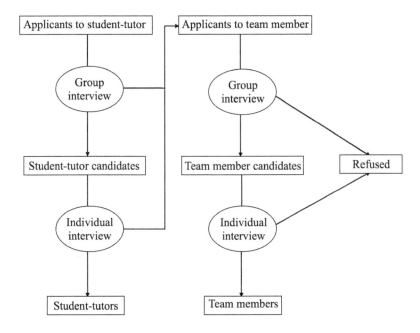

Figure 11.1   Process of selection of candidates to 5UCV-E2

responsible for organizing the group interviews based on candidates' under-graduate studies, bearing in mind that, in each group interview, the participants should come from different degrees. This interview lasts an average of 50 minutes. For a group interview to be productive, the size should be limited to about ten students at a time. Such a group can be easily managed by two entrepreneurial specialists: one who conducts the interview and another who offers support, observes and takes notes on the whole process.

After this interview, the group of candidates who are going to be student-tutors is made up of the students who have shown leadership skills, are empathetic and have fostered a good team atmosphere during the group interview. These candidates then go on to an individual interview in order to select those whose profiles best seem to fit the requirements to be student-tutors. Those candidates who are not selected to be tutors are encouraged to re-register in the programme to become members of one of the entrepreneurial teams.

The selection of student team members also starts with a group interview with the applicants. The candidates who go through to the individual interview are those who have shown a great interest in participating. The candidates who, after the group or the individual interview, display less interest in taking part in the programme are excluded.

To form the 5UCV-E2 teams, the universities also invite local entrepreneurs to participate in the programme. They are entrepreneurs of recognized prestige in the local community with whom the universities have previously collaborated in training activities.

The student-tutor and the entrepreneur are matched in pairs after taking part in a session based on a 'speed-dating' dynamic (Finkel and Eastwick, 2008). This approach is intended to bring out the affinities between entrepreneurs and student-tutors, especially regarding the topic they want to work on in the programme. After the speed-dating session, the student-tutors state which entrepreneurs they prefer to work with and, in turn, the entrepreneurs draw up a list of preferences regarding the student-tutors. These lists are used by the university specialists to organize the teams. Priority is given to cases in which the first choices of preferences coincide, which might indicate a higher degree of affinity.

In forming the teams, diversity is sought among their members; thus, the entrepreneurial specialists prevent two students from the same degree being on the same team. This criterion ensures multidisciplinary teams. The rest of the students are assigned to a team, taking their backgrounds into account.

5UCV-E2 PEDAGOGICAL UNDERPINNINGS

The 5UCV-E2 programme was conceived as a schooling intervention to create learning environments that facilitate practice and knowledge development through real experimentation (Howlett et al., 2016). However, there are significant differences in the way learning environments are created, depending on whether the business creation is conceived as following a causal or an effectual logic (Sarasvathy, 2001). According to causal logic, students start their learning process from a clearly defined business idea and a minimally viable product and then create a business plan that will help in the selection of the optimal business creation strategy. Thus, the management of secondary information and the creation of the business plan are the main elements involved in the entrepreneurial learning process (Chandler et al., 2011). In contrast, the effectual learning approach to new business creation, suggested by Sarasvathy, 'takes a set of means as given and focuses on selecting between possible effects that can be created with that set of means' (2001: 245).

Because the future is unpredictable, entrepreneurial learning is focused on providing students with the tools they need to try different actions in the marketplace before settling on a business model (Chandler et al., 2011). The pedagogical foundations of the effectual learning approach lie in Kolb's (1984) experiential learning cycle as it emphasizes entrepreneurial framing, that is, how entrepreneurs view inputs (relevant or not), make inferences, perceive alternatives and attend to constraints (Chandler et al., 2011). Rather than predicting the future, entrepreneurs following an effectual logic are more likely to work within their means and make adjustments as necessary (Dew et al., 2009).

The pedagogical design of 5UCV-E2 lies in the effectual tradition of entrepreneurial learning as it seems to work better if the expansion of students' adaptive capabilities is an important learning output to be achieved (Chandler et al., 2011).

5UCV-E2 PROGRAMME CONTENT AND METHODOLOGY

In line with the effectual learning approach, students were assigned different learning tasks and given specific teaching–learning worksheets, covering the processes of:

1. establishing hypotheses for their business proposal;
2. sharing these hypotheses with different stakeholders;
3. transforming these hypotheses into new courses of action;
4. engaging stakeholders to move ahead in the process of business model generation.

Therefore, 5UCV-E2 uses tasks as vehicles for learning (Pedler, 1996). The teaching–learning worksheets allowed the teams to involve themselves in all the tasks associated with the process of generating and improving their ideas and business models with the stakeholders' active participation. A summary of the worksheets and the content domain of the seven sessions can be seen in Table 11.1.

Each of the seven sessions was programmed to be performed over one week and lasted three hours. Each session was organized as follows: first, the lecturer introduced the students to the content domain programmed for the session, explained the learning tasks and provided them with the necessary teaching–learning worksheets. It is important to note that students were encouraged to make relevant changes to the teaching–learning worksheets in order to adapt them to the particularities of their project. In this process, they had the help of the participating entrepreneur and, when required, the specialists in entrepreneurship from each university. Thus, the teaching–learning worksheets were thought to be an important tool to fulfil the learning tasks.

Next, the students presented the results of their learning tasks related to the content domain of the previous session. A general collective discussion followed each presentation. Then, a reflective summary conducted by the lecturer closed the session. In the time between the training sessions, the teams carried out their learning tasks by holding discussions with the market guided by the teaching–learning worksheets.

Table 11.1   *List of the sessions and the learning tasks delivered*

Session	Learning Tasks	Session Summary	Relation to Business Tools	Relation to Entrepreneurial Knowledge and Capabilities
I	Establishing hypotheses on problem analyses and market niche characteristics	Understanding first aims and means Worksheet 1. Identifying the problem Worksheet 2. Identifying first means Worksheet 3. Gathering market information from secondary data	Political, economic, social, technological, legal and environmental analysis	**Entrepreneurial knowledge** - Opportunity identification **Entrepreneurial capabilities** - Self-directed learning capabilities - Adaptive capabilities
II	Defining and targeting the business idea	Enlarging creative potential Worksheet 4. Generating an idea Worksheet 5. Assessing the potential niche market	Competitive and market analysis	**Entrepreneurial knowledge** - Opportunity identification - Business conceptualization **Entrepreneurial capabilities** - Self-directed learning capabilities. - Adaptive capabilities. - Creative skills.
III	Establishing hypotheses on the minimum viable product, and testing the minimum viable product hypotheses	Development of a first draft of a product or service and getting feedback from stakeholders Worksheet 6. Conceptualization of the main minimum viable product characteristics and creation of the first prototype Worksheet 7. Getting feedback from stakeholders	Design thinking Qualitative market research	**Entrepreneurial knowledge** - Minimum viable product - Business networks - Lean start-up **Entrepreneurial capabilities** - Self-directed learning capabilities - Adaptive capabilities - Innovative skills

Session	Learning Tasks	Session Summary	Relation to Business Tools	Relation to Entrepreneurial Knowledge and Capabilities
IV	Defining and testing the hypotheses on the competitive value proposition	Understanding the foundations of new business competitive advantage Worksheet 8. Defining and testing the competitive value proposition	Competitive analyses schema	**Entrepreneurial knowledge** - Business model - Lean start-up **Entrepreneurial capabilities** - Self-directed learning capabilities - Adaptive capabilities
V	Transforming the hypotheses into a new course of action with the lean market action plan	Developing a lean market action plan Worksheet 9. Lean market action plan.	Marketing strategy	**Entrepreneurial knowledge** - Business model - Lean start-up **Entrepreneurial capabilities** - Self-directed learning capabilities - Adaptive capabilities
VI	Completing a first draft of the Business Model Canvas	Using Canvanizer, an online tool that uses Business Model Canvas by Alexander Osterwalder to brainstorm ideas	Business model	**Entrepreneurial knowledge** - Business model **Entrepreneurial capabilities** - Self-directed learning capabilities - Adaptive capabilities
VII	Involving stakeholders and moving your network ahead	Definition of a strategy to involve stakeholders	Networking tools	**Entrepreneurial knowledge** - Business networks **Entrepreneurial capabilities** - Self-directed learning capabilities - Networking capabilities

5UCV-E2 ADAPTIVE CAPABILITY ASSESSMENT

As mentioned previously, one important element that distinguishes 5UCV-E2 is its focus on cultivating undergraduate students' adaptive capabilities. At the firm level, adaptive capability is seen as a type of dynamic capability, involving quick responses to new market potentials, the identification of new business opportunities and effective problem-solving (Wei and Lau, 2010). At a personal level, adaptive capability is a personal skill that helps entrepreneurs develop their deep cognitive structures as they confront and resolve discrepancies and contradictions in their constructed knowledge base (Krueger, 2007). Literature makes it clear that capability assessment is more than just measuring the reproduction of knowledge and requires the design of formative systems

(Béchard and Grégoire, 2005; Pereira et al., 2016). Additionally, formative assessment systems have an advantage over traditional assessment systems in that they allow students to become aware of their learning and how they can continue to develop it (Weurlander et al., 2012). Accordingly, a formative system consisting of three elements was developed: qualitative analysis; peer assessment; and self- and intra-team evaluation.

To analyse the evolution of the project, at least two specialists in entrepreneurship at each university belonging to their entrepreneurial units carry out a qualitative analysis. They focus on the coherence of the lean process and the relevance and innovation of the decisions taken to pivot the project.

To carry out the peer assessment, the teams present the results of their work at their university and answer questions asked by the other students, entrepreneurial experts and instructors. After the presentations, each team has to issue a joint score for each project, except their own. One advantage of peer assessment is that each project receives feedback not only from the evaluation committee but also from the other teams and the instructors in the form of proposals for improvement.

A self-evaluation and an evaluation by co-team members are also performed. In this case, each student answers a questionnaire based on the criteria posed by Dochy et al. (1999). Briefly, each participant is asked to use a 5-point Likert scale to evaluate their participation and that of their companions according to the following criteria: positive attitude; participation in face-to-face activities; participation in non-face-to-face activities; quality of the work submitted; capacity for problem-solving; fulfilment of the role assigned in the different tasks; and prior preparation of the material. This intra-team assessment allows the levels of commitment of the different participants in the programme to be deduced.

The application of the formative assessment system makes it possible to assess the extent to which the students have developed their adaptive capability. Generally speaking, it is clear that the training programme fosters the development of adaptive capabilities in participants. On the one hand, practically all the groups make substantial modifications to their initial proposals as a consequence of the different validation processes they carry out. In fact, three groups introduced important changes even in the problem-definition phase by posing a radically different situation to that which had motivated their participation in the programme. However, two groups found that their initial proposal did not evolve as the programme went on. In general terms, the rest of the groups proposed substantial modifications to the characteristics of their minimum viable products, their value proposition and the lean market action plan.

Likewise, the results of the self-evaluation show a high level of involvement. In fact, 79.4 per cent of the participating students score above 4 on the test developed by Dochy et al. (1999). The scores referring to the intra-team evaluation are more divergent. In some groups, they evidenced the existence of problems related to teamwork that emerged in the interviews carried out with the different participants in the programme.

REFLECTION ON 5UCV-E2

The effectual learning approach applied in the 5UCV-E2 programme focuses on providing students with specific tools to set up a new business, according to Kolb's (1984) experiential learning cycle. The results related to this approach in the 5UCV-E2 programme are satisfactory at all the universities involved in the two editions carried out to date. The information gathered through interviews with the organizers, lecturers, entrepreneurs and students shows positive points in the programme that are worth highlighting, but also aspects that need improving for future editions.

Entrepreneurial Learning, Intention and Culture

In terms of learning outcomes, the 5UCV-E2 programme stands out for its contribution to the improvement of entrepreneurial knowledge. Specifically, the tools provided through the worksheets and the learning of techniques and procedures have proved useful when launching business projects from an effectual point of view.

The students' participation in the programme also enables them to develop cross-cutting skills, such as teamwork, the ability to negotiate and manage conflicts, and the ability to find points of agreement when faced with a conflictive situation.

Students reported that their experiences in the 5UCV-E2 programme have an influence on their intention to start a new business or on the perceived ease with which it could be done. In fact, 5UCV-E2 helps some students to create start-ups in the short-term, such as one participant at the Universitat Jaume I who set up his own company dedicated to motorcycle rentals between private individuals.

Programme Content and Methodology

Working on the assigned tasks with self-elaborated worksheets allows students to focus their attention on the most relevant aspects of the creation and design of their business project. Through the worksheets, lecturers translate the theoretical concepts into tasks that bring the students closer to the reality of business than they could have experienced in formal education, even in degrees that are supposed to be directly related to entrepreneurship, such as the degree in Business Administration.

The opinions of both students and entrepreneurs seem to endorse not only the content domain but also the working methodology used, based on task assignments, teaching–learning worksheets, experimentation with real stakeholders and joint reflection sessions, which foster the enrichment of the projects with the opinions of their peers. Both the pedagogic methodology used and the concepts and tools that were addressed have proved their usefulness, and it would be interesting to replicate them in other contexts.

The dynamics of sharing projects in each session contribute to the learning generated in the shape of inputs from others. Students present their ideas not only to lecturers but also to their peers, who provide feedback from an equal-status point of view. Special mention should be made of the final evaluation, in which the students collect valuable information from other teams' entrepreneurs in order to cultivate reflection and critical thinking about their own project. These inputs are digested by the teams, who transform them into new ways of looking at their business. The results are projects with a high degree of preparation that are presented and defended with real enthusiasm.

After two editions of these sessions, a discussion among the organizers has emerged. Although it may be advisable to work with a certain level of competitiveness in entrepreneurial training programmes, experience also seems to point to the need to stress the cooperative aspect of the 5UCV-E2 programme within the dynamics of the sessions. 'Some teams approached their interventions with strategies aimed at dismantling projects that had stood out during the training sessions; this resulted in a very competitive environment among the groups and there seemed to be no fair play' (Technical manager of a company in the urban waste treatment and management sector).

Teamwork

Students and entrepreneurs emphasize working in teams. Both groups attach particular value to the experiential learning that results from working with another party. The students appreciate the entrepreneurs' help, the contribution these professionals make to their learning process and the way they help them to focus on what is important.

However, some students' perceptions of the role of the student-tutor are not as positive as might have been expected: 'I don't think my tutor was ready to coordinate the group and since I didn't like the idea we worked on, for me it was disappointing' (Universitat Jaume I student). A possible explanation for this may lie in the protocols used to select the student-tutors. In fact, after considering this point, the programme organizers suggested that it would be wise to allow the group to decide on changes to the student-tutor.

Other students also state that the level of involvement of their team mates is not always as high as it perhaps should have been and, in some cases, some of the team members do not fulfil the tasks that have been assigned to them.

> In one work session with the entrepreneur, one of the students in the team had not carried out the interviews that had been programmed and we could only work with half of the information that had been planned for the activity, which delayed the planned decision-making and evolution of the project. (Universitat Jaume I student)

Working Sessions Organization

The duration of 5UCV-E2 is adequate. It is an intense and concentrated programme, although compatible with the students' degree schedules or job timetables, which is an added value when the course is extracurricular. The pace allows participants to work on their assigned tasks in depth. However, allowing the entrepreneurs to have more time to play their role as learning coaches could be a qualitative improvement to the programme. Specifically, experience shows that they need more sessions to discuss their business project and to work on it with the teams.

What has to be Improved

The conclusion reached by the organizers as a result of the information gathered throughout both editions of the programme is that some aspects need to be polished in order to improve the effectiveness of 5UCV-E2 in the future. In this regard, it seems appropriate to reflect on the time made available to students to work on their projects with the entrepreneur, which must take into account the limitations inherent to the professional activity of entrepreneurs. There is a need to introduce formulas that allow the entrepreneurs to become more involved and for a distinction to be made according to their level of involvement. The entrepreneurs' comfort is very relevant to programmes that pursue experiential learning. Their participation in the teaching process offers students the chance to obtain tacit knowledge about the world of business that is not available by explicit means, in addition to a practitioner's perspective, which is hard to transmit by traditional pedagogical methods. When planning a programme that includes entrepreneurs, the time dedicated to working with the students should be given special consideration.

The length of extracurricular programmes is a critical factor for students studying their degree or part-time students with a job. The concern here is to find the balance between giving students enough time to mature their ideas, experiment with the market and avoid the perception of a long commitment. Students need to feel some pressure to develop their tasks but not so much stress as to make them want to withdraw before finishing the programme. Tools such as task accomplishment calendars and sessions to control that accomplishment suggested by participants could help to accompany the students in their voyage from idea to business project. This monitored design would also allow organizers to prevent withdrawals due to students' perception that confronting the market with their ideas is a Herculean task (more a result of their ignorance regarding the required steps than the actual difficulty of the path itself). The dimensions of 5UCV-E2 (seven weeks, one teaching session a week and one practical per week) have been rated very well by the students and entrepreneurs. This could be a starting point to find a good length for a similar proposal.

Another area for improvement is the methodology. A compromise should be found between promoting the necessary competitiveness of the entrepreneur as an innate characteristic of entrepreneurship and non-collaborative criticism. Cooperation and the exchanging of views have proved to be one of the strong points of the programme, and this should not be jeopardized by competition between groups. Special attention should be paid to the assessment sessions. Assessment of the students can benefit from the participation of their peers. A final evaluation session open to the opinions of both students and entrepreneurs becomes an additional opportunity to learn about entrepreneurship and pivot the business project.

Nevertheless, when implementing peer assessment of students' projects, the risk of destructive competitive behaviours arises. Entrepreneurial educators should highlight the need to adopt a cooperative role in these kinds of sessions. Excessive competitiveness could ruin the dynamics of the session and, consequently, be more damaging than beneficial.

The selection of the teaching staff involved in the programme becomes especially relevant when the experiential learning method is used. Entrepreneurship education programmes require coaches rather than lecturers, instructors capable of guiding entrepreneurs through the process of adapting their ideas to the market. This means proximity and availability. While motivating speakers are the perfect fit when the objective is to generate an entrepreneurial spirit, trainers are needed when the purpose is to transform an idea into a business. Therefore, in addition to belonging to the academic body of universities, the teaching staff must also have experience in the use of active teaching methodologies and entrepreneurship. As Penaluna et al. (2012: 172) put it, they should be 'pracademics' more than teachers. Entrepreneurial education lecturers not only need to have a wide knowledge of entrepreneurship but also be masters of active teaching methodologies to help the students match their starting hypotheses to the actual market.

The experience from 5UCV-E2 shows that, although some universities that worked with teaching staff who specialized in entrepreneurship from the CISE were wholly satisfactory when the results of the first edition were pooled, they highlighted the importance of having academic staff from each university as an instrument to legitimize their running extracurricular entrepreneurship programmes. As a result, the IEC is currently searching for alternatives that allow lecturers from each university to be involved in carrying out the 5UCV-E2. Specifically, a new initiative is being developed to merge the 5UCV-E2 programme and the 5UCV-*Aula Emprende* initiative, which is also part of the activities run by IEC.

5UCV-*Aula Emprende* is a training action targeted at research and teaching staff that aims to raise awareness about the importance of university entrepreneurship. This action provides academic staff with access to teaching techniques that can be applied in a cross-cutting manner in the classroom in order to foster an entrepreneurial culture. This new initiative would link lecturers participating in 5UCV-*Aula Emprende* to the 5UCV-E2 teams, thereby reinforcing the figures of the student-tutor and the entrepreneur, who could adopt a more traditional role as a mentor.

The joint reflection of the members of the IEC after the second edition showed that this programme also has unexplored potential related to its influence on the development of networks among its participants. In this respect, for future editions, work is being carried out to organize at least one networking event that allows participants from different universities to interact with one another and exchange their concerns, knowledge and experiences in entrepreneurship. Due to the geographical distance separating the universities involved in the IEC, an effective alternative could be to create an online community that complements and enhances the networking event. Sharing projects and experiences during the process contributes to students' learning through the exchange of ideas and points of view. More value can be added to the resulting experiential learning by exploiting the networking capabilities implicit in the interactions among students, entrepreneurs, lecturers and organizations. The activities carried out during the programme could be considered the seeds for growing business networks to be incorporated into the students' social capital.

THE UNIQUE ASPECT OF THE 5UCV-E2

The main differentiating aspect of the 5UCV-E2 is, perhaps, the methodology adopted to structure the exchange of information and knowledge between the different private and public organizations at different levels of administration: national (CISE), regional (Dirección General de Economía, Emprendimiento y Cooperativismo) and local (five Valencian universities). In short, the group of practice methodology was chosen to foster collaboration among the institutions involved in IEC, due to its capacity to enhance knowledge transfer and experiential learning among its members (Wenger, 1998; Wenger and Snyder,

2000), especially in networks among public institutions (Koliba and Gajda, 2009). A group of practice is a relational structure in which communication among different organizations can be activated, and the social construction of knowledge can be achieved (Wenger, 1998). It is an important tool to facilitate the emergence of social capital, which is, in turn, a precursor for knowledge transfer and development in interorganizational networks, especially when groups of practice are deliberate (Aljuwaiber, 2016).

An important element of the IEC refers to the mode and quality of the regular collaboration. The joint practice of the IEC is organized around seven entrepreneurial extracurricular activities. Each entrepreneurial activity is led by one of the 5UCV and linked to a different phase of the entrepreneurial value chain (awareness-raising, identification and filtering of ideas, designing business opportunities and creation). Therefore, it serves specific and different pedagogic objectives. The 5UCV activities, their objectives, the target audience, the university leader and their link with the entrepreneurship value chain are summarized in Table 11.2. The complementarity of the activities makes up a university entrepreneurship ecosystem that offers different possibilities for university students to develop their entrepreneurial concerns and illustrates the uniqueness of the 5UCV-E2.

Another important element that characterizes the collaboration of the IEC is the decisive leadership role of the Dirección General de Economía, Emprendimiento y Cooperativismo (Wenger, 1998; Wenger and Snyder, 2000). Indeed, the Dirección General de Economía, Emprendimiento y Cooperativismo takes responsibility for the participants' mutual engagement, for promoting the sense of joint enterprise, for guiding the development of the repertoire of activities, for facilitating communication and knowledge transfer, for establishing relational norms to cultivate social capital, and for providing legal and financial support to sustain the joint activities.

The Dirección General de Economía, Emprendimiento y Cooperativismo convenes at least two face-to-face meetings for all participants: one at the beginning and the other at the end of each year. At the first 5UCV-E2 meeting, a proposal is presented for the development and implementation of this activity by the Universitat Jaume I, which is responsible for the programme.

In the meeting at the end of each year, the Universitat Jaume I weighs up the results obtained from the programme at each university based on the information gathered from the participants' and hosts' experience. Using this information, work is now being carried out to define improvements that could be implemented in the entrepreneurial activities in future editions. Between the two face-to-face meetings, there is at least one virtual meeting, the purpose of which is to specify the details of the implementation of the 5UCV-E2 programme and to resolve any unforeseen issues that may have arisen.

Table 11.2   Actions related to the IEC

Action	Start Year	Aim	Audience	Link with Value Chain	Participants
5UCV – AULA EMPRENDE. Led by the Universitat de València	2013	To make teaching staff aware of the importance of university entrepreneurship. To provide them with different teaching techniques that can be applied transversally in the classroom. To foster an entrepreneurial culture among students.	Teaching and research staff	Phase 1. Awareness-raising	780 trained teachers
5UCV START-UP CONTEST. Led by the Universitat Politècnica de València	2014	To reward entrepreneurial talent based on the best business initiatives presented by students and graduates of the 5UCV.	Students and university graduates	Phase 1. Awareness-raising	136 candidates
5UCV-MENTORING. Led by the Universidad Miguel Hernández	2017	To help students analyse the initial validation of the idea with the help of an expert.	University students	Phase 2. Ident-ification and filtering of ideas Phase 3. Designing business opportunities	165 pairs
5UCV – UJIE (University Junior International Entrepreneurs) Led by the Universitat Jaume I	2014	To promote entrepreneurship and the international mobility of students who propose entrepreneurial initiatives in global sectors.	University students	Phase 3. Designing business opportunities	45 students with scholarships

Action	Start Year	Aim	Audience	Link with Value Chain	Participants
5UCV- E2 Led by the Universitat Jaume I	2017	To foster an entrepreneurial culture among students through the development of adaptive capabilities.	University students	Phase 3. Designing business opportunities	41 trained teams
Patent and knowledge bank Led by the Universidad de Alicante	2013	To value the research and technologies developed by the lecturers.	Research staff	Phase 4. Creation	262 technologies
Inclusive entrepreneurship	2015	To promote the employment and entrepreneurship of persons with disabilities.	Public administrations Universities Associations of persons with disabilities Social enterprises University students and graduates and persons with disabilities	Phase 1. Awareness-raising	535 persons attended the conferences and congresses

In the time between the off- and online meetings, the university specialists rely on the internet to share knowledge. Therefore, the usage of the internet is seen as an important tool to complement face-to-face knowledge sharing and to maintain contact among participants, which in turn increases their social capital. This working methodology is the main factor accounting for the evolution of the university specialists' entrepreneurial knowledge. In fact, if there is one thing that defines the 5UCV-E2, it is its permanent evolution and adaptation to the changing reality of the university entrepreneurial ecosystem.

In short, the IEC could be considered a sound example of how universities and public organizations can share their knowledge and learn from one another through regular interaction. One of the main factors underpinning the role of groups of practice as a networking tool is perhaps the fact that they have a number of elements in common with informal networks. These elements include the fact that participation is facilitated by the Dirección General de Economía, Emprendimiento y Cooperativismo, but is not appointed by it, and that the task mission is not mandated by the institutions or by the leader but instead results from knowledge sharing among the participants. The structure of the group of practice emerges from social interaction, but the leader is appointed by the Dirección General de Economía, Emprendimiento y Cooperativismo. This last characteristic is shared with formal networks, as well as the fact that the resources of the IEC are supplied, or funded, by the Dirección General de Economía, Emprendimiento y Cooperativismo and the five Valencian universities, not by the participants.

ACKNOWLEDGEMENT

This initiative would not have been possible without the participation of the heads of the Consellería de Economía Sostenible, Sectores Productivos, Comercio y Trabajo, the Centro Internacional Santander Emprendimiento (CISE), and the specialists and directors of entrepreneurship at the five public universities in Valencia: Universidad de Alicante, Universidad Miguel Hernández de Elche, Universitat Politècnica de València, Universitat de València and Universitat Jaume I de Castelló.

Specifically, we would like to gratefully acknowledge the work and dedication of María José Ortolá, Deputy Director General of Social Economy and Entrepreneurship; Gemma José Rico Marí, Head of the Department for the Development and Promotion of Entrepreneurship; Rafael Ruiz Bada and Elena Horrillo from CISE; Josefa Parreño, Director of the Office for Student Employment and Support; Pep Rubio of the University Observatory of Labor Insertion of the Universidad de Alicante; Abel Torrecillas of the Occupational Observatory of the Universidad Miguel Hernández; María José Ramírez and Sandra Lucas, specialists in Advice for Entrepreneurs from IDEAS-UPV at the Universitat Politècnica de València; and Santiago Miralles, specialist from the Innovation, Valorisation and Entrepreneurship Department of the Research and Innovation Service at the Universitat de València.

REFERENCES

Aljuwaiber, A. (2016), 'Communities of practice as an initiative for knowledge sharing in business organizations: a literature review', *Journal of Knowledge Management*, **20** (4), 731–48.

Béchard, J.P. and D. Grégoire (2005), 'Entrepreneurship education research revisited: the case of higher education', *Academy of Management Learning & Education*, **4** (1), 22–43.

Chandler, G.N., DeTienne, D.R., McKelvie, A. and T.V. Mumford (2011), 'Causation and effectuation processes: a validation study', *Journal of Business Venturing*, **26** (3), 375–90.

Dew, N., Read, S., Sarasvathy, S.D. and R. Wiltbank (2009), 'Effectual versus predictive logics in entrepreneurial decision-making: differences between experts and novices', *Journal of Business Venturing*, **24** (4), 287–309.

Dochy, F., Segers, M. and D. Sluijsmans (1999), 'The use of self-, peer and co-assessment in higher education: a review', *Studies in Higher Education*, **24** (3), 331–50.

Finkel, E.J. and P.W. Eastwick (2008), 'Speed-dating', *Current Directions in Psychological Science*, **17** (3), 193–7.

Howlett, C., Ferreira, J.A. and J. Blomfield (2016), 'Teaching sustainable development in higher education: building critical, reflective thinkers through an interdisciplinary approach', *International Journal of Sustainability in Higher Education*, **17** (3), 305–21.

Kolb, D. (1984), *Experiential Learning*, Englewood Cliffs, NJ: Prentice Hall.

Koliba, C. and R. Gajda (2009), '"Communities of practice" as an analytical construct: implications for theory and practice', *International Journal of Public Administration*, **32** (2), 97–135.

Krueger Jr, N.F. (2007), 'What lies beneath? The experiential essence of entrepreneurial thinking', *Entrepreneurship Theory and Practice*, **31** (1), 123–38.

Nabi, G., Liñán, F., Fayolle, A., Krueger, N. and A. Walmsley (2–017), 'The impact of entrepreneurship education in higher education: a systematic review and research agenda', *Academy of Management Learning & Education*, **16** (2), 277–99.

Pedler, M. (1996), *Action Learning for Managers*, London: Lemos & Crane.

Penaluna, K., Penaluna, A. and C. Jones (2012), 'The context of enterprise education: insights into current practices', *Industry and Higher Education*, **26** (3), 163–75.

Pereira, D., Flores, A. and L. Niklasson (2016), 'Assessment revisited: a review of research in assessment and evaluation in higher education', *Assessment & Evaluation in Higher Education*, **41** (7), 1008–32.

Sarasvathy, S.D. (2001), 'Causation and effectuation: toward a theoretical shift from economic inevitability to entrepreneurial contingency', *Academy of Management Review*, **26** (2), 243–63.

Tseng, C.C. (2013), 'Connecting self-directed learning with entrepreneurial learning to entrepreneurial performance', *International Journal of Entrepreneurial Behavior & Research*, **19** (4), 425–46.

Wei, L.Q. and C.M. Lau (2010), 'High performance work systems and performance: the role of adaptive capability', *Human Relations*, **63** (10), 1487–511.

Wenger, E. (1998), 'Communities of practice: learning as a social system', *Systems Thinker*, **9** (5), 2–3.

Wenger, E.C. and W.M. Snyder (2000), 'Communities of practice: the organizational frontier', *Harvard Business Review*, **78** (1), 139–46.

Weurlander, M., Söderberg, M., Scheja, M., Hult, H. and A. Wernerson (2012), 'Exploring formative assessment as a tool for learning: students' experiences of different methods of formative assessment', *Assessment & Evaluation in Higher Education*, **37** (6), 747–60.

12. ComoNExT iStart Academy: exploring the development of managerial skills

Chiara Cantù

DESCRIPTION OF THE INITIATIVE

Overview: ComoNExT iStart Academy

'[A] startup for starters is missing'. Recognizing the need for a new educational approach, the international consortium of a European project ideated and realized the iStart Academy. iStart is 'a lean-training, innovative, multidisciplinary digital entrepreneurship platform' that belongs to the Erasmus+ KA2 strategic partnership project.

This chapter describes the ComoNExT iStart Academy, organized by Sviluppo Como: ComoNExT (in the following ComoNExT). It was hosted in Lomazzo, Italy, from 21 to 25 May 2018.

The Academy programme was designed to guide participants through the lean start-up process (from ideation to validation, pivoting and pitching). The lean start-up method (Ries, 2011) provides a scientific approach to creating and managing start-ups and getting the desired product to customers' hands faster. The lean start-up method teaches users how to drive a start-up, when to turn and when to persevere and grow a business with maximum acceleration. The method allows users to investigate customers' point of view in order to customize a new product and improve customer satisfaction (Read and Sarasvathy, 2005). Validated learning is founded on purposeful experimentation with the effectuation principles of flexibility and affordable loss (Fredriksen and Brem, 2017).

Based on this approach, the structure of the Academy involved interactive lectures, teamwork and mentoring. During the Academy, the students had the opportunity to experience the birth of a new venture. The majority of the five days was dedicated to the active work of the team with the continuous help of mentors and tutors. The final event consisted of a pitching competition.

In particular, the Academy improved the managerial skills of young entrepreneurs. A few theoretical lectures (30 minutes each day) provided them
with general knowledge about the instruments they would use to develop
their idea (for example, Business Model Canvas, presentation techniques,
how to perform a rough market validation of the idea). All teams worked with
specific tools (for example, Business Model Canvas, budget, idea deck) and
presented their idea and team in front of an expert panel on the last day of the
Academy. The best three teams were awarded three months of pre-incubation
by ComoNExT.

The Academy sustained a learning-by-doing approach as it allowed students
to experiment during the entrepreneurial activity, improving managerial skills.
According to Katz (1955), the main managerial skills are planning, communication, decision, delegation, problem-solving and motivation. As depicted by
Koponen et al. (2019), interpersonal skills include such skills as 'knowing how
to cope with and resolve conflict and understanding, persuading and getting
along with others, ability to listen, and empathy' (Rentz et al., 2002: 15).

In addition, iSTART developed an innovative, evidence-based transnational
framework that improves the knowledge and skills of academic institutions to
produce curricula focused on digital entrepreneurship practice (DEP).

The Context: The European Project

iStart is 'a lean-training, innovative, multidisciplinary digital entrepreneurship
platform' that belongs to the Erasmus+ KA2Strategic Partnership project. The
aim of Erasmus+ is to contribute to the Europe 2020 strategy for growth, jobs,
social equity and inclusion, as well as the aims of ET2020, the EU's strategic
framework for education and training. Erasmus+ also aims to promote the
sustainable development of its partners in the field of higher education and
contribute to achieving the objectives of the EU Youth Strategy.

The project consortium is made up of key academics, investors, and incubators from different industries who co-created the DEP curriculum through
an open innovation and co-creation virtual learning environment (VLE). The
cooperation among these organizations allowed the ideation and the development of the Startup Academy.

The actors of the consortium
The actors of the consortium are located in different countries and are characterized by different core activities. A foundation university, incubators,
research centres and business angels worked together to develop the project.
The universities and centres that have worked on the project include SEERC,
Instituto Pedro Nunes (IPN), and Yaşar University (YU). Established in 2001
by one of Turkey's leading industry groups, Yaşar Holding, YU is a founda-

tion university located in Izmir (Turkey). The university offers high-quality teaching and has a strong collaboration with industry. It was selected as 'Erasmus Success Story' in 2010 and was also awarded the 'Success story in Erasmus intensive programmes projects' in 2012.

SEERC is an overseas research centre of the University of Sheffield, established as a non-profit legal entity in Thessaloniki, Greece. The centre was founded by City College, the University's International Faculty, in 2003. It develops multidisciplinary research in the fields of enterprise, innovation and development, information and communication technologies, and society and human development.

IPN (Portugal) is a non-profit organization. It promotes innovation and technology transfer and is the main link between the University of Coimbra and the business sector. Its work is done through R&D in partnership with enterprises, specialized training, dissemination of scientific and technological knowledge and start-up tech company support.

Shifting our attention from universities to incubators, two involved organizations are ComoNExT and i4G. ComoNExT (New Energy for Territory) is the first Italian technological hub, founded in the Lombardy Region in 2007 to improve the attractiveness of the local economy. Since 2010, ComoNExT has been managing the call for ideas. In 2013, the incubator and incubation model were certified by the Italian Ministry for Economics (MISE). To date, the incubator has selected over 400 proposals and over 200 extra call candidates and managed 38 start-ups, whose support includes spaces, project management, business planning and networking with university and investors (business angels, venture capitals). Since 1 January 2017, Sviluppo Como has managed the Innovation Hub. ComoNExT carries a brand related to information, assistance, advisory services and incubation for companies located both inside and outside the park and promotes the technology transfer from universities and external R&D centres to firms. The high-tech firms specialize in IT, robotics, biotech, new materials, 3D technologies and other industrial areas.

Incubation for Growth (i4G) manages the first private incubator in Greece, established in 2002. The company is also engaged in the development and management of third-party business and technology incubators and the provision of integrated consulting services for entrepreneurship and innovation in public and private organizations. The aim of i4G is to create an attractive ecosystem.

In addition, the business angel of the project is identified in the European Business Angel Network (EBAN; Belgium). The constituency is diverse, reaching all of the EU's 28 member states and representing a wide range of market players: business angels, business angel networks, business angel federations, early stage funds, business accelerators and electronic funding platforms.

The Evolution of iStart Academy

In June 2017, the first iStart Academy was held in Thessaloniki (Greece). The focus of the Thessaloniki Academy in urban solutions was on solving contemporary urban problems (for example, ageing populations, environmental regulations, transportation, refugees and so on) with state-of-the-art technologies (gamification, AI, VR, data analytics and so on). The structure was based on the lean start-up process, engaging with not only professional start-up mentors but also a start-up offering city guide services.

The focus of the second iStart Academy (Coimbra Portugal, October 2017) was smart living: life in the 21st century. The top three ideas were PRESENT4YOU (a digital platform that will help remember events, buying and delivering any kind of gift), EZEAT (an app where it is possible to order and pay for meals) and HCARE (a combined pharmaceutical and medical care service).

After ComoNExT Academy (the third Academy), another Startup Academy was organized by YU (September 2018). The focus of the fourth Academy was on solutions to solve contemporary problems related to the agro-business value chain (for example, logistics and transport, warehouse management, and ICT used in agro, such as Big Data and the Internet of Things), agro-business and management, industrial design and so on.

A digital platform was also developed, closely connected with the implementation of four academies. The entrepreneurship courses offered different training modules on start-up approach, Business Model Canvas, idea evaluation, pitching and so on. Each module had a defined structure in order to support the learners. It consisted of a short introduction followed by short videos (teasers about the topic), informative material including text, references to further readings, and online discussions with comments and suggestions that facilitated the knowledge sharing among learners. In addition, there was a chat room and a discussion area so that learners could share information and improve their knowledge through interactions with one another.

In particular, iStart supported new entrepreneurs in developing managerial skills through the courses and activities of the Academy, founded on the lean start-up approach. The main activities of the Academy included the preliminary introduction, ideation and validation, pivoting and the pitching competition.

ComoNExT iStart Academy Activities

The selection
The call for the ComoNExT iStart Academy was publicized around 12 February 2018. An email was sent to university referents (professors, assistants and so on), mainly located in the area around Lomazzo. The universities

involved were Cattolica University (Milan), Insubria University (Como and Varese), Politecnico of Milan (Milan), Bocconi University (Milan), La Sapienza (Rome) and Scuola di Como (Como).

The application process included personal, demographic and background data, some educational data and finally, motivation, entrepreneurial drive and business ideas. The committee had an overall picture of the applicants, their profiles and their applications. Based on the available data, they selected the most promising candidates. In total, there were 44 applicants. The basic selection criteria included completion of all required questions and finalization of the application, quality and richness of the data provided, and motivation and entrepreneurial drive expressed.

After the selection process, each selected candidate was called to inquire about his or her availability to participate in the Academy. Thirty students were selected; 22 attended the Academy.

Preliminary introduction
The first day of the Academy started with a brief introduction, focusing on the relevant procedures and the overall schedule. During the morning, the teams formed organically, and the professional mentor of the Academy mediated the whole process. Six teams were formed. In the afternoon, the VLE platform was presented to the participants, then the mentor explained the concept of value proposition and the use of Business Model Canvas. After the theoretical part, the teams worked to pitch their value proposition to the assembly in three minutes. The day ended with the teams formed and the initial ideas documented.

Ideation and validation
The second day started with a presentation by the Academy's mentors on the process of business idea formation and validation. The focus was to have participants think about the feasibility (technical, business, legal and so on) of their business idea and initiate a design process (for example, what is the problem they are solving? Who are the customers? Who are the users?). The goal was to encourage the teams to hit the streets and get feedback on their ideas. After the theoretical lesson, the students worked in pairs to test their ideas and the question they were going to ask to obtain market feedback.

In the afternoon, the students were free to choose whether they wanted to go to Como or Milan to test their ideas. They could also ask people in ComoNExT (which hosts 125 enterprises) for the B2B projects. The second day ended with refined ideas and canvas.

Pivoting

The third day was focused on updating previous materials: idea description, lean canvas, idea validation and business concepts. The theoretical lesson focused on the definition of the market. Some teams pivoted their idea during the Academy, and they had to update the previous material and align it with the newest business focus. Another theoretical lesson was conducted about pitching in order to prepare all the teams for testing their pitches on Thursday.

In the afternoon, the theoretical lesson focused on the financing aspects (how to draw up a budget, how to finance a start-up). Then the groups worked on their financials with the help of the mentor and coaches. The day ended with ideas pivoted and budgeting finished.

Pitching

The fourth day was focused only on pitching. The day began with all the teams doing their pitches for the other participants with a Q&A session after each pitch. The standard required that all the groups have only three minutes to make their pitch. After this common moment, every group began updating their pitches and refining the work, while the mentor called every group to have a private pitch session to provide comments and suggestions. This cycle was performed three to four times during the day. The day ended with the final pitches ready for the final event.

The lean start-up process and methodology allowed participants to combine entrepreneurial and marketing competences. In particular, the methodology allowed participants to combine theory and practice in order to identify the market and its needs, depict a customized product and identify the competitors developing a differentiation strategy and brand positioning.

Pitching competition

The fifth and final day was focused on the pitch competition. The iStart ComoNExT Academy employed a professional mentor who was fully dedicated to the Academy. The positive results of the previous Coimbra Academy pushed ComoNExT to ask for the cooperation of the mentor, who is entrepreneur, investor and business consultant. In addition, coaching to the teams was provided by the project partners who attended the event.

On this last day of the Academy, a pitching competition was organized, and teams were asked to present their entrepreneurial projects. The jury comprised three members representing the quadruple helix mix:

1. *Yaşar University*: Responsible for the technology transfer institute that includes an incubator
2. *Desktop Remoto srl*: Entrepreneur and owner of Desktop Remoto, a start-up that has grown over the past few years.

3. *The digital promoter of the Como Chamber of Commerce*: Has experience in the incubation and mentoring services.

The criteria against which the jury marked the pitching teams, consistent with the previous academies, were the following (0–5 scale): Is there a strong or weak business model? Is there a weak or strong competitive advantage? Is there a substantial market size to be addressed? From a technical point of view, is the product or solution feasible? Does the team background and skill match the development of the business project? What is the potential of the project to be financially viable? How is the quality of the presentation?

The teams were given a pitch structure and were helped to complete it appropriately. Each team presented their idea for approximately three minutes while the Q&A session from the jury lasted around five minutes per team. Each jury member had to mark each team according to seven criteria with marks ranging from 0 to 5. All the marks were selected and transferred to an Excel sheet. The marks were double-checked by the organizers, and the three best teams were selected and announced. The three best teams were awarded three months of pre-incubation by ComoNExT. The winners were Boolie, an easy, fast application to organize one's agenda and booking appointments; Bookme, a platform for students to buy their books via a fast, comfortable and filtered purchase at competitive prices; and Breathe, a biocompatible nanoclay-base additive to integrate fabric.

REFLECTIONS ON THE INITIATIVES

The ComoNExT iStart Academy improved participants' entrepreneurial and managerial competences and skills. Students came from different universities and had different backgrounds. Many students had the technical competences to develop new products, and they were interested in developing competences to depict the business model and outline the business plan. Students had a business dream; the Academy allowed that business dream to become a business plan. In addition, the Academy provided participants with the competences to manage the foundation and development of a new venture.

ComoNExT carried out two surveys before and just after the Academy. The surveys consisted of an anagraphic section and a self-evaluation section about entrepreneurial skills (managerial, communication, personal).

Focusing on self-evaluation, the students were asked to describe how comfortable they felt with the listed skills, giving points ranging from 1 (less familiarity) to 3 (high familiarity). They indicated a general improvement in confidence regarding most of the skills. In particular, findings of the surveys can be summarized in the following points:

1. After the Academy, the number of students familiar with pitching increased from 2 to 11. Moreover, all the skills denoted greater familiarity at the end of the Academy. Before the Academy, the students felt a low familiarity with their managerial skills, in particular with pitching, opportunity recognition and business planning. The other managerial skills investigated were marketing and financial projections. The session of the Academy provided involved market, product and competition analysis; idea and business model validation; market segmentation; and information on how to pitch ideas and budget, forecast and raise capital.
2. The previous consideration can be made regarding communication skills; after the Academy, there was a general increase in the number of students who answered they had a high degree of familiarity. The communication and relational skills involved communication and presentation techniques, team building and teamwork, networking techniques, collaboration and empathy. The sessions provided during the Academy were teamwork and coaching, ideas presentation, teams formation and out on the streets.
3. Concerning personal skills (idea generation, flexibility and stress management), the only area that did not denote any increase in familiarity was flexibility; in all the other areas, there was an improvement in students' familiarity with the skills. The sessions provided during the Academy were idea crash-test (pivoting) and the pitching competition.

These sessions supported participants in improving management skills that a manager should possess in order to fulfil specific tasks in an organization. The sessions encouraged learning and practical experience through which management skills could be developed.

Considering the role of the Academy in supporting entrepreneurship, all students said in response to the survey that they enjoyed the Academy. All felt the Academy increased their ambition to become entrepreneurs. They said they would suggest the Academy to a friend. The things the students most liked about the Academy were:

1. *Mentoring and coaching*: Students considered these activities to be an opportunity to come into contact with experienced professionals and other like-minded people. Mentoring and coaching were developed by an expert involved in a previous start-up academy and by tutors of ComoNExT. In addition, the founders and managers of tenants located at ComoNExT supported the students in the development of their entrepreneurial ideas through the organization of several meetings.

2. *Pitching development*: Students considered this activity essential to presenting their business plans to heterogeneous stakeholders. Students appreciated pitching development as the expert and specialized organizations provided some guidelines for this activity and allowed students to experiment with it.

3. *Team building and team cooperation*: Students considered this activity to be a chance to meet new people and discuss their ideas with professionals. In particular, team building and team cooperation allowed students to improve their ability to manage the entrepreneurial team and human resources.

It follows that the Academy allowed students to interact with experts and have professional and training experiences. The Academy could be considered to be a 'gym' where students can experiment with activities that improve their hard and soft skills.

During the training activity on the first day of the Academy, the tutors presented a digital platform ideated by the partners of the iStart project. This platform was used to share documents and information about the business plan and entrepreneurial activities with students. The digital platform was developed in the second Academy and was optimized for the fourth Academy.

ComoNExT asked the stakeholders to test the platform in order to collect some feedback in order to improve the instrument and address the users' needs. The feedback was positive, with one user labelling the 'tool' as 'very useful'. This tool requires relevant content that is well organized with two methods of communication, a well-designed structure and good quality videos. The tool should be characterized by their flexibility and customization in order to improve the quality of teaching and promote a better interaction between teachers and students.

The suggestions were also helpful. For instance, in order to improve the attendance of the modules dedicated to soft skills, young start-uppers need to understand how the skills can be improved and used by themselves; for example, how to set up a meeting, communication skills, interaction with a management approach and so on. In addition, the platform interaction could be improved by the introduction of a specific tool that can simulate the pitching event with the option of a tutor evaluation. Moreover, the tool could be integrated with other university platforms that students use.

Going into more depth, the Academy also allowed students to shift the managerial paradigm from a product-oriented start-up to a market-oriented start-up. The Academy supported the training of young entrepreneurs oriented to the identification of market needs and preferences. This is the premise to develop a solution (product or services) that can create value and satisfy the market demand. The market approach is founded on strong relationships between the firm and its customers.

The Academy allowed students to adopt a marketing orientation in entrepreneurship. Participants were invited to develop their business ideas and to test them in the market, investigating the interest of potential customers in a product concept. The analysis of the market, as the basis for new product development, involves a customer orientation approach. The latter allows entrepreneurs to identify the needs of potential customers and provide them with the right solution. This approach can initiate the scale-up stage of a start-up.

Considering the start-up life cycle, the following steps are depicted: from business dream to business idea, from business idea to business plan, from business plan to commercialization, from commercialization to scale up. The analysis of the market allowed students to depict the key features of the product and identify the right channel of communication and distribution. This approach is the premise for the birth and the evolution of the start-ups. In the past, many new ventures focused their attention only on the product, and this had critical consequences if there was no demand for the product.

The Academy is founded on strong business relationships with the actors involved in the iStart European project and the analysis of the gaps in entrepreneurial education. The format of the Academy was depicted after the first trainers' lab was held in Lomazzo in 2017 with the main business partners of the project. The trainers' labs were face-to-face meetings among the partners who were thematic experts. The specific purposes of the first trainers' lab were to study each partner's local training trends and needs and the relevant communities that wanted to facilitate entrepreneurship; to establish the trainers' laboratories as an effective mechanism manned by quadruple helix organization representatives; to create a methodology for the academies, facilitating a detailed design and its deployment.

The training needs analysis results were related to desk-based research and a roundtable discussion. The desk-based research (best practice start-up incubators and accelerators around the globe) placed a limited emphasis on active university students: university studies teach 'entrepreneurship', and incubators and accelerators train 'start-ups'. There was a focus on investment-ready ideas and solid teams. It also featured a long-term (weeks or months) training process; short and intensive training was missing.

Considering the roundtable discussions (with quadruple helix stakeholders: academia, business, government and society), the main suggestions were related to skills (closing the gap between an interesting idea and commercial success, development of team building and teamwork skills, being flexible and resilient). Furthermore, suggestions also included ongoing collaboration (academia and the business world should enhance networking practices, the business world should provide commercial validation, academics should promote entrepreneurial activity); and technological trends (Internet of Things, Big Data, social networks, digital health, mobiles, robotics and automation).

In particular, on the basis of knowledge shared during the meeting, the partners depicted the structure of the Academy. The start-up Academy allowed for the sharing of the best educational practices in entrepreneurship, related to each partner, improving the entrepreneurial path of universities. The project supported the internationalization of higher education paths through transnational cooperation involving partners located in different countries.

The feedback generated through different academies allowed the universities to identify new insights to create curricula oriented to new entrepreneurship practices. As anticipated, the project aimed to develop an innovative, evidence-based, transnational framework that would improve the knowledge and skills of academic institutions to produce curricula oriented toward DEP. In addition, the impact of the project on the academic institutions and their students involved the enhancement of university–market collaboration and a better alignment of the curriculum to fit the EU market through co-creation with the actors of the quadruple helix.

This consideration enhances the relevance of cooperation between the university and external actors, such as incubators and innovation hubs, to improve the competences of students. Entrepreneurial education requires the combination of knowledge and competences: this process can be managed by universities in cooperation with organizations oriented to innovation.

The Academy generated a relevant impact, considering the academic institutions, the students and the quadruple helix stakeholders. Higher education institutions support independent, creative, entrepreneurial individuals, who understand the inter- and multidisciplinary challenges of the socio-economic environment. It can contribute to open innovation in true convergence with technological growth. Focusing on the quadruple helix model, several stakeholders play a prominent role in the higher education path, including firms, research centres, public institutions and universities that might have different objectives and priorities, cooperating in the innovation process. The research and innovation stakeholders involve the users.

In addition, the project contributed to the transformation of higher education students into European entrepreneurs. Entrepreneurship lays the foundations of the modern knowledge-based economy: entrepreneurs exploit new opportunities and stimulate economic growth and development. Focusing on the local, regional, national and European level, the impact of the start-up Academy can be summarized in the contribution of transforming European higher education and research institutes into entrepreneurial institutes.

THE UNIQUE ASPECT OF THE INITIATIVE

Entrepreneurial orientation requires a new form of higher education that could be improved on the basis of new interactive lectures, teamwork, mentoring and a pitching competition, which characterize the ComoNExT iStart Academy. In particular, one of the main points of differentiation of ComoNExT iStart Academy is the network approach that involves heterogeneous organizations and heterogeneous resources. This heterogeneity is related to different competences that characterize the business partners: universities, incubators, start-ups, chamber of commerce, SMEs and large firms. Each organization provided specific resources: universities provided scientific knowledge, incubators provided their own network of business partners and the tutorship competences, the chamber of commerce provided information about local sources, and firms provided their core competences. This relational perspective is relevant in order to develop a cross-country project at a macro level.

At a meso level, the relational approach supported the relationships within the organization in charge of the Academy (ComoNExT) and its tenants and business partners. At a micro level, the relational approach allowed students to find potential business partners among the network of the ComoNExT Incubator. ComoNExT was considered to be an intermediary as students could identify some stakeholders and business partners for their entrepreneurial activity within the venture capital, business angels or more in general business partners of ComoNExT. Several studies recognized that connecting to an existing business network and acquiring a position in the network is a necessary condition for the survival, development and ultimate success of a business (Aaboen et al., 2017).

The Academy improved the managerial approach oriented towards multi-stakeholder relationships. The development of the start-ups is strictly connected to the relationships developed with different stakeholders, including customers, providers and universities.

The interconnections of the relationships create a value network founded on collaboration with different actors in order to share resources (Håkansson et al., 2009). The development of co-managed innovation requires continuous interactive learning based on collaboration and related to the creation, exchange and combination of knowledge (Håkansson and Johanson, 2001). In addition, the development of interconnected relationships from a long-term perspective (Håkansson and Olsen, 2011) refers to collaborative learning and collaborative entrepreneurship. In Schumpeter's view (1934), innovation is closely linked to the entrepreneur, while in the current context innovation and economic development are increasingly more united and interdependent and based on the collaborative approach (Miles et al., 2006). The members of the network become active participants in the innovation process by outlining the basis of strong relationships: a business community that helps to develop innovation (Bourne, 2009: 42).

The strong relationships among the organizations of the consortium allowed them to identify the guidelines for each academy. The members of the iStart Project outlined the format of the Academy during the first trainers' lab. The result of the Training Needs Analysis proved that stakeholders' views were in accordance with the majority of the findings of the students' survey. In response, iSTART's first DEP Academy addressed the need to provide a shorter training programme to potential entrepreneurs that do not have an investment-ready idea or a formulated solid team.

The members of the consortium decided to develop the Academy with a specific structure (from Day 1 to Day 5). It featured brief presentations of topics, ongoing support to teams, guidance to form ideas and teams, assistance to fill requirements (for example, canvas, pitch and so on), dedicated mentoring and teamwork sessions after brief presentations and maximum time for completing tasks. This shared structure was replicated in each academy. These shared guidelines reduced complexity and allowed for value creation.

The interconnected relationships improved the value of the Academy. The network structure of the Academy allowed best practices in education activities related to heterogeneous actors belonging to the project network to be shared. In addition, some resources were shared in different academies, such as the mentor of Coimbra involved in ComoNExT Academy.

From the managerial point of view, the main objective of the programme is that the participants learn about different functional areas of management in a lean and efficient way. In this sense, the iSTART academies incorporated lean planning as a basic approach. Thus, the contents delivered in iSTART academies provided delegates with the foundations of business management through the optic of the process 'build–measure–learn', emphasizing clear communication with customers to develop and test products and ideas.

In addition, the managers became mentors. In each academy, a mentoring process took place with the three resident mentors. These mentors provided a brief presentation of topics and ongoing support to teams. They provided guidance to form ideas and teams, and they assisted participants in filling in all requirements (canvas, pitch and so on). We suggest that dedicated mentoring and teamwork sessions take place after brief presentations in the morning. Mentors should be proactive by going to each team to discuss their issues, rather than just responding to participants' queries upon request. Referents from iSTART partners were also expected to visit every other academy. Referents could also act as presenters and mentors. Invited speakers could be part of the pitching competition panel and the multiplier event (accompanying the Academy).

iStart Academy combines academic and managerial approaches. In a traditional perspective, universities allow students to access knowledge while firms support students by providing a job experience. The strong cooperation within universities, firms and incubators allowed iStart Academy to provide students with different knowledge, skills and competences. An innovative lens was used to analyse the market and manage the development of a solution.

Students could learn and also experiment with real business context and the skills required to manage business relationships. The general structure of the Academy is focused on interactive lectures, teamwork and mentoring. The presentations of the lecturers and mentors were given in the early sessions of each day, allowing for the teams and mentors to work with one another as well as to offer participants stimuli on the thematic domain of each academy. This valuable integration can be deployed by actively engaging not only professional start-up mentors but also start-ups in related domains.

The Academy is characterized by a new teaching method. The methodology involves lectures as the most traditional method of teaching where the teacher disseminates information, facts and thoughts through oral presentation. This was combined with case studies that provide learning, replicating the reality and consequently enhancing the decision-making ability of the students. It was also an effective method for developing analytical skills and the ability to synthesize information. Moreover, the oral presentations helped the students in the class to develop their communication and leadership skills.

The Academy also involves games and competitions (people participated spontaneously, and it ensured wholehearted involvement of the participants) and simulate role-play (used frequently to reproduce real-life scenarios, which are entertaining, educational and motivational).

Other methodologies involve group discussion (dialogue among the students regarding an issue related to the lesson facilitating the interaction among the students, which increased their empathy, team spirit and communication skills), preparation of a business plan, canvas and creative exercises. It follows that new approaches to teaching are required to improve the students' training.

Focusing on the innovative training, the Academy incorporated and tested the use of the VLE platform at its various stages of development. As such, during the last Academy in Izmir, the pilot testing of the complete VLE platform was performed.

The Academy combines the entrepreneurial and marketing approach. The educational approach of the iSTART academies is based on the entrepreneurship training model suggested by Azim and Al-Kahtani (2015). In their model, Azim and Al-Kahtani (2015) realize the limitations of the traditional educational methods and suggest that as the main goal of any entrepreneurship programme is to prepare the participants for creating and running an innovative venture, the Entrepreneurship Education Model is based on the three key inputs: contents (what is to be taught?), approaches (how is it to be taught?) and facilitation (who should teach?) (Figure 12.1).

The content of the programme is further divided into three major components of traits, skills and knowledge. The traits relate to psycho-social forces of the entrepreneur and the cultural context that can influence innovative and entrepreneurial behaviour. Skills are expertise that can contribute to the effective performance of a task. The knowledge component relates to the content of an entrepreneurship development programme.

In addition, the approaches to teaching refer to how the traits, skills and knowledge outlined in the content are delivered to the participants. In addition, facilitation refers to the characteristics of the teacher of an entrepreneurship course. This model provides a recipe with the most crucial ingredients of an entrepreneurship development programme in terms of trait, skill and knowledge content as well as approaches to teaching and the essential features of the facilitators (Azim and Al-Kahtani, 2015: 124).

The iSTART academies have been developed based on the following sections: content (curriculum), approach (teaching methods), and facilitation (mentors).

Focusing on the content (curriculum), the first set of skills involves closing the gap between an interesting idea and commercial success. As such, future entrepreneurs must train their opportunity recognition skills (understanding the needs of the market) as well as their market validation skills (effectively communicating an idea to the market).

Besides technical knowledge grounded in the specific characteristics of each industry, the knowledge delivered by the academies includes business management knowledge applied to entrepreneurial activities, with a particular focus on market needs and idea validation. It also includes soft skills training, such as team building and teamwork, presentation skills, decision-making and flexibility.

The Academy supported the transformation of universities in entrepreneurial universities. Entrepreneurial universities are considered key to competition, stimulation of economic growth and wealth creation. Universities can activate relationships through which they increase their impact within regions, engaging several organizations in third mission activities, such as licensing and knowledge transfer. The role of universities is technology transfer (that is, patents, spin-offs and start-ups) and contributing to and providing leadership for entrepreneurial thinking. Some researchers have highlighted the fact that network relationships can play a significant role in building entrepreneurial activity.

In addition, regarding Entrepreneurship Education/Training, Fiet (2000) highlights the critical role of the teacher in the pedagogy of entrepreneurship training as a facilitator to bring about attitudinal and behavioural modification

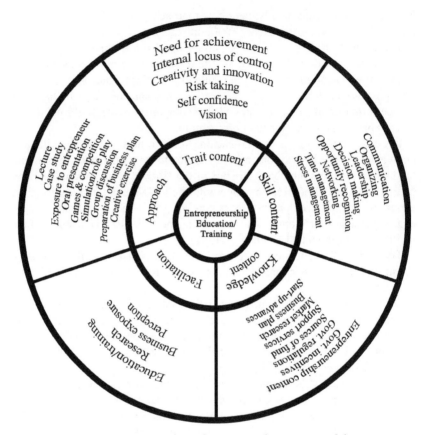

Figure 12.1   Entrepreneurship education and training model

Source: Azim and Al-Kahtani, 2015: 124

in the participants for business start-ups. In this respect, academies' facilitators can be regarded as mentors.

The Academy supported the modernization, accessibility and internationalization of higher education in partner countries. Focusing on the project Erasmus+, organizations are engaged in a number of development and networking activities, including strategic improvement of the professional skills of their staff, organizational capacity building, and creating transnational cooperative partnerships with organizations from other countries in order to produce innovative outputs and exchange best practices. The benefits for the organizations involved include an increased capacity to operate at an international level, improved management methods, access to more funding opportunities and projects, increased ability to prepare, manage and follow-up projects, as well as a more attractive portfolio of opportunities for learners and staff at participating organizations.

The second key action of Erasmus+ is designed to develop the education, training and youth sectors through strategic partnerships to support innovation in the sector, joint initiatives to promote cooperation, peer-learning, and the sharing of experience, as well as knowledge alliances to foster innovation in and through higher education together with businesses.

The skills alliances sector ensures better alignment of vocational education and training (VET) with labour market needs to modernize VET, exchange knowledge and best practices, encourage working abroad and increase the recognition of qualifications.

ACKNOWLEDGEMENT

The author wish to thank the key informants of ComoNExT for their support for this chapter.

REFERENCES

Aaboen, L., La Rocca, A., Lind, F., Perna, A. and T. Shih (2017), *Starting Up in Business Networks: Why Relationships Matter in Entrepreneurship*, Basingstoke: Palgrave Macmillan.

Azim, M.T. and A.H. Al-Kahtani (2015), 'Designing entrepreneurship education and training program: in search of a model', *Journal of Economics and Sustainable Development*, **6**, 112–27.

Bourne, L. (2009), *Stakeholder Relationship Management: A Maturity Model for Organisational Implementation*, Farnham: Gower.

Fiet, J.O. (2000), 'The pedagogical side of entrepreneurship theory', *Journal of Business Venturing*, **16**, 101–17.

Fredriksen, D.L. and A. Brem (2017), 'How do entrepreneurs think they create value? A scientific reflection of Eric Ries' lean startup approach', *International Entrepreneurship and Management Journal*, **13**, 169–89.

Håkansson, H. and Johanson, J. (2001), *Business Network Learning*, Amsterdam: Pergamon.

Håkansson, H. and Olsen, P.I. (2011), 'Innovation in networks', Naples Service Forum.

Håkansson, H., Ford, D., Gadde, L., Snehota, I. and A. Waluszewski (2009), *Business in Networks*, Hoboken, NJ: John Wiley & Sons.

Katz, L. (1955), 'Skills of an effective administrator', *Harvard Business Review*, **33**, 33–42.

Koponen, J., Julkunen, S. and A. Asai (2019), 'Sales communication competence in international B2B solution selling', *Industrial Marketing Management*, **82**, 238–52.

Miles, R., Miles, G. and C. Snow (2006), 'Collaborative entrepreneurship: a business model for continuous innovation', *Organizational Dynamics*, **35**, 1–11.

Read, S. and S.D. Sarasvathy (2005), 'Knowing what to do and doing what you know: effectuation as a form of entrepreneurial expertise', *Journal of Private Equity*, **9**, 45–62.

Rentz, J.O., Shepherd, C.D., Tashchian, A., Dabholkar, P.A. and R.T. Ladd (2002), 'A measure of selling skill: scale development and validation', *Journal of Personal Selling & Sales Management*, **22**(1), 13–21.

Ries, E. (2011), *The Lean Startup: How Today's Entrepreneurs Use Continuous Innovation to Create Radically Successful Businesses*, New York: Random House Digital.

Schumpeter, J. (1934), *The Theory of Economic Development*, Cambridge, MA: Harvard University Press.

Index